NOW THE WAR IS OVER

Now the War Is Over

A Social History of Britain,

1945–1951

PAUL ADDISON

faber and faber

To Rosy and James

This edition first published in 2012
by Faber and Faber Ltd
Bloomsbury House, 74–77 Great Russell Street
London WC1B 3DA

Printed and bound by CPI Group (UK) Ltd, Croydon, CR0 4YY

A CIP record for this book is available from the British Library

ISBN 978-0-571-29629-3

CONTENTS

Preface   vi

1 Goodbye to All That   1

2 Making Do   26

3 A Home of Our Own   55

4 From Cradle to Grave   86

5 Living It Up   113

6 Schooldays   140

7 Britain Can Make It   171

8 Festival Times   197

Notes   211

Picture Credits   216

Index   217

PREFACE

This book has been written to accompany the BBC television series of the same name, to which I have been the historical adviser. The eight chapters reflect and enlarge upon the themes of the eight programmes concerned. My aim in the book has been to link the content of the programmes, and the original research of the production team, with my own treatment of the period.

In terms of research this has been an exercise in historical journalism. Years of patient academic inquiry have not gone into it. But much else has. Ten years ago I published a study of British politics in wartime. The theme was the swing to the Left between 1940 and 1945 – the origins, in other words, of the Attlee governments of 1945 to 1951. For me, therefore, the present book is a sequel: an opportunity to revisit the 1940s and, perhaps, to revise former impressions.

The past ten years have been a great education for us all. Industrial decay, the revival of bitter social antagonisms and the polarisation of politics have prompted new questions about the social history of modern Britain. When the Marxist Left and the radical Right emerged in the 1970s there was one point on which they were agreed: that many of the seeds of decline were planted in the immediate post-war years. According to the Marxist Left, this was because socialism and the class struggle were betrayed. According to the radical Right, it was because free market forces had been stultified by the Welfare State and the managed economy. Both rejected the social democratic legacy inherited by the Conservatives from Labour in 1951.

I do not believe that either of these theories is plausible as a reading of post-war history or workable as a means of governing Britain. I believe they will and should give way in time to a radically revised version of the spirit of 1945. Yet each theory illuminated a disturbing corner of reality neglected by conventional opinion. The Marxist Left drew attention to the fact that the sources of industrial conflict were just as explosive as ever. The radical Right drew attention to the fact that the public sector sheltered powerful vested interests whose claims for greater resources were theoretically boundless. These were truths and remain so in spite of the fallacious ideological baggage with which they are mixed up. Neither problem reached critical proportions between 1945 and 1951, but with hindsight they cast a shadow over the period.

Hindsight can also distort by reading the present back into the past. What most impresses me about the post-war years is the heroic scale of social reconstruction and economic recovery. To have introduced the National Health Service, for instance, while increasing the Gross Domestic Product by 15 per cent, and diverting most of the extra resources into exports and investments, was no mean feat.

This is not to imply that by taking thought in the 1980s the performance could be repeated. During and after the Second World War British society still drew strength and inspiration from the class loyalties and robust social ideals forged in late Victorian times. The Labour ministers of 1945 expected, therefore, to preside over a yet more earnest Britain of austere public purpose. They created a new and enduring State: what they did not anticipate was the new consumer society, emancipated from deference and old class ties, in which the new State would have to function.

As readers will realise, this book is not intended as a history of politics and government, but as a wider social history of the post-war years. As the main object of the Attlee governments was to change society, they loom large in the story. But social history directs one's curiosity beyond Whitehall and Westminster to the workings of the economy, the nature of social conditions, and the actions and reactions of fifty million people.

The Attlee government was lifted into office in 1945 on the crest of a wave of economic and social change. I have tried to describe how that wave swept over Britain and transformed the landscape, but then lost momentum and gradually fell back into the sea. Two main themes present themselves: the embattled resistance of sections of the middle classes to the restrictions on personal liberty associated with 'socialism'; and the divergence of working-class reality from the ideals of citizenship conceived by social reformers. Then as now, it was a fiction that governments make society. Society makes governments, and unmakes them too.

In telling the story I have had the great advantage of being able to draw freely on the memories of people who were at the time. The BBC production team has assembled, in the course of making the series, an archive of about 200 filmed interviews. A minority are with politicians. The remainder are with articulate and observant members of the public.

The interviews have been arranged and conducted according to the rules of television, not according to the rules of social science. I will, however, skip a host of arguments about the value and methodology of oral history and simply remark that I have found the interview transcripts invaluable. They have flung open many a window on the period and I only wish I had been able to quote more of them. In addition to the interviews, the original film sources employed in the series are of great interest for the slant given by newsreels or government films to the issues of the day. From time to time I have indicated this in the text.

As will be clear from the remarks above, my greatest debt on the research side is to the production team of *Now the War is Over*. In addition they have given me practical help and advice of many kinds. Special thanks are therefore due to Angela Holdsworth, the executive producer of the series; to Maggie Brookes, Nikki Cheetham and Peter Grimsdale, the other programme producers; to Christine Whittaker as Film Researcher; to Sandra Jones as Interview Researcher; and to Maureen Hardman, Sheila Johns and Irene Hahn as production assistants.

My debts to the work of other historians and writers are indicated mainly in the footnotes. But I must single out two masterly interpretations of government policy for the indispensable guidance they provide: Kenneth Morgan's *Labour in Power 1945–1951* (1984) and Alec Cairncross's *Years of Recovery: British Economic Policy 1945–1951* (1985).

I am much obliged to Mr Ian Campbell for efficient research on my behalf at the Public Record Office. My thanks also to the following friends and colleagues for stimulating comments in the course of conversation: Dr Tony Aldgate, Dr Robert Anderson, Dr John Brown, Dr Angus Calder, Dr John Campbell, Mr Terry Cole, Miss Ella Duffy, Miss Inyang Ebong, Professor Percy Johnson- Marshall, Dr Nicholas Phillipson, Dr John Ramsden, Dr Jeffrey Richards and Mr Alistair Thomson.

In the preparation of the manuscript for the press Valerie Buckingham has been the most thorough, critical and constructive of editors. June Leech-Guiness, as picture researcher, has matched the text with a splendid set of illustrations, many of which tell their own story of the period. My thanks are due to them both as well as to Liz Calder and Tony Colwell of Cape for their personal support.

For permission to reproduce Crown Copyright material I am grateful to the Controller of Her Majesty's Stationery Office. For permission to reproduce material from the Woolton Papers in the Bodleian Library, I am grateful to the Rt Hon. the Earl of Woolton.

My greatest debt, to my wife and son, is expressed in the dedication.

Paul Addison
July 1985

1

GOODBYE TO ALL THAT

There were two leading topics of conversation in Britain during the Second World War. One was the war itself: the latest news, the latest rumours of what was to happen next, the question of how long it would last. The other was the peacetime future at home: the kind of life, the kind of society and the kind of government there ought to be when the war was over. The second was in some ways a very personal question, a matter of where to live, what kind of work to look for, whether to marry and, at times, whether to stay married. But it was a social and a political question, too. The pros and cons of social change, the high hopes of some for a more just world, and the scepticism of others, were perpetual talking points. The issues were debated in air-raid wardens' posts, in factory canteens, at mothers' meetings, on trains and buses when strangers fell into conversation. Most of all they were discussed, with the blessing and encouragement of the authorities, in the forces.

By June 1944, as D-Day approached, there were four and a half million men and half a million women in the British armed forces. Around their future the complex of hopes and fears was woven. Months of bitter fighting lay ahead in Europe and the Far East, and some would never return but would go to join the quarter of a million war dead suffered by the armed forces. But all hoped to survive, and all but a few yearned for the day when they would be free to quit the forces and return home. But what then? When Ernest Bevin, the Minister of Labour, went to Portsmouth to visit the men of the 50th Division on the eve of their embarkation for France, he was asked, 'Ernie, when we have done this job for you, are we going back to the dole?'

Hindsight supplies the answer. They would not have to return to the dole. A new deal for the working classes was already in the making, and not for the working classes alone. The hopes of soldiers and civilians for a better life, and the plans of social reformers for an all-embracing Welfare State, were converging. In the general election of July 1945 they met, and the Labour Party was returned to power in a sweeping victory.

Germany had already surrendered on 7 May 1945. Japan, terrorised into submission by the atom bombs dropped on Hiroshima and Nagasaki, followed on 14 August. Now at last the war was over and all the participants, the victors as well as the vanquished, could begin the task of rebuilding a peacetime economy and society. But the lessons to be learnt from defeat were very different from those to be learnt from victory.

In Germany and Japan, the values and institutions embodied in the war effort lay buried in the rubble of catastrophe. There was no alternative but to start afresh. In Britain, however, victory had ratified the spirit as well as the machinery of the war effort. Vera Lynn, Tommy Handley, J. B. Priestley, the Ministry of Food with its tips on how to make an omelette, the Ministry of Works with its monopoly of bricks and mortar, were all carried over in triumph from the war to the peace. Sometimes names were changed as when the BBC Forces Network became the Light Programme, or the Council for the Encouragement of Music and the Arts was reborn as the Arts Council. But continuities abounded. The Labour government itself rested on foundations constructed during the war by Labour ministers in the Churchill coalition. For a few critical years after 1945, the home front ran on without a war to sustain it, and Britain was reconstructed in the image of the war effort.

War did not revolutionise the British, but it radicalised them. There was never a serious prospect that the social structure would collapse: Ealing Studios would have been lost without it. But the relationship between the classes began to shift in favour of manual workers. The supreme crises of Dunkirk and the Battle of Britain induced a new sense of tribal solidarity, triumphantly put to the test in the Blitz on London and other major cities. In the common predicament social distinctions lost some of their force. Sir Tom Hopkinson, at that time the editor of *Picture Post*, recalls:

> In any office such as ours, besides the day's work we would go on to fire-watching at night and a managing director would fire-watch with the office boy and the junior typist, five or six people, and then they'd all doss down in great discomfort in one of the offices with the rugs that were provided for the purpose. And then the visible signs of any kind of difference in class disappeared.

Professor Arthur Ling, an architect and planner then working for the City of London, remarks:

> People were much more together. They met in the air-raid shelters, in the tubes at night, they were in the Home Guard, or they queued for spam or whatever it was they could get hold of, one egg a week. Everybody really lost a lot of their inhibitions about talking to their next-door neighbours. When the raids were over they used to almost celebrate in the early morning and this was the spirit that I think a lot of people hoped would continue after the war ...

In the heroic imagery of 1940 we see little groups of citizens gathered in the Home Guard or the air-raid warden's post, the bank manager and the factory worker shoulder to shoulder against the might of the enemy. The images are true of a moment in time but it would be sentimental to portray the psychological exhilaration of 1940 as the mainspring of social change in the long years of endurance that were to follow. Political and economic necessity were the long-term driving forces.

The moment the war began in earnest, the State came to depend upon the active assistance of the whole working and fighting population. As manual workers and their families constituted about 70 per cent of the population, their welfare and morale became a matter of the highest priority. On the political level it was no longer possible for the Conservatives to rule alone. In May 1940 a Coalition government was formed under the leadership of Winston Churchill. One episode in the making of the government illustrates the new basis on which the State was now to rest. Churchill invited Ernest Bevin, the Secretary of the Transport and General Workers' Union, to become Minister of Labour. Bevin did not immediately accept, but wrote a letter stipulating four conditions on which he would agree to serve. He knew the chance had come to reverse the defeats inflicted on trade unionism in the era of the general strike. And as Martin Gilbert writes, 'Churchill accepted the conditions, to the anger of many Conservatives.'[1]

The Coalition was the first clear signal of a shift in the balance of advantage between the classes. The governors still governed, managers still managed and officers still commanded their men. Authority itself was not in question. But, now that popular morale was regarded as a crucial factor in the war effort, the system began to adapt to accommodate working-class needs and expectations. The BBC, for example, introduced a range of programmes intended to entertain factory workers and servicemen. The social services were expanded primarily for the benefit of working-class mothers and children. Standards of health and nutrition were raised so effectively that the infant mortality rate fell more rapidly during the war than it had in peacetime. By 1945, five-year-old boys in Glasgow were on average 2·2 lbs heavier and 1·1 inches taller than their predecessors in 1930.

Much has been written about civilian life in wartime but the social history of the armed forces has yet to be explored in depth. Provided he had the good fortune not to be captured and shut away in a German or Japanese prisoner-of-war camp, the British soldier of the Second World War was more closely attuned to civilian life than his predecessors in the Great War. This was partly due to the fact that between the retreat from Dunkirk in May 1940 and the D-Day landings of June 1944, the main body of the Army was in training in camps in Britain. But there was also a conscious realisation by the Army authorities that the working classes of 1939 expected higher standards of life than the conscripts of 1916. Hence the introduction of the NAAFI, the Navy, Army and Air Force Institute. To quote Correlli Barnett:

> Every camp had its NAAFI: a club room with bar, hot meals, cigarettes and sweets, toilet requisites on sale, and often a piano. Mobile NAAFI shops served outlying units or troops in the field. In large base areas like the Middle East the NAAFI provided splendid leave camps, complete with gardens, swimming pools, shops, restaurants, dance-halls and bars. In service clubs in cities like Cairo soldiers enjoyed all the comfort and facilities of a good hotel.[2]

A parallel phenomenon was the rapid development of Army education, of which more will be said later.

One very interested witness of change in the Army was Stan Henderson, a member of the Communist Party. His impression is of a great contrast between 1939 and 1945:

> When I joined the Army it was still the old traditional British Army and the officers regarded themselves as being very distinct and apart from the other ranks. When after three and a half years as a prisoner of war I met the Army as it then was in 1945 it was a very different situation, there was a very democratic situation, particularly for an army. When a private or an NCO would say to an officer, 'Shift over, mate, I want to get at this job,' the officer shifted over.

A decline of deference in the ranks is, no doubt, something that an observer with a Communist point of view might be expected to report. But it is confirmed by other voices speaking from a background of deeply conservative experience. One such was Philip Masheder, who joined the Royal Navy after a strict northern upbringing in which the principal influences were Christianity, Kipling and the Boy Scouts:

> I'd been brought up in the Church and in the catechism – my duty towards my neighbour is to love him as myself ... to love, honour and succour my father and mother, right, but to honour and obey the King and all who are put in authority under him. To submit myself to all my betters. Now when I'm in the Navy I'm finding that people I've got to submit myself to are not my betters. They aren't my betters. Some of them in my opinion weren't fit to fasten my bootlaces because some of the decisions some of these officers used to make, and some of the remarks they used to come out with, they alter you completely ...
>
> When I came out I was an entirely different person, I wasn't going to be pushed around, I realised that the people that were immediately above me were no better than me in every respect and I was going to make sure that I found my proper station in life and I wasn't going to be dictated to unless it was somebody that I could respect.

Similar testimony, this time with a definite political twist, comes from Mrs Winnie Whitehouse, who joined the Auxiliary Territorial Service (ATS) as a girl fresh from domestic service in a country district where labourers were accustomed to follow their masters. As a woman she experienced the greater freedom enjoyed by women in general in wartime, and began to feel a sense of class consciousness focusing on the person of Winston Churchill. Asked whether she was surprised by the Labour victory of 1945, she replies:

> Not surprised at all because a lot of us in the forces, we were on rations, we queued in the NAAFI for five cigarettes ... and yet Churchill always had his cigar, he was always looked after, he was always well fed. An Ack-Ack site is rough, you know, with it being a small camp we didn't get a lot of the comforts you did on the larger ones. We were happy on it, but we didn't see why he should have everything ...

It was a decisive feature of the Second World War that the qualities and aspirations of men and women like Mr Masheder and Mrs

Whitehouse made a deep impression on sections of the traditional governing class. They came to regard the poverty and unemployment of the 1930s, and the pre-war division of Britain into two nations, as deeply reprehensible. One such was Sir Antony Part, later one of the driving forces in post-war educational reform. In 1939 he was a young civil servant fresh from Harrow and Trinity College, Cambridge:

> What did influence me a great deal was my time in the Army. I spent a certain amount of time in the ranks to start with, and that was very formative, and of course you don't lose touch with people when you become an officer. So those four or five years in the Army were very influential and they were part of one's determination really to try to understand what everybody was on about, what their circumstances were, what their hopes and fears were. That is the kind of thing that gets very deeply ingrained in you ... A whole lot of us said, 'Things must not be the same after the war as they were before the war,' and it was in that determination really that the seeds of success lay.

The change in relationship in the classes was forcibly underwritten by the economics of scarcity. With peacetime industry contracting, and imports restricted to essential war supplies, there was a shortage of consumer goods. To ensure a fair distribution of basic foods and commodities, which would otherwise be snapped up by the better off, rationing was extended.

Food rationing had begun early in 1940 with sugar, meat, bacon, ham and butter, and other items were added as the siege economy intensified. To stabilise the cost of living index, food subsidies and price controls were applied to a variety of other foods in short supply. How far the principle of 'fair shares' worked in practice was debatable. The rules governing meals in restaurants were generous and there was much criticism of 'luxury feeding'. But factory workers too were encouraged to supplement their personal ration with canteen meals, and 'British Restaurants' were established for the general public. Surveys of opinion showed that rationing was popular because it was regarded as fair. But just in case it was too fair, there was always that other popular institution, the black market, to relieve the situation.

In reducing the advantages normally enjoyed by the higher income groups, economic controls also lessened visible social distinctions. In June 1941, the rationing of clothes was introduced on the new principle of 'points rationing', with a basic entitlement for adults of sixty-six coupons or points per person per year. Instead of exchanging them for a standard weekly quantity of goods, the coupon holder could purchase over the next twelve months as much as the points value of different items of clothing allowed. A lady's winter overcoat, for instance, required fifteen points. For a pair of men's trousers, or a kilt, eight coupons had to be surrendered. The effect was to cut down the consumption of clothes to a level adequate for a working-class family. About the same time, the Board of Trade began to standardise the design and production of clothes, reducing the number of materials used and obliging manufacturers to concentrate on a limited range of designs. The 'Utility' scheme, as it was called, employed materials of high quality and the best fashion designers but, like clothes rationing itself, it tended to introduce a standardised look in men's and women's clothing. Later, the principle of Utility was extended to a variety of other goods, including furniture.

In industry, the vital scarcity was of labour. In January 1939, there were still more than two million people out of work, the legacy of industrial decline and a world slump. By January 1944, unemployment was down to 84,000, a statistic that makes one blink in disbelief. When large-scale rearmament started in the late 1930s the trade unions began to re-establish a powerful position in the manufacturing industry and the wartime labour shortage naturally reinforced this trend. Between January 1939 and January 1944, the total membership of the trade unions increased from six million to eight million. In Whitehall, Bevin established a trade union empire with a claim to representation on a great variety of committees dealing with social, economic and industrial policy. At works level, meanwhile, a measure of power returned to the shop floor with the establishment throughout war industry of Joint Production Committees representing management and shop stewards. Not that the decisions of trade union officials were necessarily satisfactory to the rank and file. Though strikes were illegal after June 1940, they multiplied rapidly from 1941 onwards. Between 1941 and 1945 there were more stoppages in each year than had taken place in any year during the 1930s. As these were mainly trivial and short-lived episodes, the number of working days lost was still very much lower than in the previous decade. Yet the number of industrial disputes in wartime is perhaps the best evidence of a surge of confidence, following on a greater sense of bargaining power, from below.

A new assertiveness was apparent among manual workers. Mrs June MacDonald, who was plunged into wartime London from a traditional middle-class background, recalls:

> From the moment I left secretarial college and went into a job, I think one was acutely aware that, for the first time in my life anyway, everybody during the war was more or less equal. Of course, one was aware of a hierarchy in the job, but the moment you got outside and you were confronted with a clippie in charge of a bus, she was in control and you did what she told you, and shop assistants were suddenly very powerful people because things were in short supply and all these people who, before the war, had been rather subservient sort of people and always terribly polite, were just the same as everybody else.

There was no great redistribution of property during the war. Rather there was a steady squeeze on income differentials. The gap between salaries and wages was reduced, and so was the gap between skilled and unskilled workers. Douglas Jay, who was a civil servant at the Board of Trade, sums up the situation:

> There was a huge erosion of class differences. There was some of course in the 1914–18 war and indeed people at that time thought it pretty startling then, but it was certainly much greater in the second war. In terms of income, in terms of consumption of food, in terms of jobs and hours of work, in terms of taxation, there was a tremendous levelling which reached, I suppose, its extreme point in 1944–5, and the fact that it worked I think did have a great effect on public opinion. People felt that if these things could be done in wartime, why shouldn't they, at any rate the best of them, be done in peacetime.

The social changes of wartime were of themselves temporary. They were the response of a government and a people to a prolonged emergency. Though politicians and the press held out visions and promises of a new deal for the working classes after the war, social surveys revealed a high level of pessimism. It was widely feared that the promises would come to nothing: the Tories and the bosses between them would restore the conditions of the 1930s. There was, of course, no guarantee that the wartime spirit of social change would be carried over into the peace – unless conscious efforts were made to translate the mood of the hour into a programme for the future.

Efforts were, indeed, made. In the summer and autumn of 1940 there began to form in Britain a broad alliance of forces in favour of social reform. Though the alliance depended very much for its influence on the power of organised labour, it was never the property of a single party. Socialists were active in the campaign, but so were non-party reformers such as Sir John Reith, Liberals such as J. M. Keynes, and a minority of forward-looking Conservatives such as R. A. Butler. The common denominator among them was 1940s collectivism: the belief in the capacity of the State to reduce social injustice, expand the economy and create a fuller and more spacious life for all. Coming as they did from a variety of political traditions, the reformers differed over the limits and purposes of State intervention. But working closely together across party boundaries, they envisaged a new society in which the most conscientious elements of the old order – the benevolent squire, the philanthropic industrialist and so on – would rally to the ideal of a new society.

The first to spread the word to a popular audience was the novelist and playwright, J. B. Priestley, in an artful series of Sunday evening radio talks broadcast between Dunkirk and the Blitz. A jovial Yorkshireman, the ideal England to which he directed his listeners' imagination was a land of good companionship overflowing with cakes and ale. The radical press, spearheaded by the *Daily Mirror* and *Picture Post*, took up the theme, calling for a declaration of war aims. In 1941, the New Year edition of *Picture Post* was devoted to a series of articles outlining 'A Plan for Britain'. As Tom Hopkinson later wrote:

> The plan – for its day – was revolutionary. A job for every able-bodied man. Minimum wages. Child allowances. An all-in contributory system of social insurance. A positive health service. A bold building plan – to start immediately war ended – to root out the slums. The same kind of education for all up to fifteen, with the public schools brought into the general system. Holidays for all ... and much more which today [1970] we take for granted ...[3]

Among the prophets were some, like Sir Richard Acland, who sought a religious regeneration of society. A Liberal MP converted to Christian socialism, Acland founded with Priestley in 1942 a new political party, Common Wealth. Priestley, who was an artist rather than a political organiser, soon dropped out. But Common Wealth went on to defeat three Conservative candidates (unopposed by Labour because of the party political truce), in wartime by-elections.

The Common Wealth party never had more than about 10,000 members. But its very existence is a reminder of the strand of socialist utopianism, to be found mainly among the professional middle classes, that ran through the 1940s. Explaining his own ideas, Acland says:

> Very briefly, my argument was that we had run our society under the system of private property, of individual initiative as it was called, but that in fact this meant that we were saying to every man, woman and group that they should go hell-bent for his, her, or its self-interest. I said there was no doctrine which could possibly be more dead contrary to the second law of our supposed religion and that there was no reconciliation except in a system of common ownership of all the major productive resources.

Acland and his party were operating on the fringes of politics. Meanwhile, reformers of a more conventional stamp were busy in the nooks and crannies of Whitehall. For a long time their endeavours were wrapped in obscurity but then came the publication of the Beveridge Report in December 1942. The main body of the Report consisted of a scheme for the abolition of poverty through comprehensive social insurance. That in itself was enough to make the headlines. But attached to the main scheme were additional 'assumptions' that gave it a wider significance. Beveridge argued that the success of the social security scheme would depend upon three other changes: the introduction of family allowances, the creation of a National Health Service and the maintenance of a high level of employment. And with a metaphorical flourish to capture the ideal of a new social order, Beveridge declared that Want (i.e. poverty) was only one of five giants on the road to reconstruction. Disease, Ignorance, Squalor and Idleness had also to be met and mastered. Wisely, Beveridge made no mention of the sixth giant – Winston Churchill.

The Beveridge Report was the most publicised document of the Second World War, and also the most popular. It compelled the War Cabinet to appoint a Reconstruction Committee to review and determine the priorities for post-war policy. Out of the Committee's deliberations there began to flow a series of White Papers defining the role and obligations of the post-war State. Though none of the rest achieved anything like the popular acclaim of the Beveridge Report, the passage of time has lent them historical fame.

A hundred years ago no British history text was complete without the names and dates of the battles that won the Empire. Today no history is complete without a list of the wartime White Papers, each one a victory for the massed ranks of social democracy. *Educational Reconstruction*, published in July 1943, proposed a system of secondary education for all and laid the groundwork for the Education Act of the following year. In February 1944, *A National Health Service* envisaged a free and comprehensive service covering every branch of medical activity. The White Paper on *Employment Policy*, published in May 1944, announced in its opening sentence that henceforth it would be the duty of the State to maintain 'a high and stable level of employment'. *Social Insurance* in September 1944 marked the government's acceptance, with minor changes, of Beveridge's insurance scheme. Strange to say, a coherent plan was lacking in one of the most important areas of all, housing. When at last a White Paper entitled *Housing Policy* appeared in March 1945, it was a vague and feeble document of barely eight pages, with no clear target for the number of homes to be built in the post-war period.

The agenda for the new Britain was the work of overlapping circles in the universities, Fleet Street, the civil service and the House of Commons. Considering that so much of the impetus came from the Left, it may seem surprising today that so much of the argument was couched in patriotic and military terms. It was as though the spirit of Kipling or Rupert Brooke had migrated into the souls of social reformers. Tories of the old school habitually regarded the new patriotism of the Left as bogus, since the very people who were now throwing their hats into the air to celebrate the deeds of our gallant soldiers, sailors and airmen had only a few years previously been strongly opposed to rearmament. True, and the propaganda for a new Britain was carefully crafted. But the pride of the reformers in Britain was authentic, more so at times than the radical credentials. Traditional Tories were slow to recognise that patriotism could express itself in different ways.

In the old Tory conception, the sole test of patriotism was readiness to do one's duty for one's country on the field of battle and the only true patriotic object was military victory. But against this, social reformers set an alternative vision. They argued that with the coming of the Blitz the civilian population was now in the front line of the battle: the old distinction between soldiers and civilians had lost its force. The armed forces, too, had changed their character with the introduction of conscription, and Britain was now defended by a citizen army. War, then, was no longer a conflict fought by a warrior caste for the benefit of civilians at home but a people's war that would have to be fought in harmony with the needs and aspirations of the people – meaning, for the most part, the working classes. If victorious commanders were to be honoured and decorated, the military participation of the rank and file should be rewarded by the extension of social and economic rights. The new test of patriotism was, therefore, to be loyalty to the needs and aspirations of the people of Britain: 'social patriotism', as it may be called.

Social patriotism corresponded more closely to popular feeling and the needs of the war effort than the traditional Churchillian variety. The belief that men or women fighting for their country were entitled to a fair share of the fruits of victory was in accord with natural justice. Explaining his decision to vote Labour in 1945, Philip Masheder says:

> You see, we'd just fought a war. Now if we'd lost that war, all the landowners in Great Britain would have lost all their land, it would have gone to Germany. Now here you've got millions of lads coming out of the forces, literally hundreds of thousands of them getting married, they go into a house. That house is costing them extra money because somewhere along the line someone had to pay for that land. Now that ground that those houses were built on belonged to me and you, shouldn't really belong to the landowners. We'd just fought for England, and Scotland, hadn't we? This is one of the ideas that were in our minds, we felt very strongly about this ...

The most remarkable victory of social patriotism over patriotism of the traditional variety took place in the very stronghold of military tradition – the Army. Following the evacuation from Dunkirk, the military authorities began to consider the problem of morale among troops who would have to remain in Britain. An expansion was decreed in the activities of the Army Education Corps, and under the guidance of education officers, thousands of part-time civilian lecturers were employed and short courses arranged, dealing with every variety of topic. But in August 1941 there was a fresh departure. The new Adjutant-General, Sir Ronald Adam, authorised the creation of the Army Bureau of Current Affairs.

ABCA was the brainchild of William Emrys Williams, an adult educationalist and director of Penguin Books. Under ABCA, Army education became compulsory for at least one hour a week in the form of group discussions. These were to be led by platoon commanders with the aid of bulletins issued by the Bureau. Half the bulletins dealt with the military course of the war but the other half were ostensibly neutral surveys of current social, economic and political affairs. The printed material distributed by ABCA was not radical in itself, nor could it have been. But free political discussion in the Army was a major innovation. And whereas it was estimated that eight out of ten soldiers had taken no part in the classes arranged by the Army Education Corps, six units out of ten had organised compulsory ABCA classes by early 1942.

A number of Conservatives were highly suspicious, then and later, of the work of ABCA. In December 1942, Maurice Petherick, the MP for Penryn and Falmouth, wrote to Churchill's Parliamentary Private Secretary:

> I am more and more suspicious of the way this lecturing to and education of the forces racket is run ... for the love of Mike do something about it, unless you want to have the creatures coming back all pansy-pink.

Looking back in 1985, at the age of ninety, Maurice Petherick is convinced that he was correct to write as he did, except that he should have written in stronger terms:

> During the war, you see, every kind of heretic about policy would start up and think they'd a jolly good chance to infect the nation, arrange not only the conditions of the peace, but the conditions in the country afterwards, and I thought that was very dangerous: the thing is to concentrate on the war and that's that. This ABCA was set up with a large number of officers lecturing to the forces and I think it had a very great influence on the post-war conditions ...
>
> They were probably not very effective academicians, and to let a whole lot of those people loose was somewhat unsafe, and everything that I then thought I'm sure was justified ...

Dr Jacob Goldman, in civilian life a general practitioner in Manchester, was his unit's ABCA officer:

> I think that some of the ABCA booklets were tending to be slightly more left-wing than one would expect, but how one used them was the really important thing and if you had a desire to interpret the facts given in the ABCA booklet in such a way that they demonstrated and added to left-wing points of view, the ABCA officer could really make almost any type of material out of it ...
>
> An ABCA lecture was almost a free period for the other ranks. And if they had any relationship with the ABCA officer, it would provide them with the opportunity to

discuss almost everything from their girl-friend to what life was going to be like after the war. In my unit in particular, it was a great safety-valve for men's submerged feelings as well as being informative to them in the political changes that were going on ...

The ABCA lectures were very much enjoyed by my other ranks, and there were some stalwart political figures amongst them, like Welsh ex-miners, and Scottish trade union men, and they thoroughly enjoyed this return to the political fray – and led the discussion, often.

Political discussion in the Army was by no means confined to ABCA. The film star, David Niven, at that time an officer in the Commandos, happened to mention to Ernest Bevin the problem of the soldiers' boredom. Bevin urged him to get them to use their 'noggins' by getting some debates going. The debates, writes Niven, proved to be a great success, the liveliest of them sparked off by an article in the *Daily Mirror* abusing the generals as 'brass-buttoned boneheads'. Niven comments:

> One thing stuck out a mile in these debates – the vast majority of men who had been called up to fight for their country held the Conservative Party entirely responsible for the disruption of their lives and in no circumstances would they vote for it next time there was an election – Churchill or no Churchill.[4]

Still more bizarre than Niven's contribution to Clement Attlee's landslide was the affair of the 'Cairo Parliament'. Cairo was, of course, the main wartime base of British forces in the Middle East. In November 1943, on the initiative of a number of politically-minded servicemen including Aircraftsman Leo Abse, later a Labour MP, a mock Parliament was established. Abse takes up the story:

> We had to take care, there were King's Regulations which clearly prevented active political discussion from going on within the forces, so we decided as a group, those of us who were involved, that the Parliament should only discuss events of after the war. We projected, as it were, the Parliament into a post-war era and we therefore put proposals before this Parliament, which fluctuated, but always had 600 to 1000 men present, always had a Labour majority. We put forward proposals as though we were living in the yearned-for peace ...

As it built up, so the blimps resented it, they didn't like this idea of citizens in uniform as we saw ourselves, and when the Germans read about it in the English-speaking Egyptian press, they put out nonsense from their radio stations suggesting that the forces of the Middle East were in rebellion and we'd set up our own Parliament. This gave the blimps the excuse to intervene and they sought to close it down. I don't want to speak of the whole saga, it led to my arrest, since I was the Chancellor of the Exchequer in this Parliament, and it led to my being sent back to Blighty after interventions in the House of Commons to prevent me being sent to an island in the Persian Gulf. So I was certainly involved in what was a politicisation of the forces. But, you know, we were only the catalyst, those of us who were already politically aware before the war, and who came into the forces. The mood was there – there was a desire for change and the old order was going – and all we were doing was in fact hinting to the forces how it could be done, and it could be done above everything else through the ballot-box.

Most of the anecdotes about Army education confirm that it tended to work in a left-wing direction. It was almost bound to do so, for any discussion of post-war social and economic conditions was likely to result in speculation about the possibilities of a better life for all. The expectations of men and women in the forces were being raised. The point is well made by John Macey, later the chairman of the LCC housing committee, who tells how he made his acquaintance with ABCA while second-in-command of a unit of engineers in Yorkshire:

> I had ATS girls as well as men in my units, and they had quite brisk discussions about what sort of kitchens they wanted and how many bedrooms and whether it should have a garden and this kind of thing ... Very few council houses before the war had central heating systems and they all dreamt of the day when they would have hot water at the sink and hot water for a bath ... Similarly they dreamt about refrigerators, for example, which were very much a luxury at that time ...
>
> I'm quite sure it [ABCA] had quite a considerable influence on the troops. The only thing that used to worry me at the time was that we were going to raise their expectations much higher than would be realisable after the war.

Talk of kitchens brings us to one of the most important side-effects of the war, the impact on the family. The family is the smallest and most private of social institutions, the State the largest and most public. Hence it has often been argued that the family and the State are natural antagonists. The family is seen as the last bastion of privacy, independence and self-reliance, the State as an encroaching force seeking to regulate and control by sending officials into the home.

In wartime, the relationship was the other way round. The family, in effect, turned to the State for support. The war tended to break up the family, separating husbands and wives, and making the care of infants and children much more difficult to organise. The evacuation of women and children to the reception areas, the direction of labour from one part of the country to another and, above all, the call-up of men into the armed forces, all tended to make mothers and children more vulnerable. As Sheila Ferguson and Hilde Fitzgerald have written:

> The family in wartime was increasingly unable to cope with such normal emergencies of life as childbirth, the illness of a mother of young children and the sickness of elderly relations. Moreover as the demand for woman-power grew and even mothers with children under school-age were encouraged to work, there were fewer friends and relations able to look after the children during working hours.
>
> What the family and the neighbourhood could now no longer do for themselves, the State had to help them to do. The social services, therefore, far from being reduced in wartime had to be expanded.[5]

The dynamics of the family also exercised a powerful influence over the future. Of the four and a half million men in the armed forces by June 1944, more than half were married. Many more, an unknown number, were engaged or planning to marry when they returned home. Inevitably a number of marriages collapsed under the strain. Arthur Egerton-Savory, whose own marriage broke up during the war, recalls the troubles of others:

> I was second-in-command of a company for quite a long time and the second-in-command was the officer with whom soldiers spoke about their problems. I was frequently having soldiers coming to me because they thought their wives had gone off with the milkman or somebody or other. Very often this was a figment of their imagination, but very often, of

course, it was true and many marriages were on the rocks, which wasn't surprising really. Men had been away from their homes, especially abroad, for years and years and years and there'd been an influx of Americans and Poles and so on, all of whom were only too keen to get themselves involved with various ladies who were around.

In England and Wales the number of divorce petitions rose from 9970 in 1938 to 24,857 in 1945, and reached a post-war peak of 47,041 in 1947. But in the 1940s marriage was still a far more durable institution than it is today. The overwhelming majority of marriages survived. But more than that, the prospect of peacetime family life was a hope that sustained servicemen through the horrors, boredom and deprivation of war.

The ambition of millions of separated husbands and wives, servicemen and girl-friends, was to reconstruct the family. An intimate project, but also a project with many demands to make on society. Millions of couples would be looking for the privacy of their own home, but would the houses be available? Since the traditional idea of the male as the breadwinner still prevailed, married women would be leaving the labour market and returning servicemen looking for jobs. But would there be full employment? Would there be a National Health Service to see the family through the emergencies of ill health? Would there be greater educational opportunities for the children after the war? On such issues, especially on housing and employment, popular opinion turned, and the Labour Party was returned to power.

The war radicalised significant minorities of the upper and middle classes, an effect also demonstrated in the armed forces. Mrs June MacDonald was by this time a member of the Labour Party and serving on her constituency management committee. She recalls her surprise at the types of people who were putting themselves forward as candidates:

> We had a Tory member of Parliament and he had a 10,000 majority and I don't think anybody in the room ever thought for one moment we could possibly win that seat, but what was so fascinating was the names that came up ... Air Commodores and Wing Commanders, that sort of thing, were suddenly applying to be the Labour MP for Uxbridge and that was a revelation to me because I had been brought up to believe that people like that were always Conservative.

Denis Healey, then a Major in the Royal Engineers serving in Italy, was a committed left-winger before the war. But he remarks on the political outlook of the officers with whom he served. They were, he says:

> Overwhelmingly Labour – and not only young officers, but quite a lot of older officers ... and I remember my General in a landing I did in southern Italy, called Urquhart, who later led the Arnhem parachute landing, he was sympathetic to Labour and recognised that most of us on his staff were Labour supporters. I think the things that were decisive with us, especially those of us who were abroad in the Army, were contact with the resistance movements and the feeling that a revolution was sweeping Europe, a rejection of course of appeasement which many of us as students had fought against just before the war, and above all, of course, a determination not to go back to the mass unemployment of the 1930s.

The emphasis placed on the services in this chapter is not intended to suggest that the service vote alone determined the result of the election in 1945. The service vote, though known to be predominantly Labour, constituted just under 7 per cent of all votes cast and the majority of people in the services did not vote at all, being otherwise engaged. But many were the parents, brothers, sisters, wives and girl-friends who are likely to have voted with the welfare of a serviceman in mind. And the radicalisation of the forces provides the clearest demonstration of the wartime fusion between the ideals of patriotism and equality. It was this movement of opinion – strongest among the working classes, but carrying with it sections of the middle and upper classes; strongest in the Labour Party but influencing the Liberal and Conservative Parties – that dominated the general election of 1945.

This is no place for a detailed account of the election campaign, with its diverting Churchillian fireworks. The Coalition government ended on 23 May, a fortnight after VE Day, and was replaced by a 'caretaker' administration consisting of Conservatives and assorted independents loyal to Churchill. The greatest measure of the impact of war was that all three main parties shared a basic platform of commitment to the programme of reconstruction worked out between 1942 and 1945. The Conservatives were pledged to carry through the Beveridge plan of social insurance, to implement the Butler Education Act of 1944, to establish some form of National Health Service, to launch a major programme of State housing, and to maintain a 'high and stable level of employment'. All these pledges were set out in the Conservative election manifesto of 1945, *Mr Churchill's Declaration of Policy to the Electors*. Churchill, however, did his best to disguise the most attractive features of his Party's policy, and in this he was representative. As most Conservatives saw it, the Coalition programme had been wished on them by the Left and the planners and, while they regarded it as inevitable, their commitment was lukewarm and somewhat unreliable. The Labour Party, by contrast, played the social reform card for all it was worth, and added a wedge of socialism: the nationalisation of coal, gas, electricity, the railways and iron and steel.

The most controversial issue, if rhetoric was to be believed, was the future of all the State controls imposed on the economy in wartime. The Labour Party expressed its determination to retain them long enough to ensure that basic social needs such as food, housing and full employment were met. Churchill produced much bombast, five years ahead of its time, about scrapping controls, and warned that socialism would entail the introduction into Britain of some form of Gestapo.

On 5 July 1945 the electorate went to the polls. There followed a period of suspense. The ballot-boxes were sealed up for three weeks to allow for the collection of postal votes cast overseas by men and women in the armed forces. But on 25 July the results came pouring through. The Labour Party was in with an effective majority of 183 over all other parties combined. That evening, Churchill left Buckingham Palace in a chauffeur-driven Rolls-Royce after submitting his resignation to King George VI. A few minutes later, the Attlees arrived with Mrs Attlee at the wheel of their Standard Ten. Ignoring the advice of colleagues who had warned him for years, and up to the very last minute, that he was unfit for the job, Attlee accepted the King's invitation to form a government.

The first great operation of the peace was demobilisation. Here was a delicate and potentially explosive affair. The spectres of mutiny and social unrest, vividly recalled from 1919, were never far from the minds of the authorities. But the preparations already made by Bevin, as wartime Minister of Labour, showed a thorough grasp of the practical human problems involved, and a determination to solve them. Working in association with the services, he set in motion a great variety of schemes to ease the transition from war to peace.

Instead of granting early release to key occupational groups, the plan which had given rise to the mutinies of 1919, Bevin decided that with few exceptions priority should be determined by age and length of service. In the incoming Labour government of July 1945, responsibility for demobilisation passed to the new Minister of Labour, George Isaacs, who was much criticised for delays in the programme. In January 1946, a series of mutinies took place at RAF bases in India and the Middle East. Impatience for release and a sense of grievance were quick to flare up. But given the relatively slow pace at which demobilisation was bound to proceed, the operation as a whole was carried through with great success. By the end of 1946 some four and a half million men and women had found their way back home and were picking up the threads of civilian life.

One of the practical problems of release from the services was the lack of a wardrobe. Old clothes had vanished or no longer fitted, and new clothes could only be obtained on the ration. Men and women leaving the forces had, of course, to be given a clothes rationing book. But since a man's wardrobe required 223 coupons and a woman's 219, the current ration of four coupons a week would have left them almost stark naked. Women, therefore, were given a money grant and 146 coupons to go with it. Men, who got a smaller bonus of coupons, reported to their local barracks to be fitted out with a free set of clothes.

Arthur Egerton-Savory, who had been photographed by *Picture Post* on the day he joined the Territorials in 1939, was photographed again on the day he left the Army in 1946 and went to pick up his demob suit in the clothing depot at Olympia. Contacted again by the BBC in 1984, he is well on the way to becoming a symbol of the 1940s, but his recollections, already cited, are matter of fact and tinged with disenchantment. Of his day at Olympia, he says:

> The procedure was that you joined a great big long queue where first of all you were measured, your height taken, your chest size and so on, the size of your shoes, was all put down. Then you proceeded to the stores where you drew two pairs of socks, a pair of shoes, underclothes, a hat, which I never wore, and a range of demob suits. There were three or four different types as far as I remember and I chose a conventional pin-stripe which would serve me for office wear. They were made by the fifty-shilling tailors as they then were called ... if one wanted to go out in the evening for something special it would hardly have been a very distinguished type of suit.

Bob Errington, an electrician who had served in the Eighth Army, was issued with his demob suit at Guildford:

You were given a suit, a hat, shoes, a shirt and a cardboard box to put it in. Quite good, really. Everybody used to say that when you got outside there were touts outside waiting for you to come out and they'd give you a couple of quid for your box, but nobody did that where I was, everybody wanted the clothes because most of the people had been away for some years and there was clothes rationing on and it was really the only clothes that some people were going to have.

Apart from the ritual of release from the services, there was one other very great event to which millions of people had been looking forward. The reunion of servicemen with their wives, fiancées, and girl-friends, now that the risk of death or mutilation in battle was past, and peace stretched ahead as far as the eye could see, was at its best a moment of supreme joy and delight – love's victory over all the enemies in the world. Mrs Jenny Parkinson, as she now is, had got engaged during the war and still remembers the precise date, 16 January 1946, when she set off to meet her boy-friend on his return:

I had a train journey, you know, from work, and down a little dark lane, and there was a street lamp at the bottom of the lane, and it was very dark even though the blackout was lifted. I ran all the way down the lane and then this dog and the soldier stepped out from the lamp. It was Bill and our spaniel dog. I don't think we even spoke to each other, you know, we didn't even kiss one another, just put our arms round each other, and we walked home and all I could think of was that he'd never have to go away again and that it didn't matter what happened in the future, there was nothing could ever be as bad as the times we'd gone through, and quite truthfully nothing's ever been as bad, and we've been very, very lucky.

Mrs Marjorie Crane had been waiting three and a half years for the release of her husband, Peter, from a Japanese prisoner-of-war camp. There had been little news of him, only a few postcards stating that he was still alive.

I didn't tell any one of the family, I just went by meself to Liverpool, and when I got there, there was a big crowd of girls all going mad, and they couldn't get through the dock gates and seemingly you had to have a special pass ... so I thought, well, I've not come all this way not to get through, so I got me handbag and I walked up to this policeman, he looked a bit formidable you know, but anyway I walked up to him and I started fumbling in me bag and I kept saying, 'Oh, I can't find me card, I did have one, I did, but I can't find it,' and I tried to cry, you know, and he must have fell for it because he said, 'Go on, go through.' I went through and I went into where they disperse and I saw him. He was eating a currant bun actually – and it doesn't sound very romantic, does it? – but he was and I couldn't help it, I just rushed up to him and I got half of the currant bun in my mouth and he said, 'Hang on, you're choking me.'

After the first sensation of joy, couples often had to work through a long phase of adaptation. After years of separation and different experiences there might well be a sense of estrangement. Peter Crane admits that for many years after the war he felt at a distance from reality, 'It took a long time before it started breaking away and dissolving.' Another complication was that his children no longer recognised him. As Mrs Crane recollects:

They just stared at him, round-eyed you know, and when he kept saying, 'Don't do this,' and 'Don't do that,' they said, 'Mum, who's that man that keeps coming in our house and staying all night?' I said, 'It's your father.' 'Well, we don't know him – who is he? Tell him to go away.' And it seemed terrible to me, that, you know, and they didn't like him.

Husbands who had been linked as blood-brothers to comrades in the forces now had to forsake one kind of emotional loyalty for another. Mr Francis had married during the war and seen little of his wife, whose experiences in the Portsmouth Blitz had been more gruelling than his own. When the time came to leave the Army, he says:

I missed very much the idea of going back to my unit, you know, because before, on leaves, there had been absolutely marvellous, hectic, euphoric times, but we knew they would come to an end, so one lived on a tremendous 'high' as it were and then went back to the unit and got on with the job. Now that was all gone and it was different, a different style altogether, one had to settle down and get a job and get to know the children very well. But they came to accept me. It was the little things, I think, of setting up home, staining the floor, getting the carpets down, hanging curtains – all those kind of things which began at last to make it all seem worthwhile, and gradually the tremendous affection that we had for each other in the unit, all became something that was in the past.

To tide them over while they were looking for work, service personnel were entitled to a lump sum, payable in instalments through the Post Office, which varied according to rank and length of service. A private with three years' service would receive £83 if single and £99 if married. For a major the equivalent figures were £177 and £196. At a time when a well-paid manual worker could expect to earn £5 a week, the gratuity was a sum larger than many young people had ever handled before. To James Rochford, whose first job after leaving school had been for a wage of under a pound a week in a cotton mill, his gratuity of £80 seemed 'a vast sum':

> I was only twenty-one, I wanted a good time first. I wanted girls and a good drink, you know, I didn't think of a job ... they gave you a book, you see, if you took it to the Post Office they gave you £3 a day. Well, a full week's wage was only £5, till eventually you got that way you was going to the Post Office every day. But it didn't last long, then you had to find a job then ... No more boozing, no more going to race courses, no more going to Blackpool with a couple of girls, taxis here, taxis there.

The next step, to get a job, was usually not too difficult. All those conscripted since May 1939 had the right, laid down in the 1944 Reinstatement in Civil Employment Act, to their old job back on the terms and conditions that would have applied had the war not interrupted their employment. If this were not practical, the employer must offer an alternative, and where disputes arose they would go for arbitration to reinstatement committees. At a time of widespread popular fear of another great slump after the war, this was as fair a guarantee as legislation could provide of a job to go to.

Arthur Egerton-Savory had been working with a firm manufacturing cement. His former firm carried out its legal obligations by offering a job, but as they were only prepared to offer him a salary increase of £100 after six years' absence, he took it as a hint to look for a job elsewhere. Those who had remained in the firm during the war had, he remarks, 'advanced considerably and now had all the plum jobs and I think they rather resented persons coming back from the services who might be a threat to their own future advancement'.

Needless to say, there was no pressure on ex-service personnel to return to their previous job. That would have been far too static a plan for restless young men or for the economy. In all kinds of ways encouragement was given to make a fresh start. Towards the end of the war six compulsory hours a week of Army education were devoted to the business of mental preparation for civilian life. Soldiers could opt either for a vocational or a cultural type of class, each offering a great variety of subjects from which to choose. Later, the Army followed up with a voluntary scheme of four-week residential courses at 'Formation Colleges', as they were called, where students could start learning about any subject, 'from Russian or philosophy to market gardening and domestic science'.[6]

After demobilisation, a variety of vocational training was available. In about thirty industries free training was provided in government training centres, with the assistance of employers and trade unions. Those wishing to attend university or embark on a professional career were eligible for financial assistance. There were resettlement grants of £150 for those intending to set up their own business, together with a three-month course in business methods. Bevin, in fact, had done his level best to ensure that it was almost impossible for a demobbed person in search of a job not to get one. If, within three weeks of signing on at a Labour Exchange, a man or woman did not have a job, they were to be offered alternative employment or a place on a training scheme.[7]

Jobs there were but, to judge by the recollections of some of those returning home, Britain in 1945 or 1946 was far from the land of exalted popular idealism sometimes hinted at in the political histories. James Rochford describes his return to Salford:

> I went back to Salford and I walked down the same streets I'd left three and a half years before. Nothing had changed, same old pubs on the corner, same old corner shops, same old terraced streets ... Everything was just the same, dismal, grim, people were fed up, tired out, and when you went in the pub you got the same atmosphere: 'Oh, here they are, here's the lads with the demob money,' and they seemed to feel a kind of resentment to the serviceman that was returning.

Of his first impressions of post-war Britain, Arthur Egerton-Savory remarks:

> I think I hoped for a different world from what I found because it seemed to me, and my experience was mostly in

London, it seemed to me that it was the age of the spiv and the get-rich-quick type of person who was ready to do anybody else down if they had the opportunity.

Mrs Winnie Whitehouse also remembers a sense of disappointment:

When we left the services we expected at first a lot was going to be different, a lot was going to be better. Of course it wasn't possible when you stop and think about it, because we'd got the other countries to see to, we'd to get back on, but I think a lot of us were disappointed in the Britain that we came back to ... nobody could make it change overnight into the Britain we wanted.

2

MAKING DO

Though the war ended in 1945, the wartime economy went marching on into the peace. If there were popular expectations that drab, run-down Britain would suddenly be transformed into a land of plenty, they were swiftly dashed. Clothes, petrol and basic foodstuffs remained on the ration. But these items at least were usually in supply. More frustrating were persistent shortages of unrationed commodities. The first peacetime Christmas was a festival of scarcity. As Harry Hopkins writes:

> In Trafalgar Square the children could be taken to admire a new feature of the London Christmas, a magnificent spruce newly arrived by ship from Norway, the gift of the Norwegian people. But filling the stockings was difficult. In one shop 200 surplus RAF kites, price 24s. 6d., were sold in an hour; model planes used in training the Observer Corps, and ex-RAF rubber dinghies, were bringing £5 each.[1]

For a variety of reasons, shortages were to prevail until the early 1950s. For Britain, the price of total war was a massive deficit in the balance of payments with the dollar area. Export markets had been lost, export industries turned over to war production, and one-quarter of overseas investments sold in order to pay for imports. During the war the deficit was made good by supplies delivered free of charge from the United States under President Roosevelt's programme of 'Lend-Lease'. But immediately after the defeat of Japan in August 1945, President Truman announced that Lend-Lease would be suspended forthwith. For the time being the crisis was staved off by the hurried negotiation by Keynes of an American loan. But in the long run, it was estimated, exports would have to be increased by 75 per cent above the pre-war level in order to finance the volume of imports Britain required.

Ironically, Britain could only recover from dependence on the

United States by turning to the United States for essential supplies. The USA was an oasis of prosperity in a world of want. Without supplies of food, fuel and raw materials from North America, Britain, like the other states of western Europe, would be unable to restore its industrial output. Dollars, therefore, were a precious commodity, and food imports from the dollar area would have to be kept to a minimum. Nor could food easily be obtained elsewhere. Over great expanses of Europe and Asia the war had ruined or damaged agriculture and it was to be several years before production returned to pre-war levels. There was no danger that the British would starve. But with food in short supply, rationing would have to continue to ensure a fair distribution.

The other main consequence of Britain's economic plight was that goods for export were a higher priority than goods for home consumption. In addition to the rationing of consumer goods, the Labour government inherited from the war years a vast panoply of controls over the supply of raw materials to industry and the production and distribution of goods. These controls were employed to divert labour and materials into the export trade while holding back production for the home market. In the pottery trades, for example, all coloured and patterned wares were reserved for export and only plain white china was allowed to be sold at home. As timber was so scarce, the sale of new furniture was at first restricted to newly married couples, or families bombed out of their homes. A licence had to be obtained before a firm could manufacture an item as humble as a cricket ball.

It was frequently alleged that the Labour government was doctrinally wedded to controls as a means of socialist planning. There was some truth in this, yet the government never conceived the restrictions as permanent. They did, however, intend, as the Cabinet resolved in August 1945, to maintain controls during a five-year period of transition from war to peace, thus, it was hoped, preventing a recurrence of the cycle of boom and slump that had followed the First World War. The timetable was impossible to foresee precisely. But five years later, after another general election, the Labour government was indeed rapidly dismantling economic controls. On 3 June 1950 *The Economist* observed:

> The leaders of the Labour Party have always said that the restrictive controls, especially those which are unpopular, would be removed as soon as it was possible to do so without running any risk of the rationing of necessities 'by the purse'

or of creating unemployment. That time, in many lines, has come. It may very well be that the Labour Party, so long as it had a secure majority, had a bias towards making these relaxations later rather than sooner ... [but] the government are, in substance, only doing what they always said they would do.

The 'age of austerity' lasted into the early 1950s, longer than even Whitehall expected. With hindsight, the most striking aspect of it all was the governability of the British people. Victory had removed the imperative of national unity and no one could seriously pretend that a 'financial' Dunkirk was the moral equivalent of the real thing. There was much grumbling. There was much protest on behalf of the middle classes, fanned by the Conservative Party and its allies in Fleet Street. Yet there was no popular revolt.

One potentially subversive force was the black market, which might well have wrecked the system had the wealthier classes decided to appropriate it for their own ends. But no such counter-revolution took place: the black market was a classless institution entitling every imperfect citizen to an extra tin of salmon or bottle of Scotch. The working-class electorate, though said by the Opposition to be undernourished, stayed remarkably loyal to the Attlee governments and the Labour Party obtained a slightly higher share of the total vote in October 1951, when they lost the election, than they had when they had won in July 1945.

The fact that everyone was entitled to the same bacon ration after the war, or the same meagre allowance of petrol, may suggest that everyone had a common experience of austerity and its frustrations, but this was not the case. Some people were better off than in 1939 and others worse off. For the underdogs of the 1930s, the unskilled and the unemployed, post-war Britain was a great improvement. Rationing did not involve a tightening of the belt but guaranteed a fair share. In other respects there were positive gains. Rent control and price subsidies held down the cost of living at a time when full employment was boosting the real purchasing power of wages. On a broader view, the working classes in general were enjoying a higher standard of living. The average real wage in 1949 was 20 per cent higher than in 1938.

The sense of post-war deprivation was sharpest among the middle classes. The figures for salaries, professional earnings and the profits of the self-employed show that all were several percentage points down in 1949 by comparison with 1938. The Attlee governments maintained the higher levels of income and surtax introduced during the war and perpetuated controls over profits and rents. The journalist and author J. L. Hodson, who spoke for Labour in the general election campaign, was quick to complain. In his diary for November 1945 he wrote:

> Men grow restive under the burden, for how is the middle-class man to send his children to the university and save for his old age? A friend described the middle classes last night as 'the suffering classes'. He has a house he wishes to sell but cannot because the local authority has put a bombed-out tenant in at a rent of £90. It is worth much more than £90.

No less disturbing was a sense of diminished status in a hostile environment, one in which the Minister of Fuel and Power, Emanuel Shinwell, could utter the following words: 'We know that the organised workers of the country are our friends. As for the rest, they don't matter a tinker's cuss.'[2]

The other main contrast of experience was between the sexes. At work conditions were improving, a bonus for working women as well as men. But the role of housewife, the principal occupation of married women, was more onerous. Shopping entailed hours waiting in queues. Cleaning had to be done with soap on the ration. Cooking was the art of turning tasteless and inferior food into something palatable for the family. The maternity services were developing rapidly but children's clothes, toys, prams and cots were in extremely short supply. No wonder that the most articulate popular protest against austerity was organised by housewives.

Food was the most sensitive issue. The Ministry of Food was responsible for buying imports in bulk and distributing them through some 1500 local Food Offices to the retailer. For the customer, the system was relatively simple. Everyone over five years of age was issued annually, through the local Food Office, with a buff-coloured ration book containing coupons for the next fifty-two weeks. Children under five had a separate green ration book entitling them to smaller rations, but including coupons for welfare foods such as orange juice and cod-liver oil. A supplementary ration book was issued to expectant mothers.

There were two main types of food rationing. Basic foods were rationed according to a fixed quantity per person per week, and coupons for these items were included in the ration book. Also included were 'personal points', as they were called, exchangeable for a month's ration of chocolates and sweets. Milk and eggs, though not actually covered by coupons, fell into the same general category since they, too, were distributed according to a fixed quantity per person. When the Attlee government first took office, the basic ration per person per week was as follows:

1s. 2d. worth of meat
3 oz. bacon and ham
8 oz. sugar
2½ oz. tea
2 oz. butter
2 oz. cheese
4 oz. margarine
1 oz. cooking fat
1 egg per fortnight
2½ pints liquid milk
12 oz. sweets per month

To obtain the basic fixed rations, a customer had to register with a particular shopkeeper for a period of twelve months. But the ration book also contained a set of much more fancy-free coupons known as points (and not to be confused with the personal points for sweets and chocolates). Points were, in fact, a form of currency restricted in quantity by the government, and exchangeable for a list of foods which could be varied in points value according to the supply available. Points covered a very large number of canned foods including fish, meat and vegetables, as well as dried fruits and odds and ends. Unlike the standard ration coupons, points could be exchanged at any shop. The retailer then cut out the coupons and presented them to the local Food Office which replaced the stocks. In July 1945, everyone with a buff ration book had an entitlement of twenty points a month.

Hotels, restaurants, boarding-houses, and factory and works canteens were, like the individual consumer, subject to rationing, and had to obtain permits from the Ministry adjusted to the number of meals served. In commercial catering there were also restrictions on the scale and price of the menu. Meals were limited to three courses and the maximum price that could be charged was five shillings. Coffee was extra and had to be charged at a reasonable price.

The regulations applied to the Ritz or the Savoy no less than anywhere else, but they did not prevent 'luxury feeding'. Five shillings was a substantial price for a meal in the 1940s and enabled clubs and restaurants to serve expensive items that were off the ration, such as game. The chef at Boodle's Club, Victor Ceserani, tells how this made his job easier:

I was very lucky working in such a club because many of the members went to Scotland on holidays, they hunted, they shot, they fished. And so overnight the train would come back from Scotland and arriving at the club the following morning would be the British Rail carrier with, maybe, rush baskets of salmon. I'd sometimes have as many as ten salmon coming in in the morning weighing from seven pounds to fifty pounds ... and whole carcasses of venison would arrive, they'd been shot, they'd been gutted and skinned and they would arrive at the club ... huge hampers used to come, and again members used to shoot and just pitch them all in, so in the appropriate season out would come tumbling pheasants, hares, rabbits, grouse, snipe, woodcock, partridges and so on, that all helped us considerably.

From the housewife's point of view the first main problem occurred when she went shopping and found that she had to join a queue. As Mrs Vera Mather remembers:

It was queues for everything, you know, even if you didn't know what you were queuing for ... you joined it because you knew there was something at the end of it. You didn't often queue for rationed stuff, the stuff you were queuing for was non-rationed, therefore you knew that it was something special ... I've known myself to queue up at a butcher's shop when doing the shopping for the family and when I've got to the counter they'd been queuing up for lights for an animal, you know, the dog food or the cat food, very disappointing.

Terry Alford's mother would send him out with his sister, who was two years older, to queue for bread or meat:

I had to get up ... about 7 o'clock in the morning and get into a queue, and then about 9 o'clock she [his sister] would come along and relieve me while I had a cup of tea or a piece of toast or something, and then if we still hadn't got what we wanted by 11 then I had to go back again and queue up, and normally my mother arrived when we were just about to get into the shop door ...

Next on the housewife's agenda of difficulties was the meagre quantity of the food allowed on the ration. In the opinion of Mrs June MacDonald:

Most sensible people realised that there was still a shortage of food and I don't think anyone expected that rationing would be ended straight away, they just realised it wasn't possible, but I think a lot of people hoped that we would get more food on the ration, so we would get actually more butter, more sugar, more meat and more of the things which we had been very short of for five long years.

Mrs Mary Blakey, who lived in Essex, recalls the advantages of having a garden:

Personally I found living on the rations was very difficult. I worked very hard physically, but actually because I lived in the country, I was more fortunate. I think we were more fortunate because anyone with a good garden could grow fresh vegetables and have fresh fruit and also run chickens and ducks. I kept rabbits, breeding rabbits. Kept three goats. Made cheese, which was helpful. But it really meant working from the moment one got up to when one went to bed.

Naturally enough, housewives passed on the pressures to shopkeepers like Mr and Mrs Mucklow, who set up a grocery shop in Stratford-on-Avon in 1945. Mr Mucklow describes the tactics customers used to adopt:

They were always trying to ask for that little bit extra, yes. Of course we used to get a little margin on our supplies, for example you had a cheese which in those days you had to skin, well you got an allowance for wastage on that, a side of bacon, you'd get an allowance for wastage on that. Well you could gradually build up a little extra stock so that when it came to re-registering you could say to Mrs Jones, 'I can let you have another couple of ounces this week.' And they'd appreciate it, you didn't do it on the day you'd got to register, that was too obvious. But that's how you looked after your customers in those days. We would have nothing to do with things like the black market.

Last but not least of the housewife's complaints was the monotony of the diet when there were so few alternative foods available off the ration. Nutritionally, food was adequate but the taste was often unappetising. To assist the housewife, the Ministry of Food continued to operate its Food Advice division, set up during the war, which distributed recipes to the press and arranged demonstrations of cookery. One of the staff of the division was Marguerite Patten, who ran a food advice bureau at Harrods:

> People [would] often say to me afterwards, 'Well, why were you demonstrating?' But you've got to remember that all the time there was a cry, 'What could I do when I have no meat left this week, when I can't get sausages, when I'm running out of sugar?' and so all the time one was looking for something new to make the rations interesting and palatable.

It was a time for experiments in the kitchen. Victor Ceserani used to call in every morning at the butcher in search of treats and tasty morsels for the members of Boodle's Club. One morning the butcher produced a plump and delicious-looking animal which he identified as a beaver. Having ordered one to be sent round to the club, Mr Ceserani set to work with his assistants to prepare it for the table:

> We dug around the cold room and got some bits and pieces, some onions, some bread, some herbs, and made a stuffing and stuffed it, we found some whole bits of fat bacon and we coated it. We put it in the oven and gave it a nice, slow, steady roast, and it smelt quite nice. Well, from twelve o'clock some of our old members who lived in grace-and-favour residences by St James's Palace used to come tottering up St James's, and we had one dear old chap, nearly ninety, who always aimed to try and get into lunch first because he knew if he got in first he got the pick of the menu. So he got to his table, the Steward presented the menu, he said to the Steward, 'What have we got today, Sharpe?' And the Steward said, 'Roast and stuffed beaver, Sir.' Well, I'd like to tell you his reply, but I couldn't repeat it. And that was the end, we sold two portions. The name beat it. I had some for my lunch and it was quite nice, it was a tender one. But I don't think I'd want to repeat the experience.

Post-war preferences in food were traditional. The British in general were as yet unaware of such smart delights as Moussaka, Boeuf à la Bourguignonne, or even lychees for pudding. There was a pent-up yearning for the old familiar flavours of Great Britain. As Mrs Vera Mather says:

> I adored chocolate and of course you never saw it during the war at all. My dream after the war – or one of my dreams – was to buy a quarter-pound block of milk chocolate and eat it all up myself, all at one go, I didn't care if I would be sick.

I think it was just that you were deprived of these pleasures and to me it was a big thing missing out of a growing child's life ... I did know about these things, but younger ones didn't because they'd been brought up on sweet coupons, but I did know what a block of chocolate looked like.

It was a measure of the dearth of minor luxuries in post-war Britain that the arrival of a banana boat should be a cause for celebration. No bananas had been imported since 1940: to adults they were a fond memory, and to children an exotic mystery in a picture book. When the first shipments arrived at Avonmouth on 31 December 1945, the Lord Mayor of Bristol was there to bid them a ceremonial welcome. Anecdotes suggest that the subsequent arrival of the banana in the home was also attended by a certain amount of ceremony. Victor Ceserani, the chef at Boodle's, remembers:

I arrived home from work one evening – ten o'clock was my usual time – to be greeted by my wife saying, 'I've got a wonderful surprise for you tonight, darling.' She wouldn't say what it was. So I got cleaned up and sat down in the kitchen ... and full of pride she produced out of the cupboard a banana. We looked at it with reverence, it was the first time we'd seen one for years. So we peeled it very carefully and ceremoniously. We then got two small plates and knives and forks and we each then carried on and ate our banana, cutting it as thinly sliced as possible so that we could really enjoy it to the full. Looking back now it sounds stupid, but that's absolutely true.

Terry Alford, who was a schoolboy at the time, says:

The first time I ever heard of a banana was when my sister came home from the theatre. She was a junior dancer on the stage in Covent Garden theatre ... and she'd spoken to one of the porters in Covent Garden market and he said there was a consignment of bananas coming in to the market next day and she said that he'd promised to give her one. So anyway she went off to the theatre that night and I sat at home waiting and waiting and getting excited about this prospect of seeing a real banana, because up to that time I'd only seen them on a film. And eventually she came in and as the door opened she had this piece of cloth ... then she took off this cloth and revealed this banana and we both stared at it and we put it on the table and it was to us, it was like a piece of sculpture, it wasn't a piece of fruit, we was touching it and moving it around. But my mother, because she'd seen bananas before the war, she came in and she says, 'You're not eating all that on your own,' and she chopped it in half and destroyed the whole image of it.

Unlike the first cuckoo of spring, the first banana did not herald the approach of better days. While the public were habituated to wartime levels of consumption, they were not expecting further reductions. But in the first half of 1946 came a series of announcements by the Ministry of Food of curtailments in the ration.

Labour's first Minister of Food was Sir Ben Smith, a former official of the Transport and General Workers' Union. He was an appropriate choice owing to his experience during the last two years of the war as the British minister resident in Washington with responsibility for the procurement of supplies from the United States. But Smith was out of luck. Early in 1946 the food experts in Washington began to predict a world wheat shortage, aggravated by a shortage of rice. Famine threatened Germany, where Britain was now one of the occupying powers, and Asia, where Britain was still directly responsible for the welfare of India, Burma, Ceylon, Malaya and Singapore. To meet its own requirements as well as those of dependent peoples, Britain had to import grain from the United States, a land of abundance free of rationing. In February, Smith shouldered the White Man's Burden and announced that in order to divert supplies to the threatened areas the British government would henceforth reduce its imports of wheat for consumption in Britain. To conserve grain stocks, the extraction rate of flour from wheat would be increased to 85 per cent, darkening the colour of a loaf that was already grey, reducing the volume of animal feeding stuffs, and restricting livestock production. High hopes of breakfast tables groaning with plates of egg and bacon, and a chicken in the pot for all, were dissipated. As will be seen later (p. 41), Smith also stirred up a housewives' revolt by threatening to discontinue supplies of dried egg – the lifebuoy of many a drowning cook.

In the spring and summer of 1946 the politics of bread came to the fore. Herbert Morrison was sent as special emissary to Washington to persuade the administration to adopt a more generous policy towards Britain. Morrison cut a bold figure in the United States as a cockney Palmerston, but cabled the Cabinet with the astonishing news that he had agreed to a further reduction in supplies of grain for this country, on the understanding that the Americans would share the burden in Germany and India. The rate of extraction was to be stepped up to 95 per cent and bread rationing, which had never been known before, was now a distinct possibility.

Bread was actually more nutritious as the extraction rate increased. But the darker loaf was unpopular with a public for whom the snow-white slice was the ideal. Douglas Jay, who was then working as an economic assistant in the Prime Minister's office, explains:

> What it amounted to was that when we were faced in the first year after the war with actual famine in three places in particular, with Germany, India and Malaysia, which has a huge population, you could keep more people alive out of a given ton of wheat by raising the extraction rate from what I think it normally is, 60 per cent or 70 per cent, this is how the millers express it, to 95 per cent, with the limited amount of wheat we had in the world. That was done and I think as a result of that, probably famines in those areas were avoided.
>
> There was great opposition from the whole milling industry ... their doctrine was that white bread was better and everybody liked white bread more. Ernie Bevin held very strongly that the British working man liked white bread – he liked white bread himself and particularly disliked brown bread – and therefore he grumbled a great deal about the proposals, but of course Ernie Bevin, in the last resort, unlike some people, knew when to give way ... and so we got our 95 per cent extraction rate in the early months of 1946.

Also extracted was Sir Ben Smith, struck down by the complaints of housewives and the decision of Attlee to remove him. On 27 May 1946 Attlee appointed John Strachey in his place. Renowned as a leading marxist theoretician in the 1930s, Strachey had begun to have second thoughts by the outbreak of war. In September 1939 he sold his £1000 worth of Russian Five-Year Plan bonds, and reinvested in General Motors. Disillusioned with communism, he became a democratic socialist on the left of the party. But no doctrinaire calculations inspired his decision to ration bread: in this he was persuaded by his officials against his better judgement. On 27 June it was announced that with effect from 21 July adults would receive nine ounces of bread a week unless they were factory workers, in which case men would receive fifteen ounces and women eleven. Children, of course, were to receive lesser quantities.

A brief storm in a bread-bin ensued. The bakers protested against the extra paperwork involved in collecting and accounting for 'bread units' as bread coupons were called. The British Housewives' League, of which more will be said shortly, took to the warpath. The Conservative Party and press hung around Strachey's neck a garland of abuse, depicting him as the apotheosis of bungling and intrusive bureaucracy.

Bread rationing was probably unnecessary. The threat to grain supplies proved to be less severe than expected and, since the rations allowed proved adequate, there was little reduction in the consumption.

In August 1947 a sterling crisis resulting from the American loan agreement of 1945 shattered the authority of the government and led to a drastic reappraisal of economic policy.

Almost on cue, a saviour was found in the person of Sir Stafford Cripps. On 29 September 1947 Attlee appointed him to the new post of Minister of Economic Affairs and, following the unexpected resignation of Hugh Dalton on 13 November, Cripps became Chancellor of the Exchequer. In assuming overall responsibility for economic policy, Cripps also took on the job of explaining his policies to the public. The word 'austerity' had been introduced into general circulation by a Conservative President of the Board of Trade, Oliver Lyttelton, in 1941. Now it stuck to Cripps, a tall, gaunt Wykehamist, known to delight in a cold bath at five o'clock in the morning, sleeping only three hours a night, never touching alcohol, driven by an evangelical conscience. While announcing cuts in the standard of living, Cripps preached work and sacrifice as though they were spiritual ends in themselves – as indeed they were to him – rather than means of material enrichment. Cripps had a Christian moral authority that made his motives difficult to impugn, and a first-class intellect, prone to clever mistakes, devoted to the task of economic planning. One of the main thrusts of his policy was to save dollars by cutting the import programme, thus setting in motion an energetic search for substitute imports from within the sterling area.

On the 'kitchen front', as the Ministry of Food used to call it, the first consequence was further cuts in imports and hence in the butter and meat rations. On 10 November 1947 Strachey admitted in the House of Commons that as a result of the reductions the average daily intake of calories per head would fall to 2700, compared with a level of 3386 recommended by the British Medical Association in

1933. There was much alarmist talk in 1946–7, amplified by the Conservatives, of malnutrition. But an exhaustive inquiry by the British Medical Association drew the less dramatic conclusion that:

> Since 1939 the diet of the nation has, on average, deteriorated in variety and palatability, but . . . supplies of calories have been well maintained and those of most nutrients have increased. It is probable that changes in food supplies have affected differently the various classes in the population, consumption of many palatable foods increasing among the poorer sections and decreasing among the richer sections.[3]

The new pattern of stringency carried through into 1949. In May of that year, frustrated by the Crippsian regime and battered by the protests of housewives, John Strachey warned:

> Progress in improving supplies of rationed and points food since this government took office has been, on balance, non-existent. When the present government was elected, the meat ration was 1s. 2d. (it is now 10d.); the tea ration was 2½ oz. (it is now 2 oz.); the bacon ration was 3 oz. (it is now 2 oz.); the cheese ration was 2 oz. (we are only now restoring it to that level next week). Since 1945 the supply of attractive points foods, such as canned meat, canned salmon and canned fruit has vastly deteriorated. To set against these cuts, all that we have managed to do is to get some more sugar which has enabled us to increase the ration from 8 to 10 oz. and to deration jam and sweets. We have also increased the fat ration from 7 to 9 oz., and in addition there has been a slow improvement in the supplies of milk, eggs, and some unrationed foods.[4]

The Crippsian era coincided with the appearance in Britain of whalemeat and snoek. Neither of these memorable dishes can be laid directly at Sir Stafford Cripps's door, for whalemeat preceded him and snoek was a brainwave of the Ministry of Food. But whalemeat and snoek fitted well with the Crippsian scheme of things.

Whalemeat was introduced because of a delay in negotiations with Argentina over the import of meat and had the advantage that, coming from South Africa, it could be paid for in sterling instead of dollars. Imported in ninety-ton carcasses on board refrigerated ships, it proved to be cheap and acceptable, if not exactly popular.

Professor Magnus Pyke was Principal Scientific Officer at the Ministry of Food when whalemeat was introduced:

They bought some whalemeat to the UK and butchered it and I got a lovely slab of about six pounds of whale steak ... we cut it off and we grilled it and when we served it out and we looked at this ... our mouths were drooling [at this] lovely chump of juicy steak. You put it in your mouth and you'd start biting it and it tasted like steak, and then as you went on biting it the taste of steak was suddenly overcome by a strong flavour of – cod-liver oil.

As a housewife, Mrs Vera Mather tried whalemeat but regretted the experiment:

The only thing I can say about whalemeat is that there was a lot of it and it was very smelly, terribly smelly and it didn't taste like anything, it was neither fish nor meat. I think we had it once in our house but you could smell it right through the house for the whole week afterwards.

Whalemeat received a mixed press but was tolerated for two or three years for want of anything better. Snoek, first introduced in May 1948, was also an import from South Africa, but never won favour. As Magnus Pyke explains: 'If you analyse it it was full of protein, it was a highly nourishing food, but it was rather salty and rank in flavour and the British public did not take to it at all.'

Mrs Vera Mather comments:

I never tried snoek, it was the label on the tin that did it, with this horrible blue fish – it was a most hideous fish and I wouldn't eat it, none of my family would, we just refused to try it, but a lot of people did eat it. I can't say they enjoyed it, but they did eat it.

Snoek was a mistake, but one that added to the gaiety of nations. Hampered by its funny foreign name and ugly mug, it was well worth importing as an infallible source of humour. The Ministry of Food's recipe for 'snoek piquante', featuring four spring onions and two teaspoons of syrup, was a master-stroke and the celebrated essay of the same title, by Susan Wilson, is not to be missed.[5]

Snoek was famous but another innovation, horsemeat, led a shadowy existence. Movietone News told cinema audiences in 1948 that two million people a week were eating horsemeat, but only half of them realised it. One who did realise was Terry Alford, who remembers buying some:

My mother sent me one day to queue up for some meat and it wasn't at the normal butcher's shop ... it was near where I used to get the coal, and I was queuing there and this lorry pulled up and out the back there was all this blood and these horse carcasses, and they was sort of unceremoniously thrown off this lorry into this yard where a man started cutting them up and weighing them into sections and I was sort of pushed forward ... I had to ask for a piece of steak and he carved off a piece of this horsemeat and put it in newspaper and just dumped it into this shopping bag and I took it home.

While rationing may have been popular in principle as the guarantee of fair shares for all, there is much to show that housewives in general complained loud and long about queues, cuts in the ration, mediocre food, shortages, and the inferior quality of essential items such as children's clothes. *Picture Post*, one of the government's best friends in Fleet Street, none the less ran in April 1947 a scathing article by Anne Scott-James on the economic crisis as the 'woman in the home' saw it. The housewife, she wrote, did not blame the Labour government, but the mysterious body of officials 'from the booby at the Board of Trade who says there is no pram shortage to the snappy spinster at the Food Office'.[6] The government's own Central Office of Information produced in 1948 a fictionalised documentary film, 'What A Life', in which a complaining wife is seen dumping in front of her long-suffering husband a plate containing a morsel of bacon, with the words, 'And you'd better enjoy it, that's your bacon ration for the week.'

One of the most curious phenomena of the post-war years was the eruption of an organised protest movement of housewives: the British Housewives' League. The League has generally been dismissed as a front organisation for the Conservative Party, which to a great extent it became. But it started as a spontaneous women's movement concerned with the grievances of the housewife, and its feminism was perfectly genuine.

In the course of a long history, feminism has taken many forms, some of them markedly conservative. When school meals were first introduced into Edwardian Britain, they were often resisted by working-class wives as undermining their role within the home. In the 1920s, Jane Lewis tells us, the Mothers' League 'opposed all intervention in the working-class home on the grounds that it threatened to undermine the working-class wife's responsibility for the welfare of her family, and reduce her to a servant and a drudge'.[7] During the Second World War, as was seen in the previous chapter, the family became increasingly dependent on the State, and its daily life subject to the regulation of officials. But this time the expansion of social welfare proved very acceptable to working-class mothers, and for the time being rationing, too, was popular as a means of ensuring a fair distribution of goods. Lord Woolton, the wartime Minister of Food, was an outstanding success as the human face of State control.

But with the end of the war, and still more as the regime of iron rations tightened, a reaction began to set in. In June 1945, Mrs Irene Lovelock, a parson's wife from Selhurst in Kent, spent a long cold morning in the rain, queuing for food in the company of old women and mothers with babies in prams. Returning home in a state of anger at the ordeals women had to endure, she persuaded her husband to lend her the church hall for a protest meeting. Though she had never addressed a public meeting before, she was soon in full flow, pouring out the grievances of women against shopkeepers. A paragraph in the local newspaper released a spate of publicity and letters of support. The League itself was founded on 18 July 1945, as a specifically non-party organisation, before the result of the general election was known.[8]

For the first few months there were only a few hundred members of the League and it concentrated on a campaign against queuing, with the shopkeeper as main villain of the peace. According to Mrs June MacDonald, an early member:

> Women were very cross, they were very cross with how they were being treated by shopkeepers. They'd had a very raw deal during the war, there was a great deal of queuing and some shopkeepers such as fishmongers had made a habit of expecting women to queue up for at least an hour before they'd even open the door and until they'd seen a nice long queue down the pavement, they wouldn't open up and then after half an hour they'd say 'No more' and bang the shutters down again, and after five or six years women were very fed up with that sort of thing, we expected that to end.

A turning-point in the League's history occurred in February 1946 when the unfortunate Minister of Food, Sir Ben Smith, decided to withdraw supplies of dried egg from the housewife, reserving them for schools and institutions. Dried egg was a kitchen stand-by of great versatility, so the move was extremely unpopular with housewives. Worse, the announcement foreshadowed other cuts in the ration. Thousands of housewives joined the League and a mass meeting was held at Livingstone Hall in Westminster. Soon afterwards, the Minister reversed his policy and restored the supply of dried egg.

No doubt the complaints of housewives reached the government through a number of channels, including the Labour Party, but the Housewives' League publicised the issues and led the campaign. It may well have been their agitation that persuaded Attlee to sack Smith and replace him with Strachey. The introduction of bread rationing, of course, was another rallying-point for protest. By this time the character of the League had clarified into a movement demanding a reduction in State control over the family. Mrs Mary Blakey, who was one of the first to respond to an appeal by Mrs Lovelock in the press, and went on to set up a branch in her own district of Great Dunmow, explains:

> Irene Lovelock was quite certain that the family and the housewife was very badly done to ... and the family was the backbone of the country and that something had to be done, to improve conditions of the housewife and the family ... in the home. Not as, for instance, was done with milk. Children got milk at school. But as soon as the holidays began they didn't get the third of a pint of milk delivered at home, it was as though you could get things via institutions but not via your father and mother ... So it was more and better food in the home, more and better clothes, more and better homes.
>
> There was a tremendous amount of government interference. It ran down to all kinds of domestic details. It was very irksome. Endless forms, endless filling in of forms, almost for everything. You had bread tickets, food tickets, clothes tickets, petrol tickets, coal tickets, coal was rationed ...
>
> And when food came into the home, it came in for the well-being of the family and it was said by some government officials that they couldn't trust mothers to give it to the children. Well if you can't trust mothers, to give milk to the children, you can't trust mothers ... Very unpleasant. My mother used to say there were snoopers everywhere and there was a ticket or docket for everything.

Mrs Blakey sturdily maintains that the League was and remains (for it still exists) non-party and technically this was so. But there was a very close match between this kind of feminism and the Conservative attack on socialism and controls. Though there were groups in other parts of the country, the backbone of the League consisted of middle-class women from London and the Home Counties. One may guess that they were the pillars of local charity and voluntary effort. With her staunch conviction that the interests of the patriotic middle class were being sacrificed for the benefit of feckless elements of the population, Mrs Lovelock – who had actually voted Labour in 1945 – was one of nature's conservatives.

While officially the League retained a non-party character, Mrs Lovelock allowed it to be blatantly exploited by the Conservative press. In February 1946 she agreed to write a series of articles for the *Sunday Graphic*, a paper belonging to the Kemsley group and firmly in the Tory camp. Shortly afterwards the League was invaded by a crusading Fleet Street journalist, Dorothy Crisp, an ultra-patriot and individualist whose opinions were well to the right of Winston Churchill. In March 1947 she was elected Chairman of the League. While the League had originally been formed with immediate practical grievances in mind, it was now a pressure-group for doctrinaire and somewhat paranoid libertarianism. Irrational fears are a recurrent element in politics and one we often pass over in retrospect. In the mid-1930s, for example, there was a genuine fear on the Left that the National government intended to introduce fascism in Britain. Similarly, there were people who feared after 1945 that the trend of events was towards a permanent socialist dictatorship with rationing and other controls maintained, not for any pragmatic purpose, but for the sake of levelling and liquidating the middle classes.

The growing overlap between the interests of the League and those of the Opposition was impossible to disguise. Dorothy Crisp, whose ambition was to become the first woman prime minister, shared platforms with leading Tory politicians. Financial assistance was received from the Road Haulage Association, a body campaigning against nationalisation and not known for its commitment to the rights of women. Local Conservative Party associations began to make applications for their women members to join *en bloc*. The drift of events prompted Mrs June MacDonald, a member of the Labour Party, to resign, as she explains:

At the time it was set up there was no question of us attacking the government as such, we were campaigning for more food on the rations and for more courtesy and generally better attention in the shops ... after about eighteen months I felt that certain sections of the Conservative press were beginning to take over the Housewives' League and using it in a way that I didn't feel happy about ... I resigned at that time. Not because I didn't like Mrs Lovelock, but I felt she had allowed the League to be used in a way that I wasn't happy about.

Though the Conservatives did exploit the League, a strand of authentic feminism remained. Paradoxically, the League propelled women out of the home and into public life. In order to defend their traditional role in the home, they had to leave the kitchen and attend a meeting or demonstration instead. The contradiction is writ large in one of the stated aims of the League: 'To encourage housewives to take their place as such as MPs, and Local Government Councillors, and representatives on other administrative bodies.' Mrs Mary Blakey, who describes herself as 'not a very demonstrative sort of woman', nevertheless took part in demonstrations. She recalls parading up and down Whitehall

> ... with a tray with a week's rations on it, except for meat – it was very hot weather and the meat would have turned ...
>
> I had a little glass pot with tea in it and I had a little brass pot with a week's sugar in it ... The fat was difficult to put in anything in hot weather, so I had the papers from butter and margarine and lard with small blocks and it was written on top how many ounces there were. The blocks were the size of the ration. And there was a very unfortunate piece of bacon that got very curly as the day went on, and then an indication as to nine pennyworth or ten pennyworth of meat, whatever it was ... There were some Australians there and some foreigners from across the Channel – they were French I think – and they were quite astonished, they couldn't believe it.

The Housewives' League tried to relieve austerity by legal and constitutional methods. Perhaps this was an approach characteristic of women who obeyed the rules. For there was an alternative method of getting round the problem. Other women, and of course men too, evaded rationing by resorting to the black market.

The black market was the inevitable consequence of the direct regulation of the production, distribution and price of goods by the State. From the consumer's point of view, it served two main purposes. The first was to supplement the quantities laid down by rationing, and the second was to alleviate the shortages of unrationed goods. In popular memory the black market is usually equated with activities of the 'spiv', a petty criminal with a barrow or suitcase of goods selling direct to the public. This may well have been the most common type of black market transaction but there were other ramifications. Often the spiv would be selling to a middle man: a shopkeeper or restaurateur. Sometimes he would be trading ration coupons rather than stolen goods. Bought illegally from members of the public, who were forbidden to sell their coupons, they could be resold to retailers who used them to obtain extra supplies. Another category of black market offence was the sale of legally obtained goods at an illegal price. During and immediately after the war the State specified not only the quality but the price of many consumer goods, as in the case of utility furniture. Wholesalers and retailers were sometimes tempted to charge their customers two or three times the fixed price.

According to Edward Smithies, a historian of the illegal economy, the black market first started up in 1941–2, appearing not only in London and other big cities, but also in market towns within easy reach of the urban areas. Thus Romford in Essex became a focus for the illicit trade in food and clothes. The goods were supplied from three main sources: 'theft and pilfering; illicit sales of agricultural produce by farmers and smallholders; and illicit manufacturing'.[9] Until June 1944 the principal suppliers of stolen goods were the personnel of US military bases; in peacetime a profitable sideline developed in smuggling from the continent.

It was a criminal offence, punishable by fine or imprisonment, to evade the regulations, and we know that in 1947, for example, 18,863 people in England and Wales were found guilty of offences under the regulations. But it is a certainty that the great majority of illegal transactions went unrecorded, so the full and precise extent of the black market is impossible to gauge.

A committee of inquiry into the evasion of petrol rationing estimated that during 1947 some 47 million gallons, or 10 per cent of total consumption by motorists, was traded on the black market. But, Smithies points out, the AA and RAC rejected the estimate and argued that the true figure was over 30 per cent.[10]

The evidence from the court cases cited by Smithies leaves the impression that most black market crime was on a relatively small scale. In 1947 a number of cases in north London involved, respectively, 'sixty pairs of socks, thirty-five tablets of soap, a single rabbit, six watches, eighty-one bottles of spirits, 130 pairs of nylons'.[11] Valentine Botwright was a policeman on duty in the Tower Bridge area, which covered parts of Southwark and Bermondsey. He recalls that it was a part of his duty to stop people in the streets and charge those found in possession of stolen foodstuffs:

> Immediately after the war, over and above normal police duty, we had a number of petty offences mainly concerned with the question of food rationing ... People had been short of certain commodities over the years and this, I think, tempted them to steal, possibly from their employers, from local warehouses, and possibly from hotels and food establishments ... The police as you may know have powers under the Metropolitan Police Act to stop and detain anyone who you may think suspect of being in possession of property stolen or unlawfully obtained ... Well, we wouldn't stop people at random, but where we had reasonable suspicion ... we'd stop the person concerned and if they had a parcel of some kind we'd politely ask them as to what they were carrying and you'd be surprised if you knew what we would find, it might be a parcel of food, or a leg of lamb ...

As Botwright's recollection suggests, there was a flourishing black market in the meat trade. Of the two markets in which farmers could sell livestock, one was under strict surveillance but the other was open to shady dealing. Livestock that was fat and ready for slaughter had to be sold direct to the Ministry of Food, whose officials paid a controlled price based on quality and the weight of the carcass. But stock for rearing or breeding went to auction at the stores market for sale to the highest bidder. There was little to prevent black market traders from stepping in, so much so that by the end of 1947 the Ministry of Food had called in the CID to assist in the quest for the vanishing pig.

The other staple of the black market was clothing, where it was usually quite basic items that were in demand. An eager customer was Mrs Clare Bond of Leeds, whose recollections, though dating back to the war, hold good for the post-war scene:

> You had the black market of food, you had the black market of clothes. Now then I found the clothing was invaluable, because you only sort of had a short supply of clothing coupons ... You could go in a public house for a drink, and somebody would ask you if you wanted to buy coupons. They'd charge you ten shillings, which was expensive, considering the wages were 31s. 6d. a week, ten shillings was a third of a working week. And then ... after about four, six

months of the clothing rationing coming in, men came round
to the door ... and they had cases full of clothes – 'Would
you like this, would you like that, would you like the other?'
Underwear was five shillings and it was mainly camiknickers,
those were the style then, so you queried, 'Well how am I
going to manage to pay for this type of thing?' So he said,
'Look, just pick what you want, and we'll fix a rate that you
can afford.' Well, at the time I could afford 1s. 6d. a week. So
for this 1s. 6d. I got three dresses, I got two camiknickers and
half a dozen pair of stockings, and no coupons ... And so, all
through the war I was kept supplied with all dresses that came
into fashion, and then it came we got coats, and then it led up
to footwear as well.

While many of the older generation freely recall the purchases
they made on the black market, it is no surprise that former spivs are
reluctant to identify themselves. But John Basnett, later well known
as a jazz trumpeter, did come forward with vivid autobiographical
testimony. He made his living in and around Stockport, Lancashire:

There's two ways of looking at a spiv. I wasn't a big spiv, I
was a very little spiv. A big spiv was someone who sold things
in thousands and didn't necessarily look like a spiv ... I
myself was more in love with the image of the spiv than
actually the spiv itself. The image of the spiv to me was
someone who patterned himself in dress on the American
gangster of the 1930s, which meant the big, wide-shouldered
suits and wide lapels, double-breasted mainly, big wide
bottoms, the two-toned shoes etc., etc.

Basnett's short life as a spiv began when he was demobbed from
the Army in 1948 and sold his demob suit and clothing coupons. All
sorts of items passed through his hands from shirts to hot-water
bottles and, on one occasion, two giant cheeses which he and a friend
stole from a dairy and lobbed over a wall to female accomplices who
stowed them away in a pram. Suspecting Basnett and his friend, the
police searched both their homes but failed to locate the cheeses,
which were then whisked away in a van and sold for £20.

For his main line of business, Basnett was indebted to clothes
rationing:

I found a way that I could buy clothing coupons, probably
from people who used to like a drink, they probably had
families, in particular women who used to go for a drink at

lunchtimes in the pub. You'd get talking to them and ask if they had any clothing coupons to sell and a lot of them had. I used to buy them off these women for sixpence or a shilling each and I had a contact in some of the better class districts and I used to sell them to people for three shillings and three and six. That lasted quite a while, twelve to eighteen months, and I made a good living out of that.

It was only occasionally that the police managed to penetrate the conspiracy of silence and catch someone in the act. One such episode is remembered by Valentine Botwright:

I can remember on one occasion seeing a woman carrying a rather bulky parcel about five o'clock in the evening and for certain reasons my suspicions were aroused and I stopped and asked her what she was carrying and she told me she was carrying some hats. This aroused my curiosity and she unfolded this parcel and I saw the most beautiful ladies' hats, each one worth several guineas a piece, and when I asked her where she got them from, she said she'd bought them in a market. I asked her what market, she was rather hesitant about that ... and she told me a certain market I knew was closed on that particular day. Her explanation was completely unsatisfactory which gave me a power to detain her, and subsequent inquiries revealed that she was a cleaner for showrooms in the West End, and she had been systematically stealing one or two hats every day. She had something like forty or fifty hats in her house, in those days worth several hundreds of pounds, and she was going round public houses selling them, making a living that way.

For the first three years after the war there was a thriving black market in petrol. The basic petrol ration, to which every private motorist was entitled, was intended to allow so many miles of motoring per month, and by August 1946 the allowance was 270 miles, or 3240 miles per annum. As this was less than half the average annual mileage of the private motorist before the war, the demand sprang up for a gallon or two on the side. Over and above the standard ration, commercial users were entitled to a supplement related to their particular needs. By one means or another, much of the petrol allocated for business use found its way into the tanks of private motorists. Another dodge was to employ a commercial vehicle for a personal trip, as Valentine Botwright describes:

At that time it was an offence to use petrol for private purposes if the petrol had been allocated for trades and commercial reasons. And frequently we'd see commercial vehicles being driven, possibly on a Sunday when it was obviously suspect. And I can remember on one occasion stopping a van travelling along the Old Kent Road towards South London and, suspecting that an offence had been committed, I asked the driver, 'Where do you come from, for what purposes are you on the road, where are you going to?' And he told me he was going to buy some antiques at an antique market. I then went to the back of the van where I saw it was filled with obvious relatives. The first person, I said to him, 'Where are you going to?' He looked me up and down in obvious astonishment and glanced at the other members and said, 'Well, we're all going to Ramsgate aren't we?' And of course there we were able to prove an offence of misuse of petrol.

In August 1947, the government announced the abolition of the basic petrol ration as a measure to save dollar imports. The Conservative Party denounced the decision as another calculated blow against the middle classes, who still formed the core of Britain's two million motorists. (As motor-cyclists also lost their ration, the accusation was wide of the mark.) In June 1948, the ration was restored at a rate of ninety miles a month and action taken to thwart the black marketeers. Henceforth petrol for commercial purposes was to be dyed red, and any private motorist discovered with red petrol in his tank was deemed to have committed an offence. The Opposition continued to allege that the government was running a vendetta against the private motorist, but the black market at least was effectively suppressed.

The word 'spiv' had tolerant and humorous overtones. While there were parts of the Continent where illegal trading overrode rationing and enabled the wealthy to exploit the poor, in Britain the black market seems to have been a genuinely popular institution for bending the rules without breaking the system. As Terry Alford remarks:

To me, you know, the spivs was just ordinary people going round wheeling and dealing and selling what they could. And there was always someone selling something, and very often I used to go round to a lady's house and as soon as she knew it was safe, out would come something from her cupboard, a few bags of sugar or some tea and a little deal would be arranged and off we'd go with whatever we could.

By comparison with the organised crime of today, the black market had a period innocence. In the 1940s, the police were more likely to be on the trail of a hidden store of gelatine than of heroin or cocaine. On 14 May 1946, the *Daily Express* reported that detectives had discovered a ton of gelatine in the back room of a hotel in Barnsley. A gang of men and women had been secretly manufacturing hundreds of thousands of illegal jellies for sale in the north of England.

Women may have emerged from war industry and the services with a greater sense of independence, and full employment encouraged a higher proportion of married women to go out to work, but otherwise the division of labour between the sexes was as sharply defined as ever. Short of clothes, and short of consumer goods for the home, women were making do, but impatient as the years passed to restore the female status quo. At the end of the war, many items of clothing for women were in short supply, and women went to great lengths to make up for the gaps in their wardrobe. Mrs Vera Mather recalls:

> It was terribly difficult to get stockings. We didn't have nylons then, they were rayon or lisle and you'd kind of listen in to the grapevine, who was having stockings delivered that week, and you just formed a queue ... often you'd just go without stockings or else, like I did and plenty others of my age, we wore liquid leg-make-up and we'd get a friend to draw a black line up the back of our legs and a heel, you know, pretending it was a stocking ... and if you couldn't get liquid leg-make-up which sometimes you couldn't ... my friends and I would have wet sand. We'd wet our hands and get a handful of sand and rub it over our legs and draw the line up just the same, you know, and it coloured it like a tanny colour. The only thing was that everything you touched with your legs ... rubbed the tan off and I remember going dancing and dancing with boys and they had dark suits on and they ended up wondering where this colour had come from down the front of their trousers ...

The one occasion on which women still felt justified in insisting on a touch of authentic luxury was their wedding day, but would-be brides were hard put to it to achieve the desired effect. Mrs Vera Mather recalls her efforts to find a long dress for her wedding in 1947:

> I, like every girl, had planned to have a white wedding, a wreath and veil and all the trimmings, and I tried for weeks. I took buses and trains in towns trying to get a dress and I think I learned a new word, and that was 'quota'. You'd go to a shop, you see, and they'd say, 'Sorry, my quota's gone,' or 'Sorry, my quota doesn't come till next week' ... and I think I'd resigned myself, very disappointed, to having a short wedding dress and a friend of mine who worked in Liverpool said, 'Oh, such-and-such a store's had a delivery,' so I took the day off work the next day and went to Liverpool ... and all they had left was one pink wedding dress ... I could have wept because I'd never wore pink in my life and my parents were rather old-fashioned and to wear anything but white suggested that you were, well, not a very good person ... My father, as soon as he saw it [said], 'What on earth will the neighbours say? A pink wedding dress?'

At the end of the war, women's clothes were plain and military in style, with skirts raised to an inch or two below the knee in order to conserve cloth. But in February 1947 a revolt began when the Parisian fashion designer Christian Dior launched his first-ever collection. The New Look lengthened the skirt to the ankle and restored pleats, bows and leg-of-mutton shoulders, recreating the romantic image of the society lady of *la belle époque*. In Britain the new fashion was roundly condemned at first as socially frivolous and a wicked waste of scarce cloth. A Labour MP, Mrs Ridealgh, put the feminist case against:

> Can anyone imagine the average housewife and business-woman dressed in bustles and long skirts carrying on their varied jobs, running for buses and crowding into tubes and trains? The idea is ludicrous. Women today are taking a larger part in the happenings of the world and the New Look is too reminiscent of a caged bird's attitude.[12]

Defying the critics, one or two women began to appear in the New Look and over the next twelve months or so glamour worked its subversive way. The *Daily Herald*, a bastion of the Transport House Look, published photographs of the new fashions, and Princess Elizabeth (having amassed the appropriate number of clothing coupons) opted for a calf-length trousseau for her marriage to Prince

Philip on 20 November 1947. The resistance of women in Britain was crumbling. Mrs June MacDonald comments:

> We were very cross about it, because there was Christian Dior, lowering the hemlines almost to the ankle with enormously full skirts and little slim tops like this and nothing that we had in the cupboard was any longer in fashion and an awful lot of us said, 'Oh we can't afford it, and we can't buy it,' but of course we did.

Few British males had any need of finery. But one exception was James Frere, a youthful country gentleman and lover of tradition somewhat out of place in post-war London. Frere managed to find the perfect niche for himself as Bluemantle Pursuivant at the Royal College of Arms. But next came the problem of obtaining the appropriate uniform:

> It wasn't easy, bearing in mind that there were restrictions on clothing immediately after the war and that the system of clothing coupons was still in force, so I had to go around to friends and relations and ask them whether they would donate some of their coupons ... the uniform of course when I had it made, was beautifully embroidered with gold oak leaves and cost a great deal of money, some £400 – a similar one these days would cost over £2000 ...

Even in court circles, the provision of ceremonial dress was hampered by shortages, as Frere explains:

> For the first service of the Order of the Garter after the war, there were five new knights who'd been appointed and who were to be installed at Windsor Castle and they were Lords Addison, Alanbrooke, Alexander of Tunis, Portal of Hungerford and Montgomery of Alamein, and again this business of clothing coupons and clothing restrictions was a difficulty, because the Knights of the Garter amongst other things wear large black velvet hats with white ostrich plumes and Ede and Ravenscroft, who are the Royal Robemakers, only had enough black velvet to make one hat for the five that were needed and they were at their wits' ends to know where to get material with the restrictions. But as luck would have it, I had a very magnificent black velvet skirt which had belonged to my great-grandmother and I offered that to them. They accepted it with alacrity and made the four extra

hats for the Knights of the Garter, and ever after that, when one looked at the Knights, one wondered which of the five were wearing one's great-grandmother's skirt on their heads.

For court and country alike, the age of rationing and austerity lasted a long time. If it got into its stride about 1941, it still had not disappeared by 1951. Stung by the complaints of the housewives, and goaded by the Opposition, ministers such as John Strachey, the Minister of Food, and Harold Wilson, who succeeded Cripps as President of the Board of Trade in September 1947, were keen to relax consumer controls as soon as market conditions allowed. The Conservative Party under the erratic leadership of Churchill had been campaigning vigorously over such issues ever since the introduction of bread rationing. While too prudent to claim that rationing could be abolished at a stroke, they implied that various unspecified restrictions could be abolished as free enterprise gradually replaced State control. As Lord Woolton, the party chairman, said in a Conservative Party film, 'The Socialists do not realise that every piece of rationing is an admission of failure. I would take a few risks and allow some items off the ration.' Churchill summed up the party line in the phrase, 'Set the People Free.'

As was pointed out earlier on, the Labour government never intended to retain wartime controls for their own sake. But they might have been kept on longer but for the groundswell of discontent. From 1949 onwards the government was resolved to abandon controls over producers and consumers as quickly as economic circumstances permitted. Bread rationing had already been abandoned in July 1948 with no ill effects. In April 1949 sweets and chocolates were taken off the ration, but too fast: supplies ran out and rationing had to be reimposed in August. After a pause the momentum resumed. On 5 November 1949 Harold Wilson pointed the way ahead when he announced a 'bonfire of controls', including the abolition of clothes rationing.

It is often supposed that Labour's association with rationing damaged the party, but if so the damage was far from spectacular. When the government went to the polls in February 1950, the average vote per candidate was down from 50·4 per cent in 1945 to 45·7 per cent. The average Conservative vote was up from 40·1 per cent to 43·7 per cent. Hardly an electoral earthquake but, given the vagaries of the representative system, enough to strip Labour down to a majority of only five seats in the House of Commons. On their return to power, Labour resumed the process of decontrol. Petrol rationing and points rationing, which still covered a vast range of canned goods, were ended in the spring of 1950. When the Conservatives came to power in October 1951 they made little change at first, recognising that for the time being the shortage of supplies necessitated a continuation of the rationing of basic foods. In October 1952 tea was derationed and, one by one, the other staples followed, but it was not until 1954 that food rationing finally came to an end, with meat the last item to be returned to the free market.

The trend towards a consumer society, arrested since 1940, accelerated once more. Motor cars, televisions, record-players, bedroom suites and fridges, wondrous toys and sweets for children, pop records for adolescents, flooded into the showrooms and supermarkets. But for many of those who had lived through the scarcities of the 1940s and, perhaps, the hardships of the 1930s as well, making do had become a way of life. The consumer boom, with its throwaway style and confidence in good times to come, never eradicated a root sense of caution and thrift. As Mrs Vera Mather comments:

> It makes you very, very careful and appreciate what you have got. You don't take things for granted ... the little luxuries that you can get if you can afford them – you do get them because you've not had them, you feel as though you've been deprived of them ... but on the whole I tend to hoard things, you know, even though they're past wearing or really old-fashioned, or shoes that you will probably never wear again. You're frightened of throwing them away in case you need them.

3

A HOME OF OUR OWN

In the autumn of 1940 the Minister of Food, Lord Woolton, made a tour of local Food Offices in the blitzed areas of the East End of London. He was full of admiration for the way in which his officials, and still more the local people bombed out of their homes, were coping. But the spectacle of street after street of damaged or ruined housing prompted forebodings about the future. He wrote in his diary:

> We are all telling them now that they are heroes for the way in which they are standing up to the strain of the mighty bombardment – and it's true. I think they will keep on being heroes, but when the war is over they will demand the rewards of heroism: they will expect to get them very soon and no power on earth will be able to rebuild the homes at the speed that will be necessary. I'm afraid there will be grave discontent. I don't believe the government machine will be capable of doing the rebuilding or of handing out the compensation that will be due to landlords and by means of which alone they will be able to finance the rebuilding.
>
> I think there's going to be grave trouble, and the danger is that if the machine of government which can spend money so recklessly in engaging in war, fails to be equally reckless in rebuilding, there will be both the tendency and the excuse for revolution.[1]

Like other prophets writing at the height of the Blitz, Woolton tended to err on the side of the apocalyptic. But otherwise his forecasts proved to be close to the mark. At the end of the war the people and the politicians did indeed inherit an acute housing crisis, to which there was no immediate solution. So great was the unfulfilled demand for housing that during the summer of 1946 about 40,000 people, taking the law into their own hands, set up home in disused service camps up and down the country.

The squatters' movement, having captured the headlines for a couple of months or so, quickly died down, and has often been written off as a mere flash in the pan. Certainly it was a long way from Woolton's revolution. The occupation of the camps had no subversive or political intent but was only another means of 'making do', sympathetically received by Government and Opposition alike. But as in the very different examples of the Housewives' League or the black market, the squatters' movement showed popular pressures at work. The post-war housing problem was only due in part to a numerical shortage of houses. It was the popular belief that the State must provide that turned a shortage into a crisis.

Very few houses were built during the war. Two-thirds of the labour force in the building trades were in the armed forces and the rest were reserved for essential war work. War industry and the services had the first claim on materials, and a stringent system of building licences virtually closed down the private sector. Meanwhile, the existing housing stock deteriorated for lack of maintenance. To exacerbate the shortage, a wartime boom in the birth rate increased the population by a million, adding hundreds of thousands of young couples with children to the potential waiting-list for homes.

All this on top of the havoc wrought by the *Luftwaffe*, and the V1 and V2 flying bombs. 'Estimates suggest', writes John R. Short, 'that almost half a million dwellings were either destroyed or made completely uninhabitable and a further quarter of a million were severely damaged.'[2] Hurling moral defiance in the teeth of the enemy, politicians and the press promised, like Lloyd George in 1918, a land fit for heroes to live in. 'Most painful is the number of small houses inhabited by working folk which has been destroyed,' Churchill told the House of Commons on 8 October 1940. 'We will rebuild them, more to our credit than some of them were before. London, Liverpool, Manchester, Birmingham may have much more to suffer, but they will rise from their ruins, more healthy and I hope, more beautiful.'

How many new houses would be needed after the war? A precise estimate was impossible, since no reliable figures had been compiled of the number of separate families already in existence, and future trends in marriage and the birth rate were a mystery. The White Paper of March 1945 trailed a figure of three to four million houses to be built over a period of ten or twelve years. The most definite pledge, and even that was blurred, was that 300,000 new houses would be built or building by the end of the second year after the war.

1   A prisoner of war returns home, 1945

2-6 *far left*, Clothing coupons; *left*, Wartime fashions; *opposite below*, The demob suit, 1945; *right*, Arthur Egerton-Savory tries on his demob suit, 1946; *below*, Municipal feeding at the Bethnal Green Museum

7–9 *above*, J. B. Priestley meets the people, 1941; *below left*, Luton Hoo, 1946: the army's university prepares soldiers for civilian life; *below right*, Class held by the Army Bureau for Current Affairs

10   Churchill's victory tour, 1945

11–13   *above left*, Sir Richard Acland, founder of the Common Wealth
Party; *above right*, Soldiers in the Middle East prepare to vote, 1945; *below*,
The Labour government assembles, 1945

TAXPAYER: "ONLY YESTERDAY, AT TEA, THE CHANCELLOR SAID TO ME,
I WONDER WHAT IT FEELS LIKE TO BE POOR?"

(From the popular old song.)

24th August, 1945

14 Peacetime austerity sets in
15 John Strachey, the new Minister of Food, 1946

16   A butcher's shop in Birmingham, 1949
17   A new delicacy, 1947

18 The leaders of the Housewives' League, 1946, *left to right*, Mrs June MacDonald, secretary, Mrs Lovelock, chairman and Mrs Landeau, vice-chairman

19–20   Mass meetings of the Housewives' League, February 1946: *above*, Teresa Billington Greig, a former suffragette makes her protest; *below*, banners and slogans

21–3   *right*, Spiv selling nylons on
the black market; *below*, Last year's
dress gets a new length, 1948

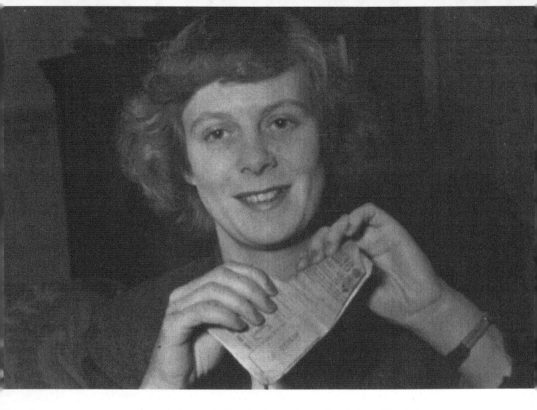

24 Tearing up a clothes ration book: Mrs Mary Wilson, the wife of the President of the Board of Trade, Harold Wilson, in March 1949

25 'Everything coupon-free', March 1949

26　The housing problem according to *Punch*, 1945

27 The consequences of the Blitz, 1940

28 Squatters move into an army camp at Crayford, Kent, 1946

29–30 The unsolved housing problem, 1949: *above*, Hermitage Buildings near the Pool of London; *below*, The private sector: Jubilee Buildings, Wapping

31 An aluminium prefab leaving a former aircraft factory, 1946
32 A prizewinning prefab garden, Camberwell, 1948

Yet the aims of housing policy were clear enough. To complete the programme of slum clearance begun in the 1930s; to rebuild the blitzed areas; to renovate and convert old housing stock; to ensure, in fact, as the government promised, a separate home for every family. Nor was a sense of urgency lacking. During the last fifteen months of the war there was a big push on the housing front. The highest priority was given to repairs. The decision was taken to go ahead with the production of temporary, prefabricated houses, better known as 'prefabs'. Many were manufactured by the conversion of the production lines in aircraft factories and by the end of the war 150,000 were on order. The only gap in the preparations was the most important: there was no plan for the efficient organisation of a housing drive.

In the general election campaign of 1945 all parties promised to tackle the housing problem, and for the Labour Party Ernest Bevin rashly promised, 'Five million homes in quick time'. But in the opening stages of the Labour government, housing threatened to become one of the major blots on its record.

Housing was the responsibility of the Ministry of Health. Attlee, in forming his Cabinet, took a gamble by entrusting the Ministry to Aneurin Bevan. Bevan, an exuberant working-class socialist and Welsh rhetorician, was fabled for his class-conscious 'extremism'. A genius of parliamentary debate, he was as yet untried in the responsibilities of office. In the Conservative Party, where fear and loathing of him ran high, his failures and mistakes were awaited with eager anticipation. During his first eighteen months or so at the Ministry of Health, so little progress was made in relieving the housing shortage that it began to look as though Bevan's head would have to roll.

With families clamouring for homes, Bevan's first line of defence was to fall back on short-term expedients. Damaged buildings were patched up. Local authorities were instructed to take over unoccupied accommodation. And much though he disliked prefabs as inferior substitutes for proper housing, referring to them in private as 'rabbit hutches', he ordered production to continue. By 1948 nearly 125,000 had been assembled.

The prefab turned out to be remarkably popular, due perhaps to the high quality of the interior fittings, and the cottage garden attached. Mr Joe Linsell, who in 1984 was still living in the prefab he was allocated in 1947, had nothing but praise for its comfort and convenience. At the end of the war he and his wife Mary and two children were living in a single room at the home of his wife's mother.

Having taken his case to the London County Council he received a fortnight later a letter inviting him and his wife to view a prefab in Royal Street. He takes up the story:

> After we looked round Mary was worried, and meself – would it be our luck to get one? When we came on the Friday, there was the council people outside with a table, there was nine families lining up. 'Course, Mary's got my hand and says, 'Oh, there's only eight prefabs.' 'Course, well, someone was going to be unlucky and as number two went, then number three, number four, so the tension was getting worse, but when it came to number eight he called my name to the table, I said, 'Yes I'll have it' ... And of course we took it and we moved in a week after but I did feel sorry for the person who was left out and she even cried. But it's the happiest day that ever happened.

Later the council tried on four different occasions to move the Linsells but each time they refused and stayed put. 'I'm on me own now,' he says, 'and I don't care if they give me free rooms in Buckingham Palace, I would not give this place up.'

Prefabs were intended as a stopgap. Bevan had a clear long-term policy. The main priority was the construction by local authorities of subsidised housing for rent. As building materials were in short supply, the only way of ensuring adequate resources for the public sector was to maintain stringent control of the private sector. A method of control was ready to hand in the wartime system of building licences, which gave the Ministry of Works the power to veto private construction. Bevan's policy was to allow one private house for every four built by the local authorities. As an emergency measure following the convertibility crisis of August 1947, all work on private housing was suspended and only resumed again in June 1948. Over the six years of the Attlee governments, 79 per cent of all permanent housing was built for local authorities, 3 per cent for government departments and housing associations, and 18 per cent for private purchase.

Lesser restrictions ran alongside the greater. To prevent the frittering away of labour and materials on less essential work, all but the most trivial private repairs were subject to control. In January 1947 George Tomlinson, as Minister of Works, announced that in future no one would be allowed to spend more than £10 on private repairs without permission from the local authority. (The figure was raised to £100 in June of the following year.)

The Labour government worked on the principle that new housing should be distributed according to social need rather than market forces. In practice this meant priority for manual workers, with generous subsidies to keep down costs and rents. Under the Housing Act of 1946 the existing subsidy of £8. 5s. per house per year over forty years was raised to £22 over sixty years. Of the new annual subsidy, £5. 10s. was to be levied from the local rates, and £16. 10s. from the Exchequer.

The machinery on which Bevan relied for the execution of his policies was cumbrous and slow to gather momentum. By his own decision, much criticised as time went by, the organisation of the housing drive was delegated to the local housing authorities, of which there were no fewer than 1470 in England and Wales. As Michael Foot writes:

> They were charged with drawing up their own programmes, preparing the sites, making the contracts with private builders or establishing direct labour departments, fixing the rents, allocating the tenants and supervising the estates thereafter.[3]

The local authorities had long experience of housing but now there were fresh hurdles to clear. Every housing programme, once agreed by the Ministry of Health, had to be passed on for approval by the new Ministry of Town and Country Planning. Once the scheme was approved, the council issued licences to the building contractors enabling them to purchase the necessary materials. But even then there might be a long delay before building could start. One of the many local authorities to experience this problem was Scunthorpe, where the expansion of the local steel industry was attracting an influx of workers. The local authority was keen to provide more accommodation, as the chairman of the housing committee, Clarrie Newlove, recalls:

> This was our main thought – build as many houses as possible. But, of course, bricks was short, timber was short, and everything you wanted in that respect was on licence. Now the local authorities were all made to give licences out to the local builders to get them going as far as building was concerned and also for the authority to get timber and building bricks. But there we came up against a snag because not only did Scunthorpe want building materials, but everybody else wanted it and so it was restricted in every way as to how many houses you could build a year. I remember

making a statement in the council that as soon as the war was over we were going to build 3000 houses a year. We never got to 300, never mind 3000, so you can imagine just exactly what the position was!

Bevan had started a competition between local authorities for resources not yet available. By the end of August 1946, the majority of local authorities had not yet completed a single house.

Apart from laying down standards of building and design, Bevan's main task was to consolidate the plans of the local authorities into an annual housing programme. But the Ministry of Health had no direct control over money, manpower, materials or the building industry. To accelerate the housing programme, Bevan had to obtain the co-operation of other Whitehall departments, each with its own special interests to protect. 'Ten cooks are spoiling the broth,' wrote *Picture Post* on 28 September 1946:

Mr Dalton, the Chancellor of the Exchequer, is responsible for providing the capital required to pay out the housing subsidies. Mr Arthur Greenwood, the Lord Privy Seal, has certain vague, overruling functions. No one quite knows what he does do. Mr Tomlinson, the Minister of Works, directs the building industry, licensing private builders, controlling building materials, and providing temporary and prefabricated permanent homes. Mr Isaacs, the Minister of Labour, has to provide manpower. The Minister of Town and Country Planning can decide against house building on any site. The Minister of Agriculture must be consulted about rural housing. The Ministry of Supply deals with materials, and especially with the provision of house components, of which there is a serious shortage. Mr Bevan's writ does not run north of the border, where the Secretary of State for Scotland controls housing. The tenth cook is Sir Stafford Cripps who, as President of the Board of Trade, is now calling upon all builders employing more than fifty men to reply to ninety questions. Everyone in this industry considers that the issue of these forms will add to the delays and costs of housebuilding.

Administrative control of the housing programme was vested in the public sector, but the bulk of the building work was carried out by private contractors. Their attitudes varied. Some were in a position to benefit from lucrative local authority contracts, handsome compensation for the lack of a free market. Others simply felt constricted by the number of forms they had to fill in and the clampdown on speculative building. Charles Mitchell was the chief executive of one of the largest building firms, Waites:

> Waites prior to the war had been very much to the fore in building houses to buy. During the war of course we turned over to aerodromes and Mulberry Harbours and all kinds of things, and we would have been very glad to get back again into what was our normal business, because we started the war with a large land bank which was still there and we were anxious to get to work on that again after the war. But we were not allowed to do that ... They introduced a control that you couldn't build a house of more than a thousand square feet and the person who wanted the house had to show a need for that and apply ... So we had to turn our hands to other things. There was a circular which permitted people, companies like Waites, to go along to local authorities up and down the country and say, 'Look, we own a slice of land here . . . we are empowered by this notice that was sent out to do a deal with you. We can sell our land to you, we can employ architects, we can design the blocks of flats and things of that kind and we can build them for you for a comprehensive price if you would like to have them.' And of course that was a busy business because the councils were very keen to rehouse people and that formed quite a big market at the time.

The frustrations of the small builder are recalled by Bob Watson, who had started his firm in the 1930s. Mr Watson owned a site at Ruislip on which he proposed to build ninety-six houses for private sale. There was no shortage of customers and some were ready to offer bribes in cash. But the local authority would only issue a licence for eight of the would-be purchasers: a cousin of Bob Watson was tenth on the list. The local authority also fixed the price of the eight houses at £1300 each. Thwarted in one direction, Bob Watson was then offered the chance to build houses to be rented by British European Airways, who were then based at Northolt and needed them for their staff. After much lobbying, BEA got a licence for fifty houses, but spread over an eighteen-month period. Bob Watson recalls:

> Well then, having got the licence to build, you then had to get a permit for certain materials, the main one being timber. We

were limited to 1·6 standards per house of 1000 square feet, that meant that we could not put a timber floor on the ground floor, we had to use pitch-mastic, and also it meant that on the direction of the Ministry we had to space the joists for the first floor and the timber rafters for the roof, they suggested thirty-inch centres. Well, the practice was, if you were a reasonable builder, sixteen-inch centres. Well this went very much against the grain and we got to the stage where it wasn't just getting 1·6 standards of timber, so that you could build to thirty-inch centres, but to get a permit to get the timber and then get it. Well, in the end I found that I could get timber with less trouble without a permit. This was irregular, but we were able to build our houses with the roof rafters sixteen inches apart and the first floor joists sixteen inches apart.

Bob Watson maintains that the many restrictions on building operations obliged builders like himself to engage in a certain amount of black market trading. Bevan, he argues, was unnecessarily strict on the private builder: 'Nye Bevan had no time for us at all. In fact he said if it was a military operation, a lot of us would have been shot.'

The necessity of rationing scarce resources was the prime justification for the retention of building controls. But whether the controls were excessive is still a debatable issue. Lord Shawcross, who was Attorney-General from 1945 to 1951 and is now a member of the Social Democratic Party, comments:

One of the matters on which we perhaps were mistaken was that our general policy was to favour State or local authority enterprise and to give that preference over private enterprise … I think we could have done better if, without neglecting the opportunity for house building by local authorities, we'd also encouraged private enterprise more in building small houses. I think we would have got a larger number of houses built. Of course it was one of the points in the Conservative programme and when they came into office they gave full rein to private enterprise and encouraged building not only by the local authorities but by private builders as well. And the production of houses in the Conservative government did increase.

In the short run, no change in the machinery could have solved the housing crisis. At first the majority of building workers were still in the armed forces. Demobilisation was inevitably a slow process and it was not until May 1946 that the labour force was restored to its pre-war level. Wages in the building industry had risen fast and costs were inflationary. The other crippling factor was a shortage of materials. A lack of timber, which had to be imported from Scandinavia or the United States, was the greatest limiting factor until the early 1950s.

The situation was aggravated by the mysterious tendency of building materials to disappear. When, for example, a site was laid out for prefabs in Dagenham, the fittings stockpiled on the spot quickly vanished. Mr Franklyn, a resident of the East End who was working at an optical factory in Dagenham, describes what happened:

> No night watchman about. It was a delight, because you could go along there and take exactly what you wanted. You could take the bathroom taps. You could take fridges. There was asbestos, everything that you wanted that you'd seen during the war but you had never had. One or two times I noticed that where they put all the goods, they put a lovely big fencing around it to stop some of the stealing. And that lasted about a day. Because the next night it was gone. All in all, everybody was on the nick shall we say. Where we lived in Bow we didn't have gardens, we had yards. And to get a bit of wood to knock up a shed so as you can do a few odd jobs in – you couldn't buy it, you had to get orange boxes and things like that. Well, when you could see all this lovely wood being unloaded and no night watchman, and no policeman about, you could go and help yourself ... I think the people as a whole thought that after six years of war, that it was theirs. They was entitled to these things. Never having anything at all they didn't steal it, as such. They just made the best of what they saw.

This philosophy of the rights of the common people was bad news for the common people who happened to be waiting for accommodation. Fortunately, other sites were better protected and in due course Mr Franklyn himself was moved into a prefab.

Popular pressures for housing after the war were strong and vocal. Expectations had been raised by several years of promises and demand was intensified by the exceptionally large number of married couples with young children, for whom shared accommodation in cramped quarters was at best a trial and at worst a nightmare. Councils were besieged by queues of people trying to get a place for themselves on the waiting-list. John Macey, at that time housing manager of the London County Council, describes the situation awaiting him at the start of a typical day:

> In those years immediately after the war, the housing manager would probably arrive at the office at nine o'clock to find a queue already there of people waiting for the doors to open ... I don't think it's generally realised that the average time on the waiting-list for a London family in those days, and probably for fifteen years after the war, was something between seven and eight years before their turn came round. So we had to impress upon everybody the need for very strict fairness and honesty in the allocation of houses and do our best to persuade these people that we were doing the best we could. It wasn't easy, as you can imagine, sometimes we had homeless families come along and there was a terrible division between the welfare services and the housing services because the welfare people wouldn't take in homeless people if they had become homeless in foreseeable circumstances, it had to be unforeseeable homelessness. So they would send them round to us and we would say, 'Well ... you've only just arrived and we've got people who've been on the waiting-list for seven or eight years, we can't put you in front of them.' And sometimes they would go away and leave the baby, a young baby, in the tray.

The Ministry of Health made no attempt to centralise the rules for the allocation of housing. Each local authority devised its own scheme. John Macey explains the system devised by the housing department of the London County Council:

> Faced with this enormous waiting-list we had to find some means of allocating the houses fairly and primarily on the grounds of need. So we would get from the family a statement of their living conditions and it worked like this. No bathroom – thirty points, shared bathroom – fifteen points, got a bathroom – nil. That sort of thing. No separate hot water supply – so many points, shared hot water supply – half that number, got a water supply – no points ... Points for each need, a physical need in the house of what was lacking for decent living conditions. And then we had a scheme for awarding up to thirty points on the grounds of ill-health. Of course there were lots of people who came in

with phoney certificates ... the doctor's certificate would say, 'This lady needs a house badly,' as if that was the cause of her ill-health, or was a state of ill-health. So there had to be some real factor of ill-health.

Many people were so desperate for a place of their own that in the summer of 1946 they began to occupy disused service camps. These camps were still the property of the military authorities and the occupations were, of course, illegal. But the movement caught on all over the country during the summer of 1946, with daily reports of fresh occupations in the press. The following, a routine item from the *Daily Telegraph* of 2 September 1946, shows how commonplace the story had become:

Squatters poured into the ATS camp at Craigentinny, Edinburgh, over the weekend. The camp was commandeered in an 'after darkness' raid last Thursday. About sixty families, comprising nearly 300 people, including children, are now living there.

Army huts in the grounds of Coxhoe Hall, near Durham, have been occupied by thirty-three families of squatters from surrounding villages.

Squatters' representatives from camps in south-west Lancashire and Yorkshire formed an area committee in Liverpool last night to amalgamate with a 'national federation' being formed in London. Mr M. Callaghan, the chairman, said, 'The committee decided that any attempt at eviction would be resisted unless alternative accommodation is provided.'

A family which moved into Woodlands Sports Club, Gravesend, Kent, and took possession of the youth section club room, has refused to be evicted. The club room was condemned for habitation.

There was nothing new about squatting itself. A good claim could be made out for Robin Hood as the first squatter; in 1945 a latter-day Robin Hood by the name of Harry Cowley was organising a band of squatters in the semi-underworld of Brighton. A brief but illuminating study of Cowley's life and times by the Queenspark oral history group in Brighton points to the conclusion that he was not a man to be lightly crossed.[4] An ex-chimney sweep and champion of the underdog, Cowley was a man of the Left who bypassed the procedures of local government in favour of street politics. Strong-arm tactics and financial pay-offs gave him the kind of influence that elected representatives lacked. Cowley had begun his career by organising the unemployed ex-servicemen of 1919 into a group known as the Vigilantes, which among other good deeds installed homeless families in unoccupied property. The Vigilantes would then 'negotiate' a fair rent with the landlord. Cowley started up the Vigilantes again at the end of the Second World War and was to be seen addressing the crowds at Hyde Park Corner.

Cowley's followers were highly organised, but squatting as a movement across the country seems to have begun quite spontaneously with the occupation in July 1946 of a disused army gun site near Scunthorpe. James Fielding had recently moved to the town in search of work, accompanied by his wife, baby and three young children. They had found nowhere to live and had spent several nights sleeping in the double seats in the back rows of cinemas. One summer's day, the Fieldings set off with the pram in search of a house they had heard was empty, but came instead upon the camp. In 1984 Mr Fielding's daughter, Mrs Thelma Ford, revisited that very spot:

> We got to the road outside the camp here, to the hedge, and we stopped for a rest and the parents decided to have a look round the camp and we were rather worried about this because as you said, army camps, you know, you don't do this sort of thing, they're out of bounds. They came back and said, you know, 'Come and have a look round, we've found somewhere to stay.'

The Fielding family moved in and soon others joined them. Then Movietone News appeared on the scene and James Fielding, as chairman of the squatters' committee, was filmed addressing the camera and showing the cinema audience around the premises:

> My name is James Fielding. I'm a married man with four children and came to Scunthorpe on a job of work and spent many weeks of searching, which was fruitless, for accommodation ... I found that several of the huts had straw in them and that evidently sheep had wandered in, or had been put in by neighbouring farmers. I felt if it was right for animals to be put in, it was much more right that homeless human beings should have them. We take the view that any right-minded man would agree with the action our desperation forced us to take.

In view of the Fieldings' experiences, it is hardly surprising that despite the absence of electricity and running water, they should welcome the chance of settling down in old army huts. Other couples were delighted to escape from cramped quarters shared with relations, or from tiny furnished rooms. Among the Scunthorpe squatters were Mr and Mrs Bill Fletcher. The Fletchers were on the waiting-list for a council house but were renting rooms in the meantime from another couple. Mrs Fletcher says:

> They had two little girls who used to steal everything that they could lay their hands on. They had two little, tiny, poky rooms – no facilities whatsoever, we had nowhere to keep coal, no pantry, nowhere to keep food, so I bought an orange-box and made curtains and shelves and coped that way to begin with until Bill was demobbed. He got a job and he came home one day and I said, 'Right, we're moving.' And I'd been down Ferry Road and nailed up this Army hut, I'd heard lots of people were doing it, and I thought, 'Right, at least it's a place of our own and we'll start from scratch.' Anything was better than where we were at the moment. The man was a drunkard and I had a two-year-old son he was training to be a drunkard even then, he would give him a pint of beer and think nothing of it. We moved down there [to the camp], we'd no water, no toilets, no electricity, no nothing, but we managed. I used to fetch water every day in a tub and keep the children reasonably clean and the place reasonably clean. Bill bought a chemical toilet and we lived there for quite a while, then the Scunthorpe Council moved us one by one to Bottesford.

Mrs Renie Lester, another of the Scunthorpe squatters, sums up: 'It was freedom, we could do as we liked, we had a place each of our own, you could have a right good row, it was heaven on earth.'

The camp fell within the boundaries of Brigham and District Rural Council, who wanted nothing to do with the squatters. Nor at first did the members of Scunthorpe Borough Council, whose reactions are recalled by Clarrie Newlove:

> I think their real view was that they were more or less like gypsies, they were living like gypsies, they were looking like gypsies in most eyes, and were making a nuisance of themselves by the fact that there was, in the early stages, neither water or anything on. Of course they were going round to the local houses begging buckets of water ...

From Scunthorpe, the squatters' movement spread rapidly around the country, assisted no doubt by the impact of the Movietone News story on cinema audiences. By the end of September the majority of camps throughout Britain had been occupied: in Scotland, only nine out of 152 remained empty. On 10 October the House of Commons was informed that some 46,335 people were in occupation of 1181 camps.

Did the wrath of the Establishment descend? Far from it. For Bevan and the government the occupation of the camps brought a measure of relief from the housing shortage. Wherever possible the camps were transferred to the local authorities, who reconnected essential services and took over responsibility for the welfare of the residents. It was generally felt that the squatters had morality on their side. As *The Economist* remarked on 24 August: 'In a country so law-abiding as Great Britain it is always refreshing when the people take the law into their own hands on an issue on which the spirit of justice, if not its letter, is so eminently on their side.'

The Fieldings were to spend three years in the Scunthorpe camp and thousands of other families were provided for in the same way. As the housing crisis eased, families were moved out, but some of the camps lingered on into the early 1950s.

One more twist in the story has yet to be added. In September 1946 the Communist Party tried to step up the agitation. On Sunday 8 September they organised the occupation of a number of blocks of luxury flats in the West End, including the Duchess of Bedford flats in Kensington. Mr Stan Henderson, who was Borough Secretary of the Hammersmith branch of the Communist Party, describes how he became involved in the protest:

> We knew literally dozens of people who were living in atrocious conditions ... I had no trouble in finding about forty families and they were presented with a single question – 'Would you like to take a chance? There is no guarantee that you will actually win a place to live in, but you may. But one thing that is certain is that we shall strike a very great blow to inspire the housing campaign which will help us all in the long run.' And it was the long-term policy that we bore in mind more than anything else.

On the day of the occupation, Mr Henderson continues:

> We joined a stream of people who were heading up through Phillimore Gardens in the direction of the Duchess of Bedford flats. And it was a scene somewhat reminiscent of the vicinity of a football crowd on a Saturday afternoon. It

seemed that thousands of people carrying all kinds of houseware, some pushing it on prams, others with it slung over their shoulders, were all heading in one direction. We joined this group and we headed to what we weren't really quite sure, but a policeman directed us and we passed a van where soldiers were serving tea and cakes, and we came to this magnificent red brick and marble looking building and there members of the Communist Party were directing people in through the doors.

The occupation of private property was a far more subversive enterprise than the taking over of the camps, and the role of the Communist Party was undisguised. The government, fearful of being outflanked from the Left, determined to call a halt. Five members of the Communist Party were arrested on charges of conspiring to incite trespass, the local authorities were instructed to disconnect services, and eviction orders were served by the High Court. The squatters, having agreed to leave peacefully, were offered alternative accommodation and the episode fizzled out. When the organisers came to trial they were treated with leniency and even respect. Sir Walter Monckton, who defended them, subsequently returned his fee. Stan Henderson rounds off the story:

> We were eventually found guilty, but Mr Stable, the judge, very kindly expressed himself at great length to the point of view that we had acted not from self-interest but with a desire to help people who were in a particularly dire set of circumstances ... We were found guilty and bound over for two years.

Looking back on the Duchess of Bedford squat, its organisers claim that it was a turning-point in the housing drive. Evidently the government was alarmed, and the incident may well have been helpful to Bevan in reinforcing the claims of the housing programme. But it so happened that the squat took place just at the point where the preparations made since 1944 were beginning to produce results, and houses were appearing in larger numbers. The housing programme was retarded on a number of occasions by recurrent cuts in capital expenditure due to crises in the balance of payments. But in 1947, 139,690 new houses were completed, and in 1948, 227,616. By the end of Labour's term in office in 1951, more than one million permanent houses had been built. The totals were relatively disappointing since lengthy waiting-lists still remained. But they compared favourably with the 1,500,000 subsidised working-class homes built over a period of twenty years between the wars.

Bevan put quality before quantity: he wanted the new council housing to be superior to the old. Determined to level the working classes up, he opted for standards that were ambitious when set in the context of austerity. He accepted a minimum specification of 900 square feet for a three-bedroom house, as recommended by the Dudley Committee in 1944. The pre-war minimum had been 750 square feet. Moreover, Bevan insisted that every house should have an upstairs as well as a downstairs toilet. He was outraged when Hugh Dalton, who succeeded him in January 1951 as the minister responsible for housing, did away with the requirement.

Besides concerning himself with the appearance and amenities of houses, Bevan had a vision of their social setting. He was against the segregation of council tenants by age or by class. 'I hope', he declared, 'that the old people will not be asked to live in colonies of their own – they do not want to look out of their windows on endless processions of the funerals of their friends.' In 1948 he removed by a new Housing Act the requirement, carried over from legislation between the wars, that housing should be provided exclusively for 'the working classes'. 'We should try', Bevan declared, 'to introduce into our modern villages and towns what was always the lovely feature of English and Welsh villages, where the doctor, the grocer, the butcher and the farm labourer all lived in the same street. I believe that it is essential for the full life of a citizen ... to see the living tapestry of a mixed community.'[5]

Bevan was an optimist. But in linking the themes of housing and community he touched on the most ambitious of all the social projects of the period: town and country planning. The Blitz was the planners' opportunity. The devastated areas would have to be rebuilt and the planners urged that central and local government should be entrusted with the power to rebuild them. The residue of urban blight and muddle, left over from the Industrial Revolution, would be swept away and replaced by comprehensive schemes of development. Shining new housing estates and community centres, schools, libraries and shopping precincts, all in the latest architectural styles, would arise amid spacious parks and gardens.

The case for planning did not stop short at the blitzed areas. Controls were urged over the pattern of land use throughout Britain, in town and country alike. The drift of population to the south-east would be checked and the congestion of London relieved by the creation of a ring of new towns. Industry would be located where it was most needed, in the depressed areas. Green Belts and National Parks would be set aside to protect the countryside. The gospel of planning ranged far and wide, and many of its implications would take us too far afield from the subject of housing. It is enough to note that in the course of the 1940s the planners obtained virtually all the powers they asked for. The wartime coalition gave rise to the new Ministry of Town and Country Planning in 1943, and the Location of Industry Act of 1945. Lewis Silkin, Labour's Minister of Town and Country Planning, carried through the New Towns Act of 1946 and – the most sweeping measure of all – the Town and Country Planning Act of 1947. The planners had won a series of famous victories.

The focal point of urban reconstruction was London. Other blitzed cities, such as Coventry, Birmingham and Plymouth, were quick to look ahead and draw up their own plans. But as the largest conurbation in the country, as the capital city, and as the first area to suffer the Blitz, London presented the planners with their greatest challenge. Politics gave the final push. The London County Council, controlled since 1935 by the Labour Party, was eager to plan. In 1941 the Council appointed the most eminent planner in Britain, Professor Patrick Abercrombie, to draw up in concert with its own architect, J. H. Forshaw, a plan for the County of London. The following year the Ministry of Works and Planning commissioned Abercrombie to produce a second report, this time covering the whole of the Greater London region, a geographical area many times the size of the administrative County of London.

The County of London plan was published in a blaze of publicity in 1943. Its purpose, as the authors explained, was to remedy four main defects in the previous development of London:

> They comprise traffic congestion, depressed housing, inade-
> quacy and maldistribution of open spaces, and finally the
> jumble of houses and industry which showed itself in a
> general tendency towards 'indeterminate zoning'. Many
> people would add a fifth defect as no less deplorable: the
> continued sprawl of London, ribboning along the roads,
> straggling over the Home Counties, and suburbanising the
> surrounding country towns.[6]

So how was urban sprawl to be checked? Abercrombie addressed himself to the problem in his *Greater London Plan* of 1944. He proposed that the Greater London area should be divided into four rings. Working from the inner ring outwards they were to be classified as the Inner Urban, Suburban, Green Belt and Outer Country areas. The Green Belt was to be preserved as far as possible from all forms of development. But from the two inner zones, more than one million people were to be dispersed into the Outer Country ring or beyond. As part of the dispersal, more than 300,000 people from Inner London were to be moved to a ring of eight new towns outside the Green Belt.

The 1940s are a long time ago. In the 1980s we live with the consequences of great urban mistakes. Working-class neighbourhoods that survived the Blitz have been broken up and scattered over high-rise waste lands far more destructive of morale than bombing. Town centres that used to inspire affection and respect have been torn down and replaced by functional complexes that nobody loves and vandals deface. In the past decade or so a profound reaction has set in and the responsibility for urban disasters has been pinned firmly on the architects and planners. The successes of planning have been overlooked and the prophets of the 1940s turned into the scapegoats of the present day. The scapegoat theory, which has the convenient effect of exonerating politicians, property developers and building contractors from a fair share of the responsibility, should be taken with a large helping of salt. But returning from current affairs to the past, the main problem is to see the 1940s clear, free of the dust cloud of controversy thrown up by more recent events.

In contrast with later decades, the planning schemes of the 1940s were architecturally modest and socially humane. There were few intimations of the high-rise housing estate or the 'new brutalism' in architecture. The tone was suburban and even traditional. Bevan's ideal council house, of which hundreds of thousands were built, had a bourgeois look. Coventry Cathedral and the Royal Festival Hall were modern architecture on a human scale. Though a high proportion of Londoners were being rehoused in flats, the LCC forbade the construction of blocks more than six storeys high.

Why, then, did 1940s planning retain the vital human perspective, for lack of which the most progressive social ideal turns to dust? Part of the explanation is that planning was still closely tied to the goals of welfare and community. The machinery of planning can be used for many different purposes. It can be used to license commercial development, to turn out the maximum number of homes in the shortest possible time, or to conduct experiments in architectural theory. 1940s planning was dominated by the ideal of the model community equipped with all the facilities of the good life.

A second factor was that planning still owed as much to the English garden city tradition, which harmonised well with popular sentiment, as to continental modernism in the manner of Le Corbusier. Stemming from the work of Ebenezer Howard at the turn of the century, the garden city school of thought was inspired by a powerful antipathy to the squalor and congestion of London. Howard and his disciples argued for the dispersal of industry and population into new towns that would bring together the best elements of rural and urban life. The garden city ideal was envisaged as a community of about 30,000 people living in cottages or terraced housing, with a low density of population. In the 1940s the garden city ideal was influentially expressed by the Town and Country Planning Association and its Secretary, Frederick Osborn.

Le Corbusier, a Swiss-born intellectual, stood at the other extreme of the planning spectrum. A prophet of megalopolis, he revelled in the possibilities opened up by the mass production of building materials. He dreamed of the technological city with a population of millions housed in soaring concrete towers of inhuman geometrical symmetry. The modern movement, strongly overlapping with Soviet and socialist ideas of planning, began to influence the younger generation of British architects during the 1930s. But it was not until the 1950s that Corbusierite radicals began to take the lead and make their mark on the London skyline. In the 1940s planning was inclined to be pragmatic, with architects borrowing something from the garden city and something from modernism.

Abercrombie himself was no revolutionary. A founding father of the Council for the Preservation of Rural England, he balanced between rival schools of thought. Similarly, he compromised with vested interests. To relieve the congestion of London was admirable in theory. But it would have been a brave man who decreed that most of London's industry and commerce should uproot itself and depart. For the rehousing of the population of central London, Abercrombie proposed three rings of population density: 200 inhabitants per acre in the central ring, 136 per acre in the middle ring, and 100 per acre in the outside ring. Measured by pre-war standards, the figures represented a considerable reduction in overcrowding. But the proposed densities still meant that a majority of the population would have to be rehoused in flats. Frederick Osborn, the champion of the garden city, was deeply disappointed. As he wrote to Lewis Mumford in September 1943:

I could not have believed that any planner could state in full the case for Decentralisation, and then produce a plan that doesn't do the main thing necessary – permit the majority of people to have decent family homes. It's all the more extraordinary because we have had, in the last year or two, every conceivable kind of opinion survey on the type of dwelling desired – housewives, men in the services, women in the services, factory workers, rural workers and cross-sections in all directions – and they all show that 90 to 95 per cent want houses and gardens and don't want flats.[7]

A radical scaling down of London was probably impossible. Abercrombie's idea was to humanise it. In his proposals for housing he saw himself as disentangling natural communities from the undergrowth in which they were trapped. First, residential areas must be separated out from industry and the heavy traffic of the main roads. Then each community must be provided with the necessary amenities of a healthy and civilised life: schools, public buildings, recreation grounds and so on. Communities were themselves to be subdivided into neighbourhoods of between 6000 and 10,000 people, a figure determined by the capacity of the local school and the number of children who would be within walking distance of it. No child would have to cross a main road between home and school.

Professor Arthur Ling was one of Abercrombie's assistants in the drawing up of the Greater London Plan, and subsequently Chief Planning Officer to the LCC from 1945 to 1955. Summing up the philosophy behind the replanning of London, he draws an intriguing parallel between the planners of the mid-twentieth century and the aristocracy of earlier days:

The government and the local authorities had been the most important elements in the war situation, giving the directions. After the war we thought, why can't they continue, why can't they be the new patrons of the arts? They are going to be responsible for the housing programmes, for planning, for many of the things for which previously the big aristocrats were the patrons. They provided the money originally for the building of great estates in London like Bloomsbury and Belgravia and now they had disappeared or were no longer active, their estates were divided up into little bits and pieces as land was sold off. But now the local authorities were coming along it was necessary for them to improve their image, their understanding of people, so that instead of building great council estates or even little estates here and there as the land became available, they had the responsibility now to think in more comprehensive terms. So that they were not just putting a little house here or a block of flats there, they were building neighbourhoods.

The Town and Country Planning Act of 1944 empowered planning authorities to define heavily blitzed areas as Reconstruction Areas for comprehensive development. In 1947 the LCC designated two such Reconstruction Areas: Stepney-Poplar and Bermondsey. While elsewhere in London planning could only be applied piecemeal, the Reconstruction Areas were miniature republics in which the planners, though never free of external constraints, had the opportunity to build from the ground up. Under the direction of the LCC Planning Division, headed by Arthur Ling, a Reconstruction Areas Group under Percy Johnson-Marshall was charged with the responsibility of preparing and executing the plans.

The pre-war population of Stepney-Poplar, an area of three square miles, was 217,000. But the Blitz had reduced this to 107,000 and the LCC now aimed for a figure of about 100,000, a density of 136 people per acre. In accordance with Abercrombie's principles, Stepney-Poplar was to be divided up into three communities and eleven neighbourhood units. Each neighbourhood would have its own churches, schools, shopping precincts, civic centres and open spaces. The parts adjoining the docks and the canals were designated as industrial zones.

The social ideals of planning were to some extent already compromised by economic factors, as Professor Johnson-Marshall recalls:

Under the Abercrombie plan the East End at that time was thought of as an area where dock work was very important and also work for different times of day and night, therefore densities were proposed that were too high in our opinion. A basic density of 136 persons per acre does mean that you've got to put a lot of people into flats. But that was excused on the grounds of the needs of work. Now what we tried to demonstrate was how to get the maximum variety for a community of people, some with large families of small children, some with small families, some without families, old people, schoolchildren, the whole range of the community and we tried to demonstrate how all these needs could be provided in one area.

The blueprints were still on the drawing board when, in 1948, the LCC was invited to contribute an 'Exhibition of Live Architecture' to the forthcoming Festival of Britain. The LCC decided that part of one of the Poplar neighbourhoods should be completed in time for the Festival and displayed to the public as a demonstration of the potential of planning. The choice fell on Neighbourhood Nine – which had yet to receive its name of Lansbury in honour of the pioneer East End socialist, George Lansbury. An area of thirty acres, comprising about a quarter of the neighbourhood, was marked out as the Lansbury estate and construction rushed forward to meet the Festival deadline. By the time the Festival opened in May 1951, Lansbury was just about ready, with residents installed and shops open.

The state of the housing stock in Lansbury immediately after the war is described for us by Professor Johnson-Marshall:

> The housing that was there of course came mostly from the middle and late nineteenth century and had almost every kind of problem in it. Some of the houses were well designed, but the standards were very poor, many had degenerated into slums, bomb damage had taken the roofs off many and made them quite irreparable; the whole area was devastating to look at and the schools were mostly in ruins, the sites were all covered with rubble or grass and weeds.

In the Lansbury estate the old Victorian terraces were replaced by a variety of housing in streets and squares, some in the shape of three- or six-storey blocks of flats. The very first residents were the Snoddy family, who moved into their new flat on a chill and rainy St Valentine's Day, 14 February 1951. Mrs Snoddy was a reluctant tenant who regretted having to move from her old home. In 1984 she recalled:

> Well, never living in a flat before, when I first saw a flat I can't say I was all that keen on it, I would have preferred to have gone and lived in a house with young children. I felt very sad about leaving the old house. We had a back yard, children could go out and play, we didn't want to leave the old house, we would have preferred to have stayed in it, but we had to get out we had no alternative so we had to plump for the flat.

Mrs Snoddy would have preferred the renovation of her old home to the accommodation she was offered. Nor was the exchange of an old home for a new flat the only source of her regrets. Separated from her previous friends, she did not find in Lansbury the old Poplar sense of neighbourhood:

> I think it was because families lived together more, children got married and they took a couple of rooms in somebody else's house until they eventually got a house of their own and everybody knew one another, they'd all gone to school together, grown up together and when they started pulling everything down we all got separated into different flats in different parts of the borough.

Mrs Snoddy's remarks remind us of the dilemmas inherent in planning. In the free market, the lower income groups have fewer choices than the higher. The State therefore intervenes to compensate the lower income groups by planning the distribution of certain goods and services. But in the course of planning, one social need has to be balanced against another: health, education, housing, all compete for finite resources. Compelled to ration the supply of collective goods and services, the paternal State has to judge what people need rather than what they want. If a democratic political system were to try to fulfil everybody's wishes, they would rapidly cancel one another out leaving a disaster that nobody intended. Similarly, in urban planning, the demand for a healthy London with plenty of greenery and open space, and the demand for a prosperous London with plenty of industrial zones to provide employment, were at odds with the demand for homes and gardens. So Mrs Snoddy moved into a flat.

It was a drawback of comprehensive development on the model of Stepney and Poplar that it took so long to produce results. By 1951, only 1197 houses had been completed there. This was nowhere near fast enough to satisfy the political pressures for impressive statistics of housing construction. The LCC, therefore, pressed on with an opportunistic policy of running up housing estates wherever it could, irrespective of high-minded principles of planning. In defiance of Abercrombie, 6000 houses a year were built on land owned by the LCC in the Green Belt.

The long-term planners were losing control of planning. As the 1940s gave way to the 1950s, communal objectives were thrust into the background by political and commercial imperatives. Party politics turned housing into a numbers game and the Conservatives, taking up the gauntlet thrown down by Labour, returned to power in 1951 pledged to build 300,000 houses a year. Harold Macmillan, the new Minister of Housing, achieved the target and was justly acclaimed for doing so. In 1954 another hole was driven through the Abercrombie conception when the government decided to lift restrictions on the building of offices in London. In all this the new wave of modern architects played their part. As Frederick Osborn observed mournfully in January 1952:

> Now that academic authority is passing into the hands of the Corbusierites, apparent support is given to the opportunist leanings of the LCC and other housing authorities, and the Ministry, and more and more block flats are being built, and density is gradually being increased in normal housing estates and the new towns.[8]

In the 1960s and 1970s Labour and Conservative governments tried to solve the housing problem through prefabricated high-rise flats, which often proved later on to have been of shoddily dangerous construction. In the 1980s the Lansbury estate, once the model of the future, is dwarfed and almost hidden from view by towering blocks. Revisiting Lansbury in 1984, Professor Ling reflected on some of the lessons to be learnt:

> It was to be a prototype neighbourhood development. Unfortunately instead of being the beginning of the whole process, it seemed in some ways to be the end of this whole conception of the new London with its human needs satisfied. This numbers game produced, as you can see on the edge of Lansbury here, these tall blocks of flats, and there's a complete change from the idea of co-ordination, of houses with stock bricks with blue-grey slates on the roofs and continuing landscape which brings all the buildings together ... if you go to the edge you see how suddenly the whole thing was abandoned in favour of just producing as many flats as possible: up they went and people were put into the sky and this is where vandalism really began since the parents can't control children if they're above three storeys, they're out of touch.

The last word on the subject may be left to Mrs Snoddy, who in 1984 was still living in her Lansbury flat and pleased that no worse fate had befallen her:

> I think this part of the estate is very nice, it's the first part that ever went up and it's still kept in decent condition as you can

see, but I think it's a lot better than what they're putting up today.

Within the County of London, the ideals of the planners went slowly down to defeat. The capital city was too vast and elemental a force to be domesticated. But the indirect approach of drawing off industry and population from Inner London, and relocating them beyond the Green Belt, proved more effective. Best of all from the planners' point of view, the experiment of creating new towns worked well. Thriving communities were planned and built where only villages or green fields had lain before.

The first generation of new towns were the direct descendants of the garden city ideal. As originally conceived, the garden city movement was an expression of late-flowering Victorian liberalism. The garden cities of Letchworth, founded in 1902, and Welwyn, founded in 1920, were experiments in private enterprise and voluntary effort. But in the late 1930s the State was drawn in. The government was alarmed by the drift of industry and the population towards the south-east. Neville Chamberlain, the unwitting source of many of the reforms of the 1940s, appointed a Royal Commission under Sir Montague Barlow to investigate the problem. Skilful lobbying by Frederick Osborn and the Town and Country Planning Association swayed the Commission strongly in favour of garden city theory and the Barlow Report of 1940 urged the creation of State-financed new towns. Abercrombie's *Greater London Plan* of 1944 was followed by specific proposals for the siting of eight satellite towns.

New towns were not mentioned in Labour's election manifesto of 1945. But when the new government took office, Lewis Silkin, the Minister of Town and Country Planning, moved with remarkable speed to frame and introduce legislation. The New Towns Act of 1946 empowered him to designate the sites and to set up Development Corporations to purchase and plan the land. Silkin proceeded to designate fourteen new towns. Of these, eight were to be satellite towns of London, closely following Abercrombie's prescription: Crawley, Bracknell, Hemel Hempstead, Hatfield, Stevenage, Harlow, Basildon and Welwyn Garden City. The remainder were to be sited in regional development areas: in the Midlands, Corby, in south Wales, Cwmbran; in the north-east, Peterlee and Newton Aycliffe; in the west of Scotland, East Kilbride; and in the east, Glenrothes. A second generation of new towns was to follow in the 1960s and early 1970s and today two million people live in the new towns.

If Rome was not built in a day, neither was Hemel Hempstead. When Labour fell from office in 1951 the new towns were still building sites with only a scattering of homes finished and occupied. Yet the new towns merit attention as a characteristic legacy of the 1940s to later times. They were, of course, prominent examples of State enterprise. Most of the capital outlay was provided by the Exchequer. The Development Corporation bought and owned the land on which a new town stood and could if necessary exercise powers of compulsory purchase. Though the machinery of elected local government remained intact, planning decisions were determined by the Corporation, whose members were appointed by the Minister of Town and Country Planning. The Corporation built and owned most of the housing stock, selected the tenants and allocated families to particular dwellings. Even the public houses were initially under State management.

As we saw in the previous chapter, there were strong pockets of resistance to Attlee's new order. The new towns in general provoked little antagonism and were later accepted by the Conservatives as admirable institutions. The great exception was the case of Stevenage, where a collision between private and public interests gave rise to a blazing row.

Intended as a prototype for new town development, Stevenage was one of the first sites to be earmarked by Silkin. But unlike some of the other new town sites, which were more or less virgin countryside, Stevenage was a well-established small town with a strongly entrenched middle class, including local farmers. Silkin's proposals meant that the town in its old form would be overwhelmed. A hundred and fifty homes were to be demolished to make way for an industrial zone, farm land was to be turned into built-up areas and the population was to be expanded to 60,000 by a predominantly working-class intake from London. Apart from the disturbance, there was much local wrath over the terms of compensation offered for compulsory purchase.

Not surprisingly, the inhabitants of Stevenage were divided over the prospect and vehement opposition crystallised into a Residents' Protection Association. When Silkin visited the town in May 1946 to address a public meeting, there were cries of 'Gestapo' and 'Dictator' from the audience. The Urban District Council organised a referendum in which a majority voted against the proposals but Silkin determined to override local opposition. Though a number of local groups registered their objections at a public inquiry, he went ahead with an order confirming the designation of Stevenage as a new town.

Next, a group of local residents challenged the legality of his decision in the High Court. The planners held their breath: a defeat might well put in jeopardy the whole process of planning, whereby extensive administrative powers could be exercised under a broad umbrella of statutory authorisation. In February 1947 Mr Justice Henn Collins ruled against Silkin and quashed the order designating Stevenage. Silkin appealed to the Court of Appeal, which reversed the judgement, a decision upheld by the House of Lords. It had been a close shave but Stevenage could go ahead. Or could it? In the aftermath of the economic crisis of 1947, Sir Stafford Cripps forbade the Stevenage Corporation to enter into any new contracts. No longer the pace-setter of the new town programme, Stevenage began to fall behind.

In the meantime, work was going ahead at another of the new town sites, at Hemel Hempstead. The chairman of the Hemel Hempstead Development Corporation was Lord Reith, a founding father of the planning movement and a glutton for hard work. He was determined that Hemel Hempstead would be the first new town, but this involved the usual scramble to obtain scarce resources. Philip Bee, the architect for Hemel Hempstead, recalls:

> We started a race to get the fastest delivery of houses that we could possibly do and when we got them on to what we call second fixings, this is when they're coming up for the plastering and the door frames and painting and that sort of thing, we used to go around with large cartons of cigarettes, saying to the plasterers and the bricklayers, 'Look if you get those off by Sunday there's twenty fags for you,' you see and we'd get through 150 fags a week sometimes doing this but we got the most houses and nobody caught us up for a long time.

As soon as a house was finished a family would be moved in. The very first tenants of Hemel Hempstead were a bricklayer and his wife, Mr and Mrs Ben Adams. With two young children at the end of the war, they were sharing a house with another young couple, and longed for privacy. Their names were on the LCC's housing list but they were told that, according to the system of allocation by points, they would need at least another sixty points before they were found a place.

Mrs Adams takes up the story:

> We'd always planned to have four children so I said to Ben, 'Well, let's have another baby, we'll get a house then.' So,

after a lot of persuasion, we decided and we had another baby. I couldn't get down there quick enough and they said, 'Well, we're very sorry Mrs Adams, but about 300 other couples did the same as you that night,' and we were back to square one, in a worse position really, with another baby on the way and no place to put it.

The Adamses did not give up. Their next move was to seek an interview with the Mayor of Wembley, who put them on to the Hemel Hempstead Public Relations Officer. He in turn passed them on for an interview with the housing manager, Mrs Penny. This was on a Thursday. By the following Monday they were installed in their new home. Priority had been given to them because of Mr Adams's trade. A bricklayer was an invaluable man to have on the spot in the early stages of a new town. For Mrs Adams, the occupation of her own home was a red-letter day:

> It was like a fairy-tale come true really, I can't really describe the feelings, and to have a cupboard and the larder was like a room to me as I'd had one shelf for over ten years and even when the Queen came she was amazed at the size of the larder you know ... Of course expecting the baby was a bit hectic at first but after the baby was born we gradually got settled, to be able to put him out in the garden was absolutely wonderful and the children loved it 'cause the cows used to come round from the fields that were there, you know they sort of rubbed their backs up against our door.

Another of the pioneer couples were Mr and Mrs Cyril Ford. They were told of the new town by friends in the Labour Party and took a bus trip out to view the show houses on the site. They were impressed but did not imagine they would have a chance of living there. But as with the Adams family, the husband's occupation supplied the key to the door. Mr Ford was a gas fitter and spotted an advertisement by the Gas Board calling for fitters to work in the new towns. At first he was offered the job without accommodation to go with it but by persistent correspondence with the Gas Board and Hemel Hempstead Corporation he won his point. When they arrived on the spot the housing manager, Mrs Penny, gave them the key and showed them around the house. Mrs Ford was astonished to find that it was a three-bedroomed home:

> We didn't realise that there were going to be three bedrooms, we thought they were allocated according to what family you

had and we had only one child, so we thought we would have a two-bedroomed house. When I went upstairs to explore there was one bedroom, and another bedroom, a bathroom and an airing cupboard and another door down the end – wonder what that is – so I went and had a look and I had three bedrooms which made me come downstairs, sit on the bottom step and howl. I wept simply because I was so happy, we had a garden for the children to run in, well a garden of sorts, because by then it was only rubble, they'd taken off the topsoil and left us a beautiful layer of yellow clay which walked into the house everywhere, but nevertheless we had a house, a home of our own and we could shut the front door and we didn't have to worry about anybody.

The early residents of Hemel Hempstead were keen to get social activities going. Mrs Adams recalls how the Reverend Stokes, the first vicar to arrive in the town, set up a church first in his garage and then in a gardener's hut. And Mrs Adams was very active herself, organising the first of twenty-two Brownie Packs she eventually ran. Mrs Ford comments:

Apart from the church organisations there was no organised entertainment at all except the two cinemas down in the town, and so we had to make our own. So we used to get together in groups and we used to have 'em once a week, all the families, all the parents would come into one house and we would have a game of housey-housey or something and we would have a sort of social evening of our own, we all used to take turns.

The first generation of new towns reflected the planning philosophy of the 1940s, with its emphasis on community. In Stevenage, for instance, there was a strict demarcation between industrial and residential zones. The residential areas were divided into six 'neighbourhood units' each with a population of about 10,000 people. On the garden city model, houses were low-rise and low-density in a leafy setting of trees and parks. In Hemel Hempstead, as the architect, Philip Bee, recalls, Lord Reith explicitly forbade high-rise flats. The planners believed that by creating the right material environment, they would encourage sociability and community spirit.

But were they deceiving themselves? The philosophy of new town planning was sharply attacked by a young and witty American sociologist, Harold Orlans, who followed the development of Stevenage between 1948 and 1950. Orlans maintained that there was no scientific basis for the theory that social behaviour could be determined by the character of the physical environment. Unwittingly, the planners were simply imposing on other people the subjective preferences of the radical middle class:

> It may be concluded, therefore, that there are no universally acceptable architectural or sociological principles for engineering the happiness and success of neighbourhood or community, but only different principles catering to the needs of different social groups and planners. Many new town planners try to understand and cater to the needs of industrial workers, but, as no full-time planner is himself an industrial worker, it is more than likely that mistakes will be made. Again, most key planners are salaried intellectuals whose outlook differs in certain respects from that of the commercial and white-collar middle classes for whom the new town will cater, so here, too, mistakes are likely. Fortunately, many planning decisions are unlikely to affect the happiness of the new town residents one way or the other, for the residents will probably be less concerned about them than are the planners and, being ordinary people and not abstractions, will be able to adjust satisfactorily to a variety of physical and social environments.[9]

Orlans was the first of a number of American critics hostile to the new towns and the garden city tradition. To them it epitomised a strain in English life of insipid, motherly, interfering liberalism, fearful of the free play of passion and conflict in the big city. This is no place for a comparative study of the relative merits of American and British values. But it has to be said that in one respect time has dealt cruelly with Orlans's scepticism. If there is one point on which planners and their critics in Britain today can agree, it is that, for better or for worse, buildings do have an influence on behaviour. They can help to alienate and demoralise; they can help to induce a sense of well-being and self-respect. Whether or not the planners got all the answers right, they were right about the problem.

Not everyone was suited to life in a new town. Several of the first residents of Hemel Hempstead complained of loneliness and left. According to Philip Bee:

The general reaction was that they liked it, they were lovely –
except for one old gentleman from the Old Kent Road ... He
came in and he said, 'I'm going back to London,' he said, 'I
can't stand the noise of these bloody dicky birdies.'

Most were happy to stay. In 1984 the Ford and Adams families
were still living in Hemel Hempstead, having seen the town grow and
expand around them. They were still glad they had come to live
there. As Mrs Ford remarks:

Hemel Hempstead now has grown an awful lot but our little
community is really sort of self-contained. We've still got
some of the neighbours we started with when we were first
here, we've had new ones of course and we've just incorpo-
rated them into the family as it were.

And according to Professor Ling:

The new towns of Great Britain were, and still are, one of the
greatest post-war successes. They have demonstrated all the
principles of town planning which were adumbrated during
the war.

4

FROM CRADLE TO GRAVE

Most people under the age of forty have grown up with the National Health Service. Born as NHS babies, they have learnt to rely on it in all the medical emergencies of life. While critical of this or that aspect of the service, they are profoundly glad of its existence and appalled by the prospect of its destruction. But however genuine, their appreciation is limited in one respect. Much as they value the NHS, they do not remember what the health services were like before it started. To grasp the full significance of the NHS one must listen to the older generation who were there at the time, and crossed the Rubicon from the old to the new.

The National Health Service came into force at midnight on 4/5 July 1948. On the evening of 4 July, Mrs Jessamine Smith, who was expecting a baby, went into labour:

> My baby arrived at a quarter to twelve on the fourth of July. And the new scheme was coming in at midnight. The district nurse was with me when the baby was born and the doctor hadn't arrived. He got there about five past twelve and did a little bit of stitching. And nurse said to him, 'Couldn't we put this through as coming after midnight?' Because it was a question of the money you see.

The doctor replied that it would be illegal to certify the child as born after midnight. The next morning he called again with a bill for £6. If the baby had been born fifteen minutes later there would have been no bill to pay for, with the start of the NHS, medical services became free of charge at the point of need.

From the patients' point of view, this was a great emancipation. In the weeks following 5 July, queues formed at the doctor's, the dentist's and the optician's as a surge of people presented themselves for free treatment and appliances. As Harry Hopkins writes, Fleet Street took a mischievous delight in reporting the bounty of goods distributed to patients:

Artificial legs, arms, eyes, surgical boots, trusses, belts, invalid chairs and other appliances, freely available now to those needing them, provided the press with an inexhaustible source of 'human stories'. But the article that appeared to exert on reporters and sub-editors a really irresistible fascination was the 'National Health' wig, prescribable for conditions which 'would unfit a person for acceptance in normal work or society'. 'GRANNY, 94, IS GETTING SILVER CURLS FROM BEVAN,' ran a typical headline.[1]

Funny stories apart, the rush for treatment was a measure of the backlog of medical neglect that had been allowed to build up under the old health services. But here we come to a problem that makes us pause. The aim of the National Health Service was to improve health, and especially the health of sections of the population that had never received proper medical attention in the past. But the relationship between the standard of health care available, and the level of health in society, has never been straightforward. Improved health services are obviously a plus, but many other factors are at work.

Much of the ill-health recorded by social investigators during the 1930s was not the result of inadequate medical care but of malnutrition and slum housing. By the time the doctor arrived on the scene the damage was done. Likewise, the NHS since 1948 has dealt with the consequences of social inequality, but cannot reach the causes. As Brian Watkin, a historian of the health services, wrote in 1978:

> It is indeed striking that in the 1970s the gap between the upper and lower social classes in terms of mortality experience was two to three times as large as in the early 1930s. Most major causes of death are now two to three times as common among social classes IV and V as among classes I and II, and the overall death rate was by the early 1970s 50 per cent higher among the lower than among the upper classes.[2]

Simple inequalities have been compounded by the fact that as a general rule better-educated people have greater foresight and persistence in getting their medical problems diagnosed and treated.

Even in a classless society, the sheer folly of humanity would tend to counteract the effects of regular medical care and education in the health problems. The determination of so many people to smoke, overeat, drink and drive, take drugs and so on, turns otherwise healthy adults into patients. The right to turn up at a casualty department late on a Friday night, dead drunk, bleeding profusely, and demanding immediate treatment, is one of our essential liberties.

The backcloth may be sombre, but it remains the case that the establishment of the National Health Service marked a dramatic advance in the organisation of health care. On the eve of the Second World War Britain had a patchwork of health services so complex that only a few experts really understand how they worked, and the more they tell us, the more baffling the detail becomes. The one certainty is that the pre-war services were riddled with gaps, anomalies and petty financial exactions. Financially, it was the middle classes who paid the highest price. Medically, it was working-class wives and children who came off worst.

Then as now there were many branches of health care but the general practitioner and hospital services were the two which dealt with the ordinary emergencies of life. As the two services were funded and organised quite independently, patients had to make separate arrangements for each.

Doctors in general practice still regarded themselves as independent professional men living on the fees they charged for their services. They were entitled to practise wherever they wished and the rewards of private practice led to an overconcentration of doctors in the wealthier regions of the country. But in practice GPs owed much of their income to the State and were half-way towards becoming employees of the public sector. A general practitioner would usually have on the register a mixture of private and, as they were called, 'panel' patients. Upper- and middle-class families still paid for the doctor's services as in the nineteenth century. But under the system of National Health Insurance, introduced by Lloyd George in 1911, general practitioners contracted with the State to provide a service for the working classes.

Under National Health Insurance, employees whose income was £250 p.a. or below were compulsorily insured. Barring a handful of excepted categories, all manual workers were covered by the scheme, and the income qualification drew in many clerical workers as well. Instead of being in the hands of a department in Whitehall, the administ ation of NHI was in the hands of a multitude of 'approved societies'. These were either friendly societies, which had pioneered insurance clubs in the nineteenth century, or industrial assurance companies such as the Prudential. The role of the commercial companies in the scheme requires a word or two of explanation. They were not permitted to make a profit out of National Health Insurance and were indeed legally obliged to set up non-profit-making sections of their companies to administer it. But through participating in the State scheme, the agents of the industrial assurance companies got a foot in the door of almost every working-class home. This gave them the opportunity to sell private insurance as a supplement to the State scheme.

In return for weekly payments, to which the employer and the Exchequer added their contributions, members of the National Health Insurance scheme received sickness benefit when off work through illness, and the services of a general practitioner. For this purpose, doctors were grouped into 'panels'. The doctor was remunerated by a capitation fee and allowed to take up to 2500 panel patients – thus ensuring a substantial basic income guaranteed by the State.

The compulsory State scheme did not include the right to dental or ophthalmic treatment, or the right to the services of a specialist. But some insurance companies did offer dental and ophthalmic services as optional extras. The benefit consisted of a subsidy on the cost of teeth or spectacles, leaving the patient to pay the rest. There was no provision for hospital treatment, which was organised separately.

No benefits were available under National Health Insurance for the dependants of the insured, apart from a maternity grant of £2 which was payable to the wife of an insured man. The scheme was, in fact, essentially masculine. Women belonged to it if they were in paid employment but, as most of them were unpaid housewives, the main effect of health insurance was to protect the male bread-winner. A survey of 1250 working-class wives on the eve of the Second World War showed that only thirteen belonged to the NHI. The gap had to be filled, if it was filled at all, by a variety of insurance clubs. So the working-class wife usually attended the doctor's surgery as a private patient, and her children would invariably do so.

The relationship between the general practitioner and the patient has to be viewed from both sides. Every general practitioner was free to determine the fees charged to private patients. And it is clear that many general practitioners operated a Robin Hood system of subsidising the costs of poorer patients out of the fees of wealthier ones. Miss Roche, a nurse whose father was a GP, describes how, as a child in the 1920s, she would listen to her father and her mother drawing up the bills:

I can remember very well as a child hearing him saying to my mother when they were making out the bills together ... 'Colonel Dowdeswell, three visits – seven guineas,' says Daddy. 'Much too much, he only had three visits,' says my mother. 'Oh, the old dear can afford it,' says Daddy, so that was that ... They always put the prices up for people who could afford to pay because a lot of people like Mrs Jones, for instance, who'd had thirty-six visits when all the children went down with measles and complications ... she was only sent a bill for five shillings because she always insisted on paying and couldn't afford it ...

Dr Ashworth, who was in practice in a working-class district of Manchester, explains the policy of his own surgery:

We divided patients into three groups. Those who were in no way creditworthy, we used to give them a prescription to take to the private chemist across the road. He could have the battle as to whether they paid or not. Then there were those we thought were reasonable payers and we charged them on the spot. And then we thought there were those who were worthy of credit and their names were entered in the great leather-bound ledger and each month we made up the account and we sent out the accounts and we used to have collectors who used to come on a Friday at half past three, ready to get the collector into the patient's home before the insurance agent arrived, because if they paid the insurance agent first, there was never any money left for the doctor's collector. And we used to pay the collectors a halfpenny in the shilling for every shilling they collected. I think the bad debts in my practice when I took it over were about £300 a year, which was about 10 per cent, quite considerable.

Though doctors very often subsidised the costs of private patients on low incomes, and were sometimes prepared to write off the debts of families who could not pay, this did not remove the financial disincentive from the patient's viewpoint. The effect on middle-class families is difficult to gauge. The effect on working-class families is well authenticated.

As Mrs Griffiths of Manchester recalls:

There was always the feeling that if you went to the doctor's you would first be thinking how much money he would want. You would pay for the consultation, and you would pay him over the desk there at his surgery, and then after that he would say that if you go round the back the chemist will give you, or the pharmacist will give you, a bottle. And then it would be 2s. 6d. for the medicine, and the 1s. 6d. for the visit. If you didn't have it, well you just wait until pay-day until you have got some money ... Definitely you wouldn't go if you hadn't got the money.

As a schoolboy in the 1930s, Len King had a part-time job working as a collector for his father's practice in Manchester. Asked whether patients dreaded his arrival on the doorstep, he replies:

People were generally cheerful but there wasn't much money about, a lot of people were out of work and I suppose with the rent man coming, the insurance man coming ... the doctor's bill was something that could be pushed to one side occasionally. So you would occasionally go to a house, walk up to the door, you could hear life going on behind the door and as soon as you knocked at the door, dead silence! Dead silence and you thought, I'm sure I heard somebody. Knock again, still dead silence. On one occasion, a little girl eventually came to the door and said, 'Me Mum says she's not in!'

As already mentioned, compulsory insurance did not include provision for dental or eye services. The dentists, whose main business remained the extraction of teeth, were still in the process of establishing themselves as a profession, and 40 per cent of registered dentists were academically unqualified. As children grew up, they would receive treatment from the School Dental Service if they happened to live in one of the areas where it was in operation. But among adults rotten teeth were commonplace. As S. Melvyn Herbert wrote in 1939:

The wealthier classes have acquired the habit of visiting a dentist regularly and looking to him to protect their teeth rather than to extract them when decay has finished its work. But the working classes generally have not come to realise the importance of dental health, and in any case many of them cannot afford regular dental treatment. Accordingly, they tend to wait until pain drives them to the dentist. By that time extraction is often the only remedy.[3]

The dentist, like the doctor, charged a fee. The predicament of a patient with a toothache but no cash is illustrated in the story told by Norman Hyland. After leaving school, he began work in Manchester and on the Wednesday of his first week in employment he suffered severe toothache. It was his afternoon off and he set off in search of a dentist:

I tried all round the district ... in those days it was half a crown for an extraction – and no one would trust me till the pay-day – and thinking the police would realise that I wouldn't try to do them down, I went to the huge police station ... A desk sergeant there – and in those days they were about sixteen stone in weight – gazed down at me and said, 'What's the complaint?' and I said, 'Toothache,' and he said, 'Are you trying to be funny with me, young man?', like Robb Wilton. And I said, 'No, I've come to borrow half a crown,' and he said, 'What makes you think this is a moneylender's?' Anyway, he was very kind, he gave me a note to St Anne's Hospital in Manchester and a young intern came and took me boots off and sat me on a couch and he made a quick extraction and that was the end of my trouble. But St Anne's Hospital had a Daisy Day [fund-raising day] every first of August when they sold a little white flower and for years afterwards I always dropped a half a crown in the box, remembering that day.

To obtain a prescription for a pair of spectacles, a patient had first to visit a general practitioner. But as most GPs were not qualified to dispense glasses, the patient would be referred to an optician. The prescription of spectacles aroused professional jealousies, with the opticians claiming a monopoly and the GPs resisting. But for most people the dispute was irrelevant. It was cheaper for them to test their own sight and select their own lenses. Just as one went into a shop to try on a hat, so one could go in and try on a pair of glasses.

Mrs Crane was still in her teens when she worked on the spectacles counter at Woolworth's in Manchester Piccadilly. Owing to the fact that every item on sale was priced at sixpence or under, Woolworth's was still known as the 'sixpenny store'. As Mrs Crane explains:

Each lens was sixpence, and then of course the frame was sixpence, and if you wanted a case that was sixpence, so altogether in the old money it came up to two shillings ... and people who couldn't afford an optician used to go there.

A visitor to the spectacle counter of the same store was Mr Law, whose father used to buy his glasses there:

Stacked on the counter were spectacles, with a large card with a large A going down to a small Z, I would think, and I can see my father now, trying on different pairs of glasses, looking at the card, putting down a pair, picking another pair up, until he got the selected pair he required, then he would look at me, he would ask me how he looked. I'd say, 'You look smashing, Dad,' and then we'd just go out of the store ...

Millions of pairs of spectacles were selected in this way before the introduction of the NHS.

There was no unified hospital service in the 1930s. Instead, there were two main types of hospital, each with its own traditions: the voluntary hospital and the local authority hospital. Hospitals of all kinds had originated as institutions for the treatment of the poor, and still bore the marks of their beginnings. The voluntary hospitals had begun as philanthropic foundations and were still self-financing and independent of government control. Many of the local authority hospitals were nineteenth-century poor law hospitals recently transferred to the local authorities under Neville Chamberlain's Local Government Act of 1929. They still had the grim aura of the workhouse.

There was an approximate division of labour between the voluntary and county or municipal hospitals. The majority of voluntary hospitals were general in character: they could treat all kinds of cases, and also catered for the bulk of out-patient work. The local authority hospitals, on the other hand, provided most of the beds for infectious diseases, maternity, and chronic cases. In 1939, there were 1000 voluntary and 2000 local authority hospitals in England and Wales.

To generalise about the voluntary hospitals can be misleading, since they varied so much. The leading voluntary hospitals, such as Guy's or Bartholomew's, were world-famous for their pioneering work in medical research. At the other end of the scale were 500 cottage hospitals with fewer than 100 beds, where treatment was in the hands of general practitioners. Of these institutions, Brian Abel-Smith, an expert on social policy and historian of the health services, has written:

It was in these small hospitals that some of the really bad medical care was provided. There were general practitioners who were prepared to attempt surgery which was beyond their competence and to attempt it in conditions which denied them the services of skilled and experienced nursing staff or a proper range of equipment.[4]

Looking back from the vantage point of the National Health

Service, it seems extraordinary that the voluntary hospitals should have supported themselves without a penny of direct funding from the Exchequer. But they did. Consultants in the voluntary hospitals usually held honorary appointments to which no fees or salary were attached. But as the recognised hallmark of a consultant, the appointment enabled him to set up a flourishing private practice in Harley Street or its provincial equivalents. The drawback of this arrangement was that since consultants depended on private clients, they naturally looked for appointments in the more affluent areas of Britain, especially London and the south-east. In the heartlands of industry, the hospitals and their patients were starved of attention.

The running costs of the voluntary hospital – including the salaries paid to junior doctors – were met by a variety of charitable devices and insurance schemes. One traditional method of raising cash was through the annual flag-day, when medical students attached to a particular hospital would go out and solicit donations from the general public. Dr Katharina Dalton, who was a medical student at the Royal Free Hospital in London, recalls:

> Collecting for the flag-days was great fun. We used to look forward to it a lot and you'd get a permit for twenty-four hours so that meant you stayed out from midnight, started technically collecting at midnight and went right through the next twenty-four hours. And after a time you knew exactly where to go. I mean you'd catch the theatre crowds and late dinner crowds and then you'd go along to the main line stations at two o'clock, three o'clock and then at four o'clock you'd go along to Smithfield Market and actually those marketeers were absolutely wonderful, they really were very generous in Covent Garden and then you'd get the crowds going to work and then you'd get the shoppers during the daytime and you went right through for twenty-four hours like this. It was grand fun.

A marked feature of voluntary hospital finance was its dependence on local loyalties, and the patronage of wealthy interests in the district. Mrs Ward speaks as a nurse who began her career in 1940 in a voluntary hospital:

> I started training as a nurse in a voluntary hospital in Lancashire which was supported by the cotton mill owners. They would give quite good sums of money to this hospital to keep it going and people would bequeath beds in memory of

patients with little plaques on the wall ... There was also a very good fund in the cotton mills themselves so that people who had to have treatment could ask for what they call 'the recommendation' and this would pay for part of their treatment. If I remember right, I think even a straightforward X-ray in those days was about two guineas, which was a lot of money out of a working man's pay. Christmas was lovely in the voluntary hospital because the Lord Mayor came round and went to every little child on the ward and gave them all a little present and of course the surgeons used to come and carve the turkeys. They used to make a good day of it, it was the patient's day, Christmas Day. Nowadays, I think everyone is sent home as far as possible.

In the voluntary hospitals, the medical attention given in the public wards was usually restricted to families with an income of under £6 a week and was technically free. In practice, however, these patients contributed according to their means, and it was the task of the lady almoner, when a patient was admitted, to conduct an informal means test. As more and more middle-class patients found themselves unable to bear the full cost of treatment by a consultant in a nursing home, private wards and pay-beds were gradually introduced into the voluntary system. But the most important new source of income between the wars was the contributory scheme. A hospital would set up its own insurance fund and, in return for a payment of a few pence a week, the contributor and his family would receive free treatment. The spread of these schemes posed a threat to the income of general practitioners, as they began to draw in the wives and children of panel patients, providing an alternative to a visit to the doctor's surgery. By 1939, eleven million people were covered by hospital contributory schemes. Fifty-five per cent of the working-class wives investigated by the Women's Health Enquiry Committee belonged to a hospital savings scheme. The voluntary hospitals were expanding: but in the long run the rising costs of health care threatened to outstrip their income.

Through the voluntary hospitals, the medical care of the lower income groups was heavily subsidised. The same was true at the local authority hospitals, which charged a small fee for maternity cases and minor operations, but waived fees for the chronic sick and the poor. For the working-class family, therefore, health provision was a patchwork of subsidised schemes with fees here and there, as Mrs Carter recalls:

My husband used to pay a stamp of one and sixpence a week, a health insurance stamp for himself only, for the doctor or any medication he would need and he also paid a scheme at work, threepence a week, which was called a hospital scheme and that covered the whole of the family for any hospitalisation that was needed, but not maternity. I paid threepence a week into a medical aid for my son, but I was in good health so I didn't bother about myself ...

In the 1930s there was little political pressure for the reform of the health services. The momentum came from within the medical profession, where an understanding of the deficiencies of existing health services was matched by the desire for greater resources, and sharpened by the rivalry of competing interests within the medical world.

Plans for change revolved around two major and widely acknowledged deficiencies in health provision. National Health Insurance covered less than half the population and was strictly limited in the services it provided. It was in the interests of the health of the population at large, and no less in the interests of general practitioners, that it should be extended. In 1938, the British Medical Association, which represented more than three-quarters of all practising doctors, published its proposals under the title *A General Medical Service for the Nation*. A revised version of a plan first put forward in 1930, the scheme recommended that the health insurance scheme should be extended to cover dependants and to include dental, ophthalmic and specialist services. This would have meant that 90 per cent of the population were included in the panel system, with the higher income groups remaining outside as a lush pasture for private practice. But for the impact of war and the return of a Labour government, it is very likely that National Health Insurance would eventually have been reformed along these lines.

The second deficiency in the health services was the lack of co-ordination between the voluntary and local authority hospitals. To make the best use of all hospital beds it was necessary to plan the staffing, equipment and budgets of all hospitals within a region. By the end of the 1930s the hospitals were beginning to co-operate along these lines and in 1939 the Nuffield Provident Hospital Trust was set up to promote the process. As general practitioners had many interests at stake in the hospitals, the BMA did not hesitate to make recommendations in its *A General Medical Service for the Nation*. The BMA urged that more hospital beds should be made available for general practitioners wishing to treat their patients in hospital, and that access to out-patients' departments should be restricted to staunch the flow of private patients away from the general practitioner. As regards the overall organisation of the hospitals, the BMA favoured greater co-operation between the two kinds of hospital, and an element of regional planning with a single authority supervising all health services within its boundaries.

The peacetime trend towards reform was accelerated by the medical emergencies of the Second World War, an event that shook the health services to the core. An Emergency Medical Service, planned before the war for the treatment of the victims of air-raids, disclosed an acute shortage of beds and equipment in the hospitals. The government had to install nearly a thousand new operating theatres and many thousands of additional beds were provided in temporary huts. Through the agency of the EMS, a national hospital service, a model for the future, was superimposed upon the old structure. Though the new service was restricted to emergency categories of patient, the categories were broadened to include service personnel and workers in war factories. A parallel expansion occurred in the maternity and infant welfare services, with the introduction of vitamin supplements for expectant mothers, the provision of free orange juice to infants, and a highly successful campaign of immunisation against diphtheria.

The EMS spotlighted the regional disparities between advanced and backward parts of the country. Dr Janet Vaughan, a clinical pathologist, explains its effects:

> The great physicians and the great surgeons from the London teaching hospitals ... went out into the periphery and for the first time saw the sort of medical services that existed in the periphery, which was something that really had to be seen to be believed in, particularly in the country districts or the slum areas of the big cities. I was only supposed to be looking after the blood transfusion service, but I can remember going to a big railway accident to take the blood and to set up the blood transfusions and being just shattered by seeing how the local surgeons from the local hospital didn't know how to handle the major accident surgery.

While galvanising the profession, the EMS stepped up the popular demand for hospital treatment. Dr Elizabeth Rose, who worked in two of the EMS hospitals in Scotland, says:

I do think the public were ready for the changes brought about by the National Health Service, really because of what went on in the war years. Because during that time, the young people of the community were accustomed to a free medical service in the forces and they were accustomed to going to hospital for investigations and so on and tests ... in the obstetric field it became acceptable to go to hospital clinics and to go to hospital to have your baby.

The medical profession was quick to appreciate the radicalising effects of war and was strongly influenced by them. In August 1940, the BMA, the Royal Colleges, the Royal Scottish Corporations and the Society of Medical Officers of Health joined forces to establish the Medical Planning Commission. Its interim report, published in May 1942, was remarkably expansive, and the BMA surprisingly enthusiastic in its response. As Charles Hill, the Deputy Secretary of the Commission, writes:

> The plan involved a National Health Service available to everyone whatever their income (the 100 per cent principle), the building of health centres at which general practitioners would work together in groups, the unification of hospitals under regional bodies, the payment of general practitioners partly by salary, and the gradual disappearance of the custom of buying and selling practices.
>
> In view of what happened subsequently, I find it difficult to believe that in September 1942 the BMA really accepted the plan in broad outline, including the idea of health centres, and the disappearance of the custom of buying and selling practices subject to adequate compensation. However, it referred back the suggestion of part-time salaries for general practitioners and totally rejected any notion of a whole-time salaried service.[5]

On the face of things, it is a paradox that the doctors were among the first to propose a National Health Service yet later fought a fierce rearguard action against its introduction. But the paradox dissolves on inspection. The Medical Planning Commission was affected by the phase of high social idealism between 1940 and 1942, when national unity seemed to be dissolving old quarrels. As the mood faded, the doctors began to take up a more hard-headed position. While still favouring the introduction of some form of National Health Service, they began to prepare for hard bargaining.

The most important factor in changing the attitude of the doctors was the intervention of the politicians. Until December 1942, the initiative in the reform of the health services rested with the medical profession. For more than a decade all the proposals had come from them. But the Beveridge Report, with its timely proposal for a comprehensive health service, delivered the issue into the hands of the government. Almost at once the British Medical Association ceased to be the pacemaker of change and took up a defensive posture as a pressure group demanding the best terms for its members.

The natural aim of every profession is to govern itself, with as little accountability to the outside world as possible. When, therefore, the doctors learnt that the planning of a National Health Service had begun in Whitehall, they began to fear that doctors would lose their professional independence and become salaried servants of the State under the direction of officials. In November 1943, a Conservative politician, Henry Willink, was appointed Minister of Health. Willink at once fell under the suspicion of the BMA and doctors began to write to the press denouncing the machinations of the Ministry. They strongly attacked Willink's proposals, published in a White Paper early in 1944.

If the BMA was fearful of a Conservative politician like Willink, the July 1945 Labour landslide and the subsequent appointment of Aneurin Bevan as Minister of Health sent a shudder through the ranks. Bevan had a long record as a left-wing rebel and had rocked the Coalition boat with insolent and penetrating attacks on Churchill's conduct of the war. Instead of carrying on where Willink had left off, Bevan wiped the slate clean and began to devise, from all the different proposals aired in recent years, a radical synthesis of his own.

One of his first decisions, put to the Cabinet in October 1945, was to nationalise the voluntary hospitals and place all hospitals under regional boards accountable to the Ministry of Health. This was Bevan's boldest stroke. It was bound to be opposed by the voluntary hospitals themselves and by the Opposition. But an important vested interest in the Labour Party was also affected. By taking the public hospitals out of the hands of the local authorities, Bevan was striking a blow against Labour's municipal base. Herbert Morrison, as the former chairman of the London County Council, led the opposition in the Cabinet. Attlee, whose support for Bevan was to prove crucial then and later, backed his Minister of Health, and Morrison was overruled.

Sir George Godber, then serving as a Medical Officer at the Ministry of Health, reflects on Bevan's decision:

Nye came into a situation in which a rather indecisive negotiation had been going on with all the specialist interests under a competent minister, Henry Willink, and he saw that you couldn't go on making the kind of compromises that had been forced on his predecessor, and he cut across it as far as the hospitals were concerned with one decisive point – you must take over the ownership of the hospitals, you must run them together as a group, not under separate ownership . . . I think myself that was Nye's great contribution to the National Health Service. If we hadn't had that we would have had far more confusion and a less efficient outcome in the first decade.

Within limits, Bevan was a very much more pragmatic politician than was generally realised at first. In the early stages of his consultations with the medical profession he abandoned, if he had ever supported, the complete socialist model of a full-time salaried medical profession. And perhaps with the aim of driving a wedge between the doctors, he took special pains to cultivate the leaders of the consultants – the Presidents of the Royal Colleges of Surgeons, Physicians, and Obstetricians. In the autumn of 1945 he decided on far-reaching concessions in their favour. They were to retain the right to private practice and pay-beds which they had enjoyed in the voluntary hospitals, and would now be able to colonise the former local authority hospitals as well. No wonder it was said of Bevan's relations with the consultants that he had 'stuffed their mouths with gold'.

Dame Janet Vaughan, however, argues that a more positive construction should be placed on events:

> I don't think it was a question so much of making it a deal . . . some of the senior men, people like Lord Moran – Corkscrew Charlie, for whom I have a profound admiration and affection, and many of the surgeons, men like Rock Carling, many of the physicians, men like Jimmy Spence from Newcastle – had seen what medicine in the periphery was and known what good medicine could be and they were prepared to fight, and fight they did to get a decent sort of service for the country and they worked in collaboration with Bevan because Bevan was a great statesman . . .

The leaders of the consultants – though by no means all of their colleagues – had been squared. Bevan, however, still had to win over the 51,000 general practitioners who belonged to the British Medical

Association. There was never any question of conscripting doctors into the service. Bevan's aim was to persuade them into accepting a new contract of service, and the proposals he formulated in the autumn and winter of 1945 were intended to be conciliatory. One of the doctors' major fears had been local authority rule. But having bypassed local government, Bevan proposed that general practitioners should be under contract to health councils on which they (together with dentists and chemists) would occupy half the seats, alongside the representatives of the local authority and the Ministry of Health. A second and related fear of the doctors was that capitation fees would be replaced by a salary, thus converting independent professionals into employees. Again Bevan gave ground, agreeing that apart from a small, basic salary doctors would be paid as before on a capitation basis.

When, in January 1946, Bevan outlined his policy to the BMA, the first response was favourable: there was less State socialism than had been expected. But there was still a large enough element of State control in the proposals to give rise in the following weeks to a vigorous backlash.

Bevan was determined to secure a more rational distribution of doctors around the country and intended to take powers to prevent doctors from setting up in areas that were already over-doctored. To the BMA, this smacked of dictatorship. Similarly, the Association condemned his proposal to abolish the old custom of the sale of the good will of a medical practice. There were even fears that once in the new health service, doctors would have no right of appeal to the courts against decisions by the health authorities.

During the three-day debate on the second reading of the National Health Service Bill, which began on 30 April 1946, the BMA's Representative Body, composed of delegates from the regions, gave the first expression to the feeling of the rank-and-file members. The atmosphere was one of mounting indignation. Resolutions were passed condemning the nationalisation of voluntary hospitals, the introduction of an element of salary into the doctors' pay, the restriction on doctors' freedom of movement, and the abolition of the sale of practices.

Specific grievances, taken one by one and debated in detail, might have been dealt with in a calm spirit of negotiation. But the particular causes of complaint were interlocked in a complex of fear and mistrust. The BMA consisted mainly of conservative and middle-class Anglo-Saxons – the 'backbone of England'. But they were dealing with a supremely agile Welsh socialist from a militantly working-class background. The doctors feared that beyond the immediate proposals, which they thought bad enough, lay undisclosed intentions for the long-term future. Why, for example, did the Bill propose a small basic salary for doctors? Bevan had remarked in the course of the debate, 'There is all the difference in the world between plucking fruit when it is ripe and plucking it when it is green.' Did this not betray ulterior motives?

But this was not all. The professional concerns of the BMA were symptomatic of anxieties among the traditional middle class. Speaking for the Conservatives in a debate in the House of Commons on 9 February 1948, David Eccles declared:

I do not think we can understand why the opposition of the doctors to the Minister has increased unless we see the Minister's recent obstinacy as one of a series of blows delivered by this Government against the middle class. Houses are not to be built for sale; the purchasing power of professional incomes goes steadily down; the basic petrol ration is abolished; university seats in this House are to disappear; and now there is talk of a capital levy which will hit those people for whom the Secretary of State for War [Shinwell] does not care a 'tinker's cuss'.

Brian Watkin is surely right to suggest of the BMA that 'the resentment they felt, as members of the middle class ... coloured and distorted their perceptions of what the government was proposing to do in the field of health'.[6]

While, therefore, Bevan entered into private negotiations with the BMA, these were accompanied by a strident propaganda campaign warning that doctors would never join the health service on the terms proposed by Bevan. The language of the doctors alternated between wild threats and allegations of dictatorship. As it was not yet quite respectable to attack the Soviet system, Bevan was represented as a would-be Führer. 'I have examined the Bill', wrote Dr Alfred Cox, 'and it looks to me uncommonly like the first step, and a big one, towards National Socialism as practised in Germany.'[7]

On 6 November 1946 the National Health Service Bill became law. The Appointed Day set for the start of the NHS was 5 July 1948. But there was nothing in the Act to compel the doctors to join and without them the service would remain an empty shell. In the month the Bill became law, the BMA proceeded to hold a plebiscite of its members, asking them whether they were prepared to enter negotiations on the basis of the present Bill: 54 per cent voted against negotiations and 46 per cent for, leaving a deadlock. But early in 1947 this was broken by the intervention of the leaders of the three Royal Colleges, and negotiations were resumed in earnest.

Lord Hill, who as Charles Hill, the Radio Doctor, and Secretary of the BMA led its Negotiating Committee, recalls Bevan's style of handling meetings:

> He was very honest in that ... when something was said with which he disagreed he said so. He didn't use the old formula, 'I'll consider that,' when he meant, 'I'm going to reject that'.

Hill goes on to say that in his opinion there was one flaw in Bevan's approach. Accustomed as he was to the insulting rhetoric of parliamentary debate, he would sometimes ridicule a doctor in front of his colleagues. At one of the sessions between Bevan and the Negotiating Committee of the BMA,

> Dr Cockshott of Hendon said something and Nye Bevan bit his head off and the Chairman of the doctors got up and protested. 'What you have said about my colleague', he said, 'is nothing but clever misrepresentation.' The last thing he repeated, 'nothing but clever misrepresentation', and Nye bent over and said, 'Doctor, it couldn't have been so clever for you to spot it so quickly!'

Negotiations throughout 1947 failed to produce a settlement. The BMA insisted that the National Health Act, as it now was, should be amended. Bevan would only offer adjustments within the framework of the Act. At the beginning of 1948 the scene was set for a showdown, with only six months and four days left before the NHS was due to begin. In February a second plebiscite produced another overwhelming vote against the Act: 40,814 against, and 4735 in favour.

Bevan had shown remarkable nerve in resisting the clamour. But with time running out he deftly played two more cards. On 7 April, after further manoeuvres with the consultants behind the scenes, Bevan announced in the House that the legislation would be amended by the addition of a clause to forbid the introduction of a full-time salaried service. The concession, accompanied by public intervention in its favour by the consultants, split the BMA. At the same time Bevan began to mobilise the doctors' patients. A publicity campaign was launched to persuade the public to obtain from their doctor the application form necessary for registering with a National Health doctor. A doctor who refused to sign an application was in danger of losing his patients to a doctor who would. A third plebiscite in April, though still revealing a large majority against the scheme, also showed the beginnings of a shift. This time 14,620 were in favour, 25,842 against. Resistance was beginning to crumble and as 5 July approached it collapsed.

One of the last to hold out against the scheme was Dr Jeaffreson Harris, a GP in Dorset, who describes the trend of opinion:

> Before the National Health Service came into being there were meetings called by the BMA at Dorchester and I very vividly remember the first of those which was attended by, I think, nearly all the doctors in the area. The room was absolutely crammed and it was interesting to see quite a lot of young doctors still in uniform having not yet been demobilised, and the feeling then was that we should under no circumstances enter a National Health Service under the suggested rules. This was followed at regular intervals by further meetings and bit by bit the numbers dwindled away until, in the end, the last meeting I attended there were regrettably only twenty doctors saying no.

By 5 July, about 90 per cent of general practitioners had entered the National Health Service. Dentists, opticians and pharmacists had also settled their terms and agreed to enter the service.

The first day of the National Health Service was a red-letter day for many families, relieving them of worries about money and health. Mrs Clare Bond of Leeds describes how, on 5 July, she and a group of friends went to the pub and celebrated by getting drunk on Farnby's wine at twopence a glass. And as she explains, there was good cause for the celebrations:

> When the National Health Service started, oh it was fantastic. My mother and dad had been having problems with their teeth for ages, and I think they were the first at the dentist, as soon as he opened, they were there for an appointment. And instead of having just a few teeth out, they had the complete set out. And free dentures. You know? Thought it was wonderful ... My sister had had school-supply steel-rimmed spectacles for ages. But many a time she used to go out without the glasses on and she used to scab like this, you know, she couldn't see properly without them. And as soon as the NHS started, she was there, [at the] optician. Marvellous NHS spectacles, you know, some style about

them. So she didn't hesitate at wearing glasses any more after that. And then I had another sister, she'd had one baby and it was rather bad, she had to pay 12s. 6d. for a midwife, no gas and air, anything like this, and just after the National Health started she had her second baby, at home, as you did have your children at home then. Then she thought it was absolutely wonderful, because besides having a free midwife, she had a nurse came in every day, you had to stay in bed fourteen days then, a nurse came in every day, bathed the baby, showed her how to look after it ...

Unfortunately the NHS arrived too late to be of much assistance to Mrs Bond's father:

Well, Dad thought it was wonderful, because he ... had a small wage, and thought with a family of four children to bring up, it was just too much for him to be able to go to the doctor ... He used to buy some concoction from the chemist at sixpence a bottle, that eased his pains in his stomach. But when he went on the National Health Service, this was thoroughly investigated, and they found out that Dad hadn't a stomach upset, Dad had a cancer. Had it been treated earlier, could have been cured but unfortunately, due to the expensive doctors, Dad had not had this looked into before, and we lost Dad, Dad died of cancer.

Another witness, Alice Law of Manchester, describes the reactions of her mother to the inauguration of the NHS:

I can remember this particular day, everything was in a radius of a few minutes' walk, and she went to the optician's, obviously she'd got the prescription from the doctor, she went and she got tested for new glasses, then she went further down the road ... for the chiropodist, she had her feet done, then she went back to the doctor's because she'd been having trouble with her ears and the doctor said ... he would fix her up with a hearing aid, and I remember, me mother was a very funny woman, I remember her saying to the doctor on the way out, 'Well the undertaker's is on the way home, everything's going on, I might as well call in there on the way home!'

Mrs Law's recollection suggests that women in particular were the beneficiaries of the NHS in the opening weeks and months. Corroborating evidence is supplied by Dr Katharina Dalton, who happened to qualify as a doctor on the Appointed Day. She began as an assistant in general practice in a poor working-class district:

> I think what I remember most is two conditions that you don't see much now but you saw a tremendous amount in the first six months. One was low thyroid, hypothyroidism, and the women just got slower and duller and falling asleep in the evenings and it was just accepted as their personality – and you know, you could suddenly change them. And then also the women with ulcers on their legs – they'd had varicose ulcers for twenty, thirty years and suddenly they could be treated ... They had to pay before the health scheme and that was too much, too expensive. I mean some of them were brought up with the idea that, you know, you never go to a solicitor, you never go to a doctor because it's always far too expensive ...

Mrs D. Chapman, a Bournemouth District Nurse, tells how she and other nurses often felt thwarted before the NHS by the difficulty of obtaining for chronic or terminal patients such elementary items as bandages and cotton wool. Of the start of the NHS she says:

> Well, it was so exciting, I think for quite a week beforehand we – there were not many nurses in those days on the district – but we talked and we wondered and the great day came ... It didn't only uplift us, it was the patients as well, it was just fantastic, it was just something that you never believed could have happened, you know, when you've struggled and tried so long ...
> If you could imagine doing extensive dressings and knowing that you – you just hadn't got anything really to do it with, you just did cope and suddenly you'd got it all, this gorgeous soft cotton wool, beautiful clean bandages, so much so that we just talked about it for weeks afterwards, it took a long time to sink in.

It is often said that problems cannot be solved by throwing money at them, but all these accounts go to show that the easing of financial constraints on patients and staff did lead to immediate practical improvements in the standard of health care.

Another factor in the raising of standards was the reorganisation of specialist services in the hospitals. Sir Francis Avery Jones, who was Consultant Physician at the Central Middlesex Hospital when the NHS was introduced, comments:

I welcomed the NHS originally because I knew how dreadful was the distribution of specialist skills around the country: whole areas with inadequate anaesthetists, paediatricians, gynaecologists, orthopaedic surgeons. All that has been straightened out. Now, the length and breadth of the country, you will be able to get first class service for any emergency ...

All to the good, but the effects of the NHS in improving the level of health must not be exaggerated. Improvements in housing and nutrition may have been just as influential. The state of medical knowledge, whether professional or popular, was another critical factor. In 1947 the BMA, as part of their campaign over the NHS, made a dramatised documentary, 'The Family Doctor', to illustrate the virtues of the traditional GP. The doctor, a reassuring elderly gentleman, is shown comforting a distraught wife whose husband has left her. To calm her down he hands her a cigarette – an irony that now speaks volumes.

What effects did the NHS have upon the careers and working conditions of general practitioners? On balance, it seems, the consequences were favourable: a more secure income, free of the hazards of debt, but with the retention of clinical freedom. Dr Jeaffreson Harris, quoted above as a last-ditch opponent of the NHS, comments:

In the end, when the National Health Service came in, it seemed to work very well. I think we were all agreeably surprised. There was very little interference and obviously the government was softpedalling to get us to comply.

The terms offered by the government in compensation for the abolition of the sale of practices were regarded as stingy. Dr Goldman, a Manchester GP, still feels that he was badly treated:

I had borrowed money to buy the share in the practice when I came out of the army, so I had a not inconsiderable loan outstanding. I knew that I would not be able to support this loan if the monies were not returned to me by the National Health, and I had the belief that the money would be returned to me in pound notes, or used fivers. But in actual fact it was returned to me as Government stock, yielding a very low percentage, much lower than I could have got by investment in other kinds of stock. In order to get that money back, you had to show special hardship of a financial nature.

This I tried to do but was unfortunately unsuccessful so I had to wait a full term before those monies were returned to me.

A fortunate consequence of the NHS was that minor operations hitherto carried out by GPs were transferred to the hospitals. Though in one or two places GPs retained a ward in a local hospital, the division between general practice and the hospital was otherwise complete. Dr Ashworth tells how he breathed a sigh of relief when the NHS came in:

> I realised that all these old implements which I'd inherited from my predecessor were no longer going to be of any use to me. So I opened the drawers and I found the amputation knife which he and his father before him had used. I thought it would have made a very good carving knife but my wife refused to have that knife in the kitchen and I had to consign it to the dustbin. And I threw away my catheters and my trocars and cannulas and my consulective guillotine, if I'd kept them now they would have been worth a place in a medical museum.

For hospital staff, there was no instant change. A unified regional administration took years to establish. Mr Mostyn Davies of Cardiff was Group Secretary for one of the Hospital Management Committees which had the responsibility, under the Regional Board, of grouping a number of hospitals together:

> My aim within the group was to make it a complete entity, with hospitals mixing together and staff mixing together and patients transferred from the smaller hospitals to the larger hospitals if necessary. Now this had never happened before. But, and it did take time, it took a couple of years for people to get used to this, it also meant that the patients had to get used to it, patients going from one town where they had had their own hospital for years and years having to go to another town albeit it was only ten or fifteen miles away but people did get used to it and you see you can't equip these smaller places with sophisticated equipment, they've got to be centred somewhere in the larger places and this sunk in all right ...

The nationalisation of the voluntary hospitals passed off with surprisingly little protest but the staff naturally regretted the loss of their independence, and perhaps a certain loss of professional status as well. As Dr Ashworth observes:

The voluntary hospital always regarded itself as the cream of hospital care, and the consultants at the voluntary hospitals were the type to whom you doffed your cap and touched your forelock ... The consultants in the municipal hospitals were rather more sweated labour: the consultants, for example, in the voluntary hospital might have fifteen female beds, fourteen male beds. The consultants in the municipal hospitals which were maintained out of the rates, often had thirty, forty, fifty female beds, fifty male beds. But, come the day of reckoning, with the introduction of the National Health Service, what happened? What happened was this, that the general practitioner who had a patient whom he wished to get into a hospital bed, thought to himself, 'Ah, if I send my patient now to the municipal hospital consultant, he's got many more beds and a damn sight better chance of getting the patient in, than if I send him to the voluntary hospital consultant, who's got a limited number of beds.' So you could imagine that these consultants at the municipal hospitals practically became millionaires overnight ...

Consultants contracting with the National Health Service had the option of working full- or part-time. One who decided on a part-time contract was Sir John Stallworthy, an obstetrician working in the Oxford area. The reason, he explains, is that he was fearful for the consequences in medicine:

I was fearful that medicine itself, the service that we were trying to give, could suffer by possible edicts from higher up from people who didn't know the areas and didn't know the problems ... I wanted independence.

Critics of the Welfare State maintain that it has been established at the price of the loss of older virtues of civic and personal responsibility. Nurse Roche, who worked in a voluntary hospital in Bournemouth before and after the introduction of the NHS, recalls a change in the attitudes of patients to the staff:

Gradually I noticed over the years that they treated us more like paid employees of the Civil Service ... very slowly over the years they were looking for things to sue for, we didn't get the gratitude and the little presents ...

Practically from the day it began, the NHS was overshadowed by controversy over the cost of the service. The estimates made in advance of the costs of medical, dental and eye services all proved to be gross underestimates. There was no cooking of the books: the information available was simply inadequate. In an appendix to the Beveridge Report the government actuary, Sir George Epps, had estimated the total cost of the NHS in its first year as £170m. Moreover, Beveridge argued in the Report that improved health services would actually reduce the number of people who were ill and claiming sickness benefit. The implication was that the cost of the health services would tend to fall in real terms. But the actual cost in the first year turned out to be £242m., growing to £384m. by 1952–3. The rising curve of expenditure falsified the more optimistic expectations present at the start of the NHS. Dr G. Jaffe, who was then a medical student, recalls:

> We were very idealistic at the time, because we were brainwashed into thinking that the Health Service would be so wonderful that everybody would be very much fitter, all serious diseases would be cured and there was a grave danger that in a few years' time doctors might become redundant because there'd be insufficient work for them.

Bevan himself, though worried, as he said, by the cascade of medicine pouring down the throats of the public, was inclined to be optimistic about costs in the long run. Lord Bruce, who as Donald Bruce MP was Bevan's PPS, observes:

> He was well aware of the financial cost but in his view, if you succeeded in Britain in establishing the correct social climate where people valued things on the basis of need rather than on sordid profitability, he thought that the expenditure on the Health Service would progressively moderate.

No one could have guessed on the eve of the NHS the extent of the hidden popular demand for its goods and services. At a press conference on 6 October 1949 Aneurin Bevan gave some of the relevant figures: 187,000,000 prescriptions had been dispensed at a cost of 2s. 9d. each; 5,250,000 pairs of spectacles had been supplied and another 3,000,000 were on order; 8,500,000 dental patients had been accepted for treatment.

There was much criticism of the NHS for tending to encourage extravagance in the use of resources. This is still the verdict of Nurse Roche on the basis of her experience in a former voluntary hospital:

The trouble is, when an invisible 'They' far away owns everything nobody bothers to economise, whereas in the old days of the voluntary hospitals, people turned off lights, turned off hot water taps ... unused dressings were sent down for resterilising, all those sorts of things, whereas today nobody bothers, they all go into the dustbin.

After the National Health started, gradually we realised there wasn't the same pressure on nursing staff and others to mind the pennies as we had to in the old days when the hospital was supported by voluntary subscriptions, and slowly the paperwork increased. In the old days if the steriliser broke down we just rang up the workshop: 'Right you are, Sister, I'll be up,' and somebody would come along and fix it. After the National Health when the paper started accumulating you had to fill in a book in triplicate, one chit to the Admin Office, one chit to the Works Office and the third chit stayed in the duplicate book ...

In a period of Crippsian austerity, when a tight deflationary rein was being kept on public expenditure, the NHS was an inevitable target for cuts. In 1949 the Treasury under Cripps was anxious to introduce prescription charges and Bevan reluctantly agreed to the introduction of a legislative clause authorising a one shilling prescription charge to be levied, if a fair and workable scheme could be devised. This was a delaying tactic by Bevan, but one that was to be quoted against him later on. In 1951 the new Chancellor of the Exchequer, Hugh Gaitskell, was determined to push through a £4700m. rearmament programme arising out of the Korean war. He insisted that £25m. be trimmed from the cost of the National Health Service by the introduction of prescription charges for teeth and spectacles. Bevan, by this time Minister of Labour, led the resistance to Gaitskell's proposals in the Cabinet. He criticised the defence estimates as overblown and unattainable, a judgement later proved correct, and attacked prescription charges as a breach in the principle of a free health service. Gaitskell, however, won the battle and announced the new charges in his budget on 10 April. On 23 April Bevan resigned from the government together with Harold Wilson, the President of the Board of Trade, and John Freeman, Parliamentary Under-Secretary at the War Office. The levy on the cost of teeth and spectacles went ahead and the following year the new Conservative government added a standard charge of one shilling for other prescriptions. Neither charge applied to needy categories of patient, who were exempt.

The scare over the cost of the NHS proved to be greatly exaggerated in the short run. In the 1950s economic growth came to the rescue. At about 4 per cent of national income, the cost of health care in Britain was much lower than in many other developed countries. After the initial bonanza of teeth and spectacles, the NHS settled down to develop at a fairly slow pace under fairly strict government control of expenditure. For a glimpse of the evolution of the NHS through the next two decades we may round off with the words of Sir George Godber, who followed events from the beginning and became Chief Medical Officer at the Ministry of Health in 1960:

> I don't think that any of us had realistic plans at the beginning. We saw what we had, we knew it had to be reconstructed, we were aware that there were scientific changes in medicine that made it potentially greater. We certainly hoped for faster movement in its development. One small point like hospital building: we had virtually no money in the first twelve years of the Health Service to do more than make good failing buildings, add a few extra facilities like the X-ray departments, out-patients departments, laboratories, operating theatres ... so we didn't begin to get the kind of building programme one would have liked to see until the early 1960s. And that meant that we'd lost about ten years' impetus in what one would have liked to see on the hospital side. We also perhaps thought there would be more changes in general practice. There had been much talk about health centres and then about the development of group practice, but it takes time to change a large body of professional people, and we didn't see clearly then the sort of group practice develop with the doctors and community nurses really working together for the same population. The thing you really should see as the great gain is the technical improvement in health care – the way that new techniques were made available to everybody through the regional district system of specialist service, and through the better development of general practice.

5

LIVING IT UP

There are stock images for every period. For post-war Britain they are black and white images of hardship and high endeavour. They conjure up a land in which it was usually winter and people were digging themselves out of snowdrifts. The middle classes had disappeared and the male population, driven on by the exhortations of the government, were all digging coal or building ships. The women, meanwhile, were queuing for offal at the butcher's. In such spare time as they had left the people were grappling with social problems and were either squatting or looking forward to a set of NHS dentures. But the cinema brought relief – with the latest Central Office of Information documentary on the progress of the social services. After six years of work and welfare it was naturally time for a break, so in May 1951 the Festival of Britain was declared: but in keeping with the spirit of the times, newsreels show that on the first day it was open to the public, the rain came bucketing down.

Only one item is missing from the received impression: the fact that there was plenty of fun to be had in the Attlee years. It was often summer and the summers were long and hot. And whatever the season, peace brought with it a sustained outbreak of pleasure. Never before in British history had so much been enjoyed by so many. Attlee himself, though few people's idea of a barrel of laughs, had his moments. Insisting on time off at weekends for tea and tennis, he took pride in the fact that he could still jump over the net in his sixties. If a buttoned-up and conscientious soul like Attlee took care to remember the pleasures of life, the broad-minded British were never likely to forget them.

It is a fair guess, though only a guess, that the leisure activities of the late 1940s tapped some very deep springs of motivation. In 1945 there were six years of grief, boredom, frustration and slaughter to make up for. The right to live in peace had been dearly paid for at the risk of life and limb, and the mere fact of physical survival was something to celebrate. Yet the conditions of everyday life were shabby and constricting. Work, though plentiful, was slow to bring the longed-for rewards of an ideal home with a chicken in the pot and a Morris Ten in the garage. Leisure, in other words, had to compensate for many other things. And fortunately leisure activities were more widely available than ever.

The post-war economy encouraged a high level of demand in the leisure and entertainment industries. An initial boost was given by the millions of returning service personnel, each with a gratuity to spend. In conditions of full employment, the collective spending power of the working classes was greater, and the relatively higher proportion of married women at work compared with 1939 gave many families spare cash to spend. But what could it be spent on? With many commodities on the ration and others in short supply, leisure was the most powerful magnet, and the leisure industry a licence to print money.

Though there was a boom in leisure activities there was little change in content. Technical innovations in the media were slight, and the technology of sport and games was temporarily at a standstill. There was no 1940s invention to parallel the introduction of the gramophone record, the talking picture, the motor bike, or the electric hare in greyhound racing. Television, first introduced by the BBC in 1936, and suspended during the war, was restarted in June 1946, but the audience at first was small and confined to the London area. The post-war boom in leisure witnessed the zenith of old or established pastimes rather than the introduction of new ones.

As families were reunited after the war, they looked forward to a traditional seaside holiday, something that had been almost impossible since 1939. In wartime the coastal resorts had only a trickle of holiday-makers or were out of bounds to civilians for defence purposes. But with the return of peace they sprang to life again in the most favourable of circumstances.

After 1945 more families than ever could afford a holiday away from home. The Holidays with Pay Act of 1938 had paved the way for the provision of paid holidays as a normal feature of wage agreements, and by 1946 some 12 million workers, about 80 per cent of the labour force, were covered. In origin, the popular seaside holiday was a Victorian creation, made possible by the railway lines built to connect the urban heartlands with the coast. Many of the features of a seaside holiday were still as the Victorians had left them: the piers, the promenades, the deck-chairs, donkey-rides, buckets and spades, Punch and Judy shows. In time, cinemas and dance-halls and many other attractions had been added but the main change was the growth in the number of holiday-makers as incomes rose and paid holidays spread.

The late 1940s marked the peak of the Victorian resorts. As the majority of working-class families did not own a car they still depended on the charabanc or train to get them to the seaside, and holiday excursions followed well-beaten paths. In July and August the queues at railway stations were so enormous that the government launched a publicity campaign to persuade the public to stagger their holidays over a longer period.

Every region had its favourite resorts, but the most famous of them all remained Blackpool. Mrs Freeman, whose family ran a boarding-house there, describes the town after the war as 'heaving':

> At a peak time you'd have about twenty-four people in with one loo, which unfortunately was in the same room as the bathroom, so it was a case of first up first served, and for washing you could cut out half the people going to the bathroom for a wash, because we delivered jugs of hot water outside the rooms every morning, and then while they were in breakfast some poor bugger had to sort of scuttle around and go and empty all the bowls out of the bedrooms.

The record level of demand for seaside holidays was an opportunity unlikely to be missed by the redoubtable Billy Butlin. Butlin – or 'Mr Happiness' as he liked to be known – was a hereditary showman. Born of English parents in South Africa, he received little formal education and, after the break-up of his parents' marriage, spent his boyhood and adolescence with his mother in Canada. It was through his mother, a member of an old fairground and circus family in the west of England, that Butlin entered the holiday business after his arrival in Britain in 1921. His first major venture, an amusement park in Skegness, became the springboard for the innovation that made his name and fortune: the holiday camp. The Skegness camp was opened in 1936 and another at Clacton in 1937.

In the Second World War Butlin came in very useful to the government, and the government came in very useful to him. The buildings and facilities of the holiday camps made them ideal for the use of the armed forces. Moreover, Butlin could build camps faster and more cheaply than the service departments. So he was commissioned to complete a third camp at Filey and build two more, for the use of the Navy, at Ayr and Pwllheli. At the end of the war, he bought the new camps back from the government and reconverted them for the use of holiday-makers. Butlin celebrated the restoration of peace with a gala opening of the Filey camp in 1946, and all five of his camps were ready for the holiday season the following year.[1]

In the summer of 1947 about half a million people flocked to Butlin's camps. The genius of Butlin was to take all the organisational worries out of a holiday and fill the holiday-maker's day with a ceaseless round of organised fun and games. In return for a single payment the camper received accommodation, three meals a day and all entertainments without additional charge. There was nothing for the campers left to spend their money on but drinks, snacks and cigarettes.

It was obvious from the demand for a Butlin's holiday, and the fact so many campers returned year after year, that the experiment was a raging success. A vivid description of the Skegness camp in the first year it was reopened is given by Joan Astelle, whose praise is mingled with realism:

> It was very, very nice ... As I recall it, we had what I thought then was marvellous food, I couldn't get over the food, rationing was still on and the food seemed wonderful, we had eggs and bacon for breakfast and fresh peaches for lunch, it was an absolute dream, but the rest of the accommodation was not at all palatial. It was wooden huts, just creosoted, there was a wash-basin in the hut, but that was cold water only. In fact I think they were very much as the Navy had left them, we even had bedspreads with HMS *Royal Arthur* on them and that had been the name of the Navy base during the war.

A visitor who looks back on a Butlin's holiday with unqualified delight is Mr Franklyn:

> I think it was 1947 that I first went to Butlin's. And I could go for a week. And I remember going there and seeing all these chalets. Everything was so wonderful after the drabness of the war ... As soon as I got there I opened me wallet up and I had eight pounds to last me for the week. I was rich! It was really wonderful. Butlin's was the best thing that happened to ordinary people. To get them a holiday outside their own areas. To go up to King's Cross. To get on a train. It was a wonderful feeling. And Butlin's cashed in at the right time, they really did.

Butlin's claimed to offer visitors the very best in entertainment. Not that Butlin himself was an infallible judge in show-business affairs. His advice to the young Frankie Howerd, who auditioned for him about this time, was brief and to the point, 'Take it from me, son, you will never get anywhere as a funny man.'

Butlin could hardly bring to the camps the stars of the cinema, who were mainly American, and as yet there were no stars of television. So the entertainers at the camps were great names from radio. Ted Young, a trainee manager at Skegness, recalls:

> We had a slogan: 'The Stars You Have Heard, But Seldom Seen' – and those were the people who were commissioned to come along and produce their shows, and give their shows on the centres. They had many of the famous names: Tommy Handley, Jack Train – they're all from ITMA – Richard Murdoch, Kenneth Horne ... I can remember Terry Scott and Bill Maynard being a double act in the revue company. Tessie O'Shea, Cavan O'Connor, the Beverley Sisters, Talbot O'Farrell, in fact we went up-market at the opening of some centres and Sir William in his keenness imported the entire San Carlo Opera Company from Italy to produce operas and the following year was the London Symphony Orchestra under the direction of Vic Oliver – though he was known as a comedian he was also a very talented musician and conductor.

As Ted Young's recollections show, Butlin was inclined to set up after the war as a patron of the arts. When the San Carlo Opera performed Puccini's *La Bohème* at the gala opening of the Filey camp, it was for the benefit of 400 VIPs invited up from London on board the Yorkshire Pullman. Later, Butlin invited the Old Vic to Filey to give a short season of Shakespearean plays. Celebrities were invited to stay at the VIP Chalet, No. A7: Anthony Eden spent a night there, and the Chancellor of the Exchequer, Hugh Dalton, was Butlin's guest for a week. The Archbishop of York, Dr Garbett, was a regular camper, gratified by Butlin's decision to introduce regular Sunday services in the post-war camps: Butlin's paternal grandfather had been a clergyman of the Church of England.

In the immediate post-war years, the Butlin camps did indeed cater for quite a broad social spectrum. The prices were too high for the poorer wage-earner, but ideal for the skilled or clerical worker, and middle-class professionals were often to be found at the camps. The habit of mixing with all types, characteristic of the Army and the Home Front, had not yet worn off.

Ted Young says:

> The greatest cross-section of the community came through
> the centres ... let us take the knobbly knees competition, it
> was nothing weird to see a barrister, doctors, and many
> professional men queuing up with the road sweeper or the
> refuse person, all getting together and having a very good
> time.

The atmosphere at a Butlin's camp was that of a continuous
party. Throughout the day, the redcoats were busy jollying people
along and organising games and competitions. So hectic and non-stop
was the activity that the Labour MP Woodrow Wyatt, who spent a
week at a camp in 1947, concluded that 'illicit sex is ruled out by
physical exhaustion'.[2] The round-the-clock schedule of fun and
games is vividly remembered by Joan Astelle:

> There was continuous dancing and there was other things that
> one could do – there was the swimming pool, the lovely
> ladies contest, the knobbly knees contest, everywhere as I
> remember it there were redcoats trying to get you to join in
> ... as a young person going there, this was marvellous, we
> needed someone to sort of push us in the pool and make us
> laugh, we were all very shy and self-conscious. This sort of
> holiday was something totally new.

Totally new? Not quite. A Butlin's camp was a Blackpool in
miniature, bringing together under one roof all the traditional
ingredients of a really good time. Yet Butlin's did have an extra flair.
The camps were ideal for parents, who could leave their children in
safe hands at the nursery or the swimming pool. And as Ted Young
explains, there was a skilful manipulation of colour to provide
psychological escape:

> Colour was essential. At Skegness alone there were 37,000
> rose bushes planted. We never could find a bloom that would
> come out somewhere round about the beginning of May and
> die in October when we closed the sites, so roses were best.
> The other gimmick we had was putting artificial flowers in
> the trees, rather large ones ... the chalets, the exteriors, had
> to be bright and cheerful, the workhouse browns and dark
> greens from the cities and provincial towns had to be done
> away with, there'd been so much mud and khaki and dark
> blues in the war, colour was essential.

Was there also a new communal spirit reflected in the post-war expansion of Butlin's? The atmosphere of togetherness can, of course, be attributed to working-class tradition, but the popularity of life in a camp with a commandant and a corps of redcoats must surely have owed something to wartime experience. Millions of service personnel and war workers away from home had become used to living in camps and had perhaps begun to enjoy living as an organised crowd. The post-war appeal of old Army camps as temporary homes, and the popularity of the harvest camps run by the Ministry of Agriculture, would point in the same direction.

Visitors to Butlin's had, of course, to take their food ration books and hand them over to the management for the coupons to be clipped out. Later, they might have to sit down to a whalemeat dinner. The days might be luxurious, with the sun beating down on the holiday lovelies competition, but complete isolation from the conditions of austerity was impossible.

The long-drawn-out delight of the English summer – and the most eternal bore for those who did not appreciate the game – was the cricket season. During the war, Test series were out of the question and the MCC, the governing body of cricket, suspended the County Championship. Afterwards, the game was quickly restored but not without many petty vexations.

Test matches resumed in 1946 with the visit of the last All-India side, captained by the Nawab of Pataudi. As the historians of the MCC record, there was great difficulty, owing to clothes rationing, in kitting out the Indians with boots and white flannels. Nor was this the only problem:

> The purchase of cricket equipment was controlled by buying certificates; new cricket balls had to be rationed, and there was a waiting list for reblading bats ... Shortages of food, which was rationed until 1952, were suggested as a possible contributory factor in the slow recovery of English cricket after the war. The 1948 Australians, conscious of their own plenty, refused the temptation to supplement their English rations, deciding that to do so would be to take unfair advantage of their opponents. Instead they brought with them 200 cases of tinned meat, which were handed over ceremonially to the Minister of Food for distribution to the people of Britain to compensate for the food the team would eat while they were here.[3]

A nice gesture, and not bad as gamesmanship either. Reputedly the best Australian team ever to tour England, Don Bradman's side went on to win four out of the five Tests and retain the Ashes.

The golden age of cricket is always in the past. In the case of first-class cricket this may well be true, for the audience reached its maximum in the glorious summer of 1947, when nearly three million people paid to watch the game. In a series of three Test matches against South Africa, Denis Compton thrilled the crowds by hitting four centuries, including one double century. In a tribute to Compton, Neville Cardus wrote:

> Never have I been so deeply touched on a cricket ground as I was in this heavenly summer, when I went to Lord's to see a pale-faced crowd, existing on rations, the rocket bomb still in the ears of most folk – to see this worn, dowdy crowd watching Compton. The strain of long years of anxiety and affliction passed from all hearts and shoulders at the sight of Compton in full flow, sending the ball here, there and everywhere, each stroke a flick of delight, a propulsion of happy, sane, healthy life. There was no rationing in an innings by Compton.[4]

Denis Compton had the distinction of playing football for Arsenal, one of the top teams in League Division One, as well as cricket for Middlesex and England. Looking back on those days, he is impressed by the size and enthusiasm of the crowds who turned out to watch first-class sport:

> Everybody in fact was absolutely starved of sport, so what was wonderful from our point of view, then you might say in our heyday, was that we played all our cricket and our football in front of capacity crowds and that to me was absolutely marvellous ... The football crowds were absolutely marvellous, I mean at Highbury, the Arsenal, pretty well every Saturday we used to get 60,000 people and we used to get the young boys, children of even eight, nine, ten, eleven, twelve all going with their parents and in fact at times not going with their parents, going on the terraces which were absolutely packed and you know you used to see them being pulled down over the heads of the crowd down to the front so they could get a jolly good seat. Nobody was ever hurt, the atmosphere I thought was absolutely electric ...
>
> The working-class people went, the middle-class people went and you might say the upper-class, the up-market class,

33–4 *left*, Replanning London, 1944; *below*, Aneurin Bevan opens a new housing estate at Elstree, 1949

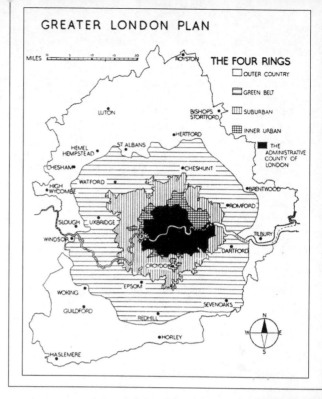

GREATER LONDON PLAN

MILES

THE FOUR RINGS

☐ OUTER COUNTRY
☐ GREEN BELT
▥ SUBURBAN
▦ INNER URBAN
■ THE ADMINISTRATIVE COUNTY OF LONDON

ROYSTON
LUTON
BISHOPS STORTFORD
HERTFORD
HEMEL HEMPSTEAD
ST ALBANS
CHESHAM
CHESHUNT
WATFORD
HIGH WYCOMBE
BRENTWOOD
ROMFORD
SLOUGH   UXBRIDGE
TILBURY
WINDSOR
DARTFORD
CROYDON
EPSOM
WOKING
SEVENOAKS
GUILDFORD
REDHILL
HORLEY
HASLEMERE

N
W   E
S

35–6 The Lansbury Estate before and after redevelopment

37–8 *right*, Sir William Beveridge; *below*, The Minister of National Insurance, James Griffiths, welcomes the first recipient of family allowances at Stepney Post Office, August 1946

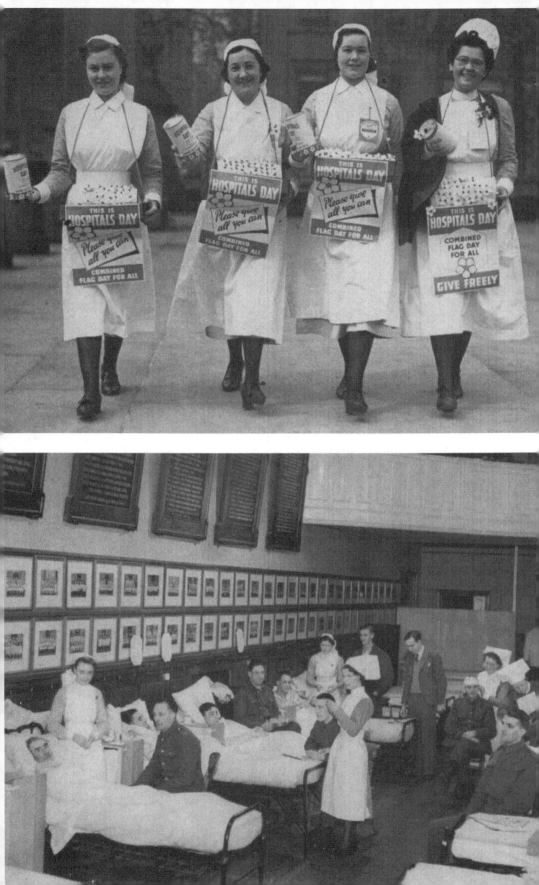

Train to be a
NURSE
*a distinguished
career for
women*

Enquire at your nearest Nursing Appointments Office or any local
office of the Ministry of Labour and National Service or write to
(Department N.R.) Spencer House, 27 St. James's Place, London, S.W.1

39–41   *opposite above*, Raising money for London hospitals, May 1940;
opposite below, Mill Hill school premises converted for use as an emergency
hospital, 1940; *above*, The post-war recruitment of nurses

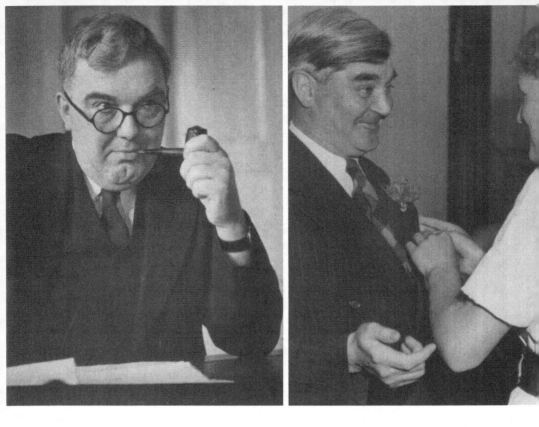

42–4 *above left*, Charles Hill; *above right*, Aneurin Bevan, 1950; *below*,
After seeing their doctors, patients queue for hospital appointments, 1949

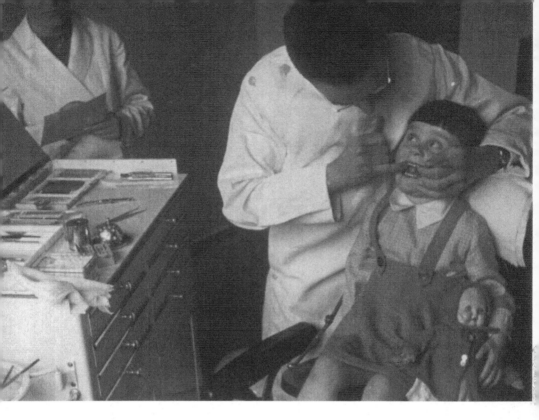

45   The way forward in dental care, 1944
46   Free spectacles from the optician, February 1951

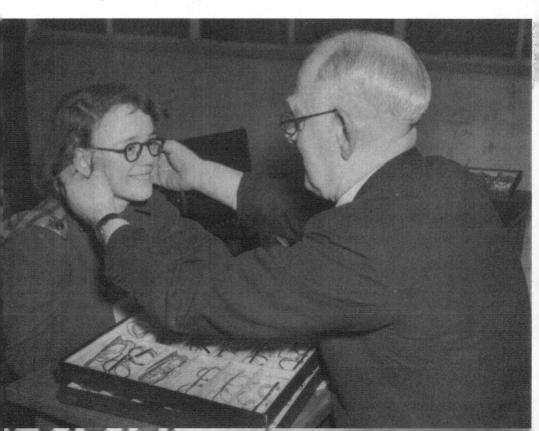

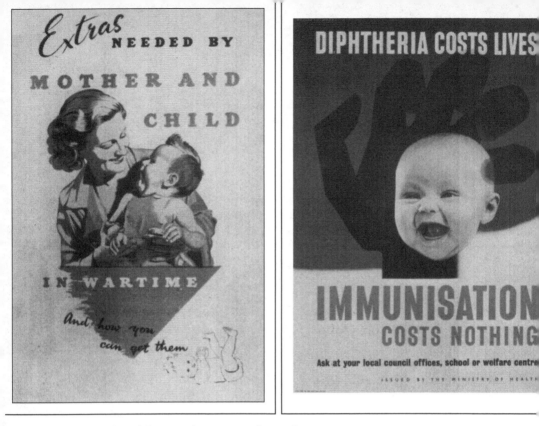

47 *above left*, A wartime message for mothers
48 *above right*, The wartime campaign against diphtheria
49 *below*, A wartime gain: free school milk, 1947

50   Whit Monday at Southend, 1950

51–4 *left*, Holiday crowds at Waterloo Station, July 1948; *opposite below*, A Butlin's holiday at Clacton; *right*, Bill Edrich and Denis Compton (England and Middlesex) going out to bat against Sussex CCC, Lord's, May 1947; *below*, Queuing at 7 am outside Lord's for a Test match, June 1948

55–60 *opposite top left*, Stanley Matthews takes a corner kick for Blackpool against Chelsea, February 1951; *opposite top right*, Tommy Price, winner of the 1946 British Riders' Championship; *opposite below left*, Fred Trevillion's greyhounds, 1948, *left to right*, Trev's Heir, Trev's Perfection and Trev's Harvest; *opposite below right*, A cycling club in 1948; *above*, Clem Attlee kicks off; *right*, Rita Hayworth and Aly Khan at the Derby, 1949

61   A day at the races: Harpo Marx and Prince Monolulu at Alexandra Park, 1949
62   Dancers at 100 Oxford Street, 1949

63   April 1949: Leicester Square lit up for the first time in nearly ten years
64   The last day of the Van Gogh exhibition at the Tate Gallery, January 1948

65–6 *left*, Gerald Campion as Billy Bunter on BBC Television; *below*, The annual Fourth of July celebrations at Eton, 1947

they all went ... they went there I think because they loved the game of football and I think the same applies to cricket.

Like first-class cricket, Association Football had been suspended during the war and replaced by regional competitions from which many star players were absent, due to military service. Football kept going but there was a thirst at the end of the war for the return of the real thing. Terry Alford remembers:

Football at that time was very popular, more so than it is today, and especially just after the war because during the war the football leagues were divided up. You had ... just a northern league and a southern league, and you never knew these famous footballers who played for the northern clubs, but after the war when they reverted back to the four divisions, or three to four divisions again, you had these really absolute megastars of football coming down from the north and playing and the crowds were absolutely fantastic ... I can remember a little Polish man taking me to see Newcastle United play, which was a team that had some fantastic players like Frank Smith in goal, Milburn, the Robledo brothers, and he took me, and it was so crowded he stood me on his shoulders 'cause I was only a tiny tot and I was watching the game but he couldn't see because he was down below me and I had to describe to him what was happening!

In England, as in Scotland, Association Football had been the national game and the king of working-class sports since the end of the nineteenth century. Crowds of over 100,000 people had been commonplace in English Cup Finals since 1901 and the largest football ground in the country, at Hampden Park in Glasgow, could theoretically hold 183,570 people. The record attendance at an English League fixture was reached in 1934, when a crowd of 84,560 watched the Cup Tie between Manchester City and Stoke City.

Crowds the size of an industrial town were nothing new in the history of football, but overall attendance at football matches was higher in the late 1940s than ever before or since. In the peak season of 1948–9, there were more than 41 million attendances as regular supporters filed week by week through the turnstiles. The professional clubs were in clover and all but a few recorded healthy profits. No less impressive was the popularity of the amateur game, with 90,000 people turning up for the 1949 Final at Wembley. (The result, incidentally, was: Bromley 1, Romford 0.)

Football was the game the British had given the world, but the world showed signs of improving on it. Since 1929, when Spain had the insolence to defeat England in Madrid, England had suffered a number of away defeats at the hands of continental sides, but victory in the Second World War, a pretty decisive reply, had sponged away the memory. In November 1945, Moscow Dynamo came to Britain and pulled off a disconcerting victory over Arsenal but football fans were still confident that British was best. As Brian Glanville explains, the myth of soccer supremacy rested on the fact that neither England nor Scotland had ever been beaten at home by a foreign team. New life was breathed into this illusion in May 1947, when a Great Britain team beat the Rest of Europe 6-1 at Hampden Park. 'Not for another six and a half years,' writes Glanville, 'when the Hungarians came to Wembley on a November afternoon, scored six goals and might have scored ten, was the island myth of British superiority at football scattered to the winds.'[5]

Football had no serious contender as the national game, but two more recent spectator sports were setting a cracking pace: greyhound racing and speedway. In its commercial form, with the dogs chasing an electric hare around the track of a stadium, greyhound racing had been introduced in the 1920s. The first track was opened in Manchester in 1926. The dog tracks were the poor man's version of the turf. Since horse-racing took place during the day and many of the meetings were out in the country, they were difficult to get to on a weekday. Greyhound-racing tracks could be laid out within earshot of the factory hooter, and the meetings took place after work.

It was often said of greyhound-racing, as of horse-racing, that it was merely a pretext for gambling. Certainly, people attended with the intention of placing a bet, and the promoters got most of their profits from this source – so much so that free admission to the stadium was a common practice. But Jack Huss, a great devotee of the dogs, argues that there were other reasons for their popularity. There was the excitement of a night out, often a family affair, and for connoisseurs there was the pleasure of studying the form of the animals:

A greyhound might have attached itself to your mind, and you'd see it to the ends of the earth. Just to go and see it run. Not because you thought it might win, but because it would reproduce its running to a 'T' and you could forecast how it would run, whether it would win or not, and the glorious thing about greyhound racing has always been the way animals reproduce their running, to within a hundredth of a second, and that's pretty good.

The post-war boom in greyhound-racing was short-lived but feverish while it lasted. In 1939 the estimated annual attendance was 24 million but in 1946, the peak year, it rose to 45 million, before levelling off and going into a decline.

The greyhound-racing tracks could also be turned over to speedway, a less popular sport which attracted a very different audience. 'The greyhound-racing followers', says Jack Huss, 'and the speedway crowds had absolutely nothing in common ... They're chalk and cheese, chalk and cheese.' No betting was allowed in speedway. The attraction was wholly dramatic and emotional: the competition of daredevil riders for stardom. As Tommy Price, who won the 1946 British Riders' Championship, puts it, 'There was a sort of gladiator effect ... a death or glory sort of outlook.' In June 1946, about 300,000 people a week were attending speedway fixtures, while a league match at Wembley, which was acknowledged to be the premier stadium in the country, attracted 71,000 people. Among the spectators at Wembley was the future Mrs Price, who describes speedway as 'a real family sport, everybody used to sort of pack up their sandwiches and leave straight from work to go and make sure of a seat because the crowds were so great'.

Speedway was a team sport, with teams competing in a league of twelve major clubs. But the reactions of the crowd focused on the performance of individuals. Tommy Price, who rode for the Wembley Lions, tells how he always felt an extra tension when he was due to ride at Wembley:

> Racing at Wembley was always very, very keen. Before you went to a meeting you had a tense feeling because you know that there's going to be a lot of people there, and I myself was very interested in the engineering side of the bikes, I designed my own machines and prepared them. But there were a lot of people going to criticise you, more so than any other track, so I suppose the adrenalin flew a lot harder than at the second division tracks.

Football, horse-racing and the dogs were the lifeblood of the gambling industry. Gambling was a long-established working-class tradition, and the amount of money lost to the working-class family budget had long been a matter of concern to moral reformers. The main legal restriction on gambling was that since 1906 off-course betting had been illegal. A bet on a dog or a horse could only be placed at the race meeting. It was also illegal to run a football betting business on a cash basis, but the law tolerated the football pools since they were conducted by post and, in theory at least, on credit. In spite of these restrictions, gambling flourished.

By the 1930s, estimates of the annual amount spent on gambling varied between £300 and £500 million, with horse-racing by far and away the greatest attraction. These figures can be compared with the post-war estimates compiled by the market researcher, Mark Abrams:[6]

	1947	1948	1949
		£m	
Horse-racing	400	350	450
Greyhound-racing	300	210	200
Football pools	70	69	67
Other	25	21	18
Total	795	650	735

One reason why precise figures are impossible to obtain is that off-course betting on horses, though forbidden by law, was commonplace. A Mass-Observation survey, carried out for the Anti-Gambling League, suggested that betting on horses was the most widespread form of gambling, with the pools running second. Most of the money spent was not lost to the gambling population but redistributed among them. Eighty per cent of the money laid out on the pools, and 90 per cent of the money spent with bookmakers, was returned to the lucky winners. Just as the social insurance system supplied guaranteed benefits, so gambling delivered irregular windfalls and compensated for the predictability of life. It was the irrational supplement to the Beveridge Report.

The comfortable view of gambling was that as the majority of gamblers were cautious types who only indulged in a 'little flutter', betting was therefore a fairly innocent pastime of responsible family men. This was largely true of the 10 million people who, according to the social surveys, filled in the football pools. There was, however, a high-spending stratum of gamblers, who did not square with this picture. Only about 500,000 people regularly attended the dog tracks but, as can be seen from the figures, they collectively staked a sum of money several times greater than the 10 million who filled in the football coupons. As Jack Huss recalls:

> I had met people who had been in the services, had been pre-war enthusiasts, they couldn't wait to get back to their love

and it was a love, it wasn't mixed up with betting, but they were betting all right ... it was nothing for them to have a thousand or two thousand on a dog, I mean in pounds, you work that out to today's standards ... I've seen a man that had £5000 on a greyhound, to win a thousand, yes. Well I mean I don't know where he got his money but it was genuine money.

In April 1949 the government set up a Royal Commission on Gambling, under the chairmanship of Sir Henry Willink, to review the law. A strong condemnation of the effects of gambling was advanced by the representatives of the churches, who maintained that it contributed to poverty, broken homes, absenteeism in industry, petty crime, juvenile delinquency and child neglect. They recommended the abolition of the football pools, the restriction of dog-racing to one day a week, and the abolition of off-the-course totalisator betting in horse-racing.

In general, the other witnesses called by the Royal Commission, including employers, policemen and social workers, argued that the churches' claims were grossly exaggerated. In its findings, the Royal Commission criticised the gambling habit as 'self-regarding and essentially uncreative' but dismissed the more serious charges against it:

We are led by all the evidence we have heard to the conclusion that gambling, as a factor in the economic life of the country or as a cause of crime, is of little significance and that its effects on social behaviour, in so far as these are a suitable object for legislation, are in the great majority of cases less important than has been suggested to us by some witnesses.[7]

Football, speedway and greyhound-racing were all sports with a strongly working-class character. Their vitality, like that of the labour movement, signalled the ascent of traditional working-class culture to a summit of influence in the mid-twentieth century. A phenomenon that received far less attention at the time was the discrete reappearance at other sporting fixtures of high society. Given the generous support received by farmers from the taxpayer, it was perhaps to be expected that fox-hunting would flourish: by 1953 there were 190 packs of hounds compared with 170 in 1939. In the green fields of England, or on the turf, Toryism could refresh itself at the wellsprings. The greatest event in the annual racing calendar was Derby Day, held every year without fail since 1780. The Derby was a national event, an annual reunion on the Downs at Epsom of society swells and the common people. During the war years the Derby was exiled to Newmarket, leaving the old course deserted and crumbling. When the Derby returned to Epsom in June 1946, the pre-war glamour of the occasion had vanished. In his record of the Derby Stakes, Roger Mortimer writes:

> The stands and the course, to say nothing of the spectators, looked rather shabby and war-worn, and there was not a single top hat to be seen in the Members' Enclosure. Strict rationing was still in operation and the facilities for eating and drinking were depressingly spartan.[8]

Written, one feels, from the heart. But within a year or two some of the traditional prestige of the occasion was creeping back. Jennifer Chorley, soon to be presented as a débutante at Court, recalls:

> I think the social scene really got going again at the race courses, Ascot and Epsom. I remember very soon after the war going to the Derby and seeing Aly Khan and Rita Hayworth and all these famous people all parading down from the paddock and Prince Monolulu, the great racing tipster, reappeared and coaches came back ...
>
> I remember very well in the war my father keeping his top hat in the attic in our house, saying after the war this would be coming out again for Ascot. And in spite of several incendiary bombs and other things falling into the attic it remained intact and was sort of symbolically brought down at the end of the war and worn quite soon afterwards.

A general view of spectator sport cannot run the whole gamut of possibilities. Swimming, boxing, tennis and athletics must fall by the wayside, and so too must the first post-war Olympics, staged in London in 1948. Far from the headlines but vital to the general picture was a world of local sporting clubs and societies, whose chief spectators were friends and relations. Angling, cycling, canoeing, rambling, mountaineering, bowls, badminton, table tennis, snooker, darts – the list runs on and begins to write itself, but is worthy of note for all that. Here was a range of active enthusiasms, pursued for no better reason than love of congenial company, pleasure in a skill, or the enjoyment of exercise and fresh air.

A reminder of this other world comes from June Kilbey, whose enthusiasm was cycling. Cycling clubs, which had been all the rage in the 1890s, were undergoing a revival due partly to restrictions on petrol. Shortly after the war June Kilbey joined a club formed by an employee of the London Electricity Board, whom she later married. 'We considered ourselves proper cyclists,' she says, explaining that the club was affiliated to the National Cyclists' Union and that members took care to wear the proper dress and generally observe the code of cycle club rules. As for the pleasures of cycling:

> A club run would be members getting together and they would say, 'We'll go Sunday,' and arrange places to meet and eat. We'd all meet up early in the morning, sometimes about eight in the morning, perhaps there would be half a dozen of us, perhaps there would be fifty of us ... and we'd just cycle off and it would be really lovely because the roads would be quiet, there was no traffic in those days you see; and you'd be going through villages and they were so unspoilt, no traffic, nothing parked by the side of the road and people would come out and see you go through, especially if you was a large club. They'd just sort of come out and you know, wave to you, and you'd wave back, and if you had a puncture they'd come out and ask you if you want a cup of tea.

The late 1940s seem to have been a good time for outdoor recreation of all kinds. The government ran agricultural labour camps to assist the farmers at harvest time, an adaptation of traditional patterns of seasonal labour in the countryside, but with a touch of Butlin's added. The National Parks Act of 1949 led to the designation of the Lake District, the Peak District and Snowdonia as areas of outstanding beauty to be protected by the Countryside Commission. For ideal images of England, writers and artists – unlike architects and planners – often turned back in time to pastoral images and this may well have helped to popularise the countryside. In post-war Britain, Kenneth Morgan writes, there was 'a renewed cult of the countryside, variously popularised in the broadcasts of Ralph Wightman; the radio play serial *The Archers* (first transmitted in the Midland region in Whit week, 1950); the success of magazines like the *Countryman*; and the writings of A. G. Street'.[9]

Thrilled by the sight of a host of golden daffodils, and awed by the prospect of Caledonia stern and wild, the British were nineteenth-century romantics about nature. But romance, in the twentieth-century sense of love, sex and marriage, was somewhat rudely handled in British music-hall comedy and popular song. Saucy postcards, mother-in-law jokes, George Formby ('I kept me ukelele in me hand'), the tearful, homely voice of Gracie Fields, the chaste vowels of Vera Lynn, all left something to be desired: sexual romance. The Mayfair musical comedies of the 1930s, all top hat and tails, were long on romance and short on sex. The comedian Max Miller's book of blue jokes was just the reverse. The spellbinding arts of erotic enchantment were, to say the least, feebly developed in British popular culture. In search of them, adolescents and young couples turned to American styles of entertainment in popular song, the dance-hall and the cinema.

In the late 1940s there were 450 permanent dance-halls in Britain and it was estimated that about three million tickets, usually costing between 1s. 6d. and 2s. 6d., were sold each week. They were supplemented by other dances in hotels or town halls, but there was no substitute for the luxury palais with a balcony, revolving bandstand, and glittering sphere suspended high above the dancers' heads.

The dance-halls were pleasure-domes where American influence was strong. The dance bands were British and there were some very British moments when the whole floor would erupt into 'Oh, the Hokey Cokey', or 'Do you know the Muffin Man, the Muffin Man, the Muffin Man?' But the bands were modelled on Tommy Dorsey or Glen Miller and the vocalists crooned in the style of Bing or Sinatra. After the entry of the United States into the war in 1941, American influence was intensified by the arrival of real, live GIs in the dance-halls, and the broadcasts of the American Forces Network.

Asked why girls liked to go dancing, Mrs Freeman, who used to go dancing about three times a week in Blackpool, puts us right straightaway:

> Oh, to pick up boys, quite definitely, everybody knew what it was in aid of, but we sat in little clans, girls up one side and boys up the other and then those clans would split off into other little groups, those that you didn't dance with ... who dressed a bit loud and a bit common, probably went to the Tower, we went to the Winter Gardens ... and it probably took you till about ten o'clock at night ... [for] the boys to ask you to dance and you to agree.

Joan Marwood adds:

> I think dancing was the main way of meeting fellows, there were no discos and you didn't go into pubs and things like that, it was mostly meeting a chap really. And also I suppose

to dress up, you see girls liked dressing up in those days, there was no hassle to spend hours experimenting with clothes, you didn't just rush into a pair of jeans sort of thing.

Mrs Freeman recollects the attention that girls lavished on their appearance:

It took about two hours to get ready with these ridiculous hairstyles, we had what we called pageboy hairstyles then, with your hair curled under and a bit of a fringe, very bouffant skirts with loads of net underskirts – you'd mind how you sat down – and very high-heeled shoes, the higher the better, whether you'd got blisters or not didn't matter, black patent if you could afford them and stockings, because tights weren't around then, stockings with patterns on the side, you really thought you were the bee's knees.

Behaviour on the dance floor was carefully supervised. 'There was an MC in the middle of the ballroom', Mrs Freeman points out, 'to make sure that there was no necking going on and that you were all going round the right way so that nobody collided with anyone.' The latest dance-hall craze, jitterbugging (or jiving as it was called later on), had been introduced by the GIs and was at first strongly resisted by the dance-halls. John Basnett, whose youth was spent in Stockport, recalls:

At [Manchester] Bellevue there was no jitterbugging allowed because of what happened during the war. The Yanks would come along and most of them in their uniforms with their Army boots on and the girls in their high heels and they were cutting the dance floor to pieces. But they found out that because there was no jitterbugging allowed their attendances were dropping, so what they did, we got a special part of the dance floor, and had it roped off, for jitterbugs only.

Talking of the major London dance-halls Joan Astelle remarks:

You were thrown out of the places if you were jitterbugging, there were notices on the walls, 'No Jitterbugging', and we used to go in and jitterbug and get warned off, you'd get the hand on your shoulder, but of course gradually they couldn't keep it out and it took over.

Apart from the wireless, to which almost everybody listened, the most popular form of entertainment in the 1940s was the cinema. As with so many other established forms of leisure, the silver screen was at the pinnacle of its fortunes: 1946 marked the all-time statistical high, with an annual attendance of 1635 million. (By 1982, the figure would have shrivelled to 64 million.) A third of the population, the Government Social Survey reported in the autumn of 1947, visited the cinema at least once a week. As yet, the competition from television was relatively slight, with only three-quarters of a million licence-holders by 1951.

The statistics run on – but a simple fact is easily lost in the telling: the cinema was first and foremost a medium for people under the age of thirty. The habit of cinema-going was usually formed at about the age of five or six and the highest frequency of attendance was among adolescents and young adults. Children, of course, would often go in the company of older people, but on Saturday mornings about half a million children attended cinema clubs run by the Odeon and Gaumont-British cinema chains.

The most compulsive cinema-goers were between the ages of sixteen and nineteen. In her study of adolescent girls, *Rising Twenty*, Pearl Jephcott printed the notes made by an eighteen-year-old shop assistant of her visits to the cinema during three separate weeks in 1945. Out of eighteen weekdays, she went to the cinema on sixteen. During one week in August 1945 the films she saw were as follows:[10]

Mon: *When Irish Eyes Are Smiling*
Tue: *Flight from Folly*
Wed: *Bride By Mistake*
Thu: *Flame of the Barbary Coast*
Fri: *Fiddlers Three*
Sat: *Medal for Benny*

Even a small country town in the 1940s would usually have two or three cinemas and the larger towns and cities offered an abundant choice of programmes. As Mrs Sylvia Stilts, who was living in Whetstone, north London, recollects:

Cinemas were quite different from today. Locally we used to have two circuits, one was an ABC cinema and one was an Odeon, so you could go to two completely different programmes during the week, and some of them even changed in the week. A lot of them had a restaurant upstairs so that leaving the office in the evening you could have a jolly good meal of fish and chips and a cup of tea and ice cream for three shillings before getting your ticket and going downstairs ... The main picture was an hour and a half and then there'd be the 'B' movie which was usually a not very good American one, and that lasted about an hour. There would be trailers for the next week's films and a trailer for Sunday – on Sunday the cinema started about three o'clock in the afternoon, and they were usually old films that were on – then there'd be slide adverts of the local traders and possibly a short documentary of some kind. It really was, you know, a jolly good one-and-ninepence worth, and you just sat round until where you came in.

In the late 1940s the more educated classes were still reluctant to come to terms with the cinema. Many of the intelligentsia took no more notice of it than of Tin Pan Alley. Those who did pay attention were, more often than not, moral and cultural improvers with an axe to grind. They wished to impose on the cinema a Reithian duty to enlighten and instruct and the more they applauded the 'best' in film – the documentary film, the drama of social realism, the adaptation of classics to the screen – the more critical they were of the 'worst'. As Norman Crosby wrote of the cinema in 1948:

> It tends to create false values, and through years of cinema-going the acceptance of such values becomes part of the concept of living. Millions of people probably owe mainly to the cinema the ideas that the acquisition of wealth is far more important than the acquisition of knowledge; that physical beauty is the passport to romantic happiness; that sex in a purely physical sense is the mainspring of life; that the ideal life is one in which there is no necessity to work and pure pleasure is the main pursuit.[11]

Much naïvety about the cinema-going audience was still in evidence. In 1948 Gordon Rattray Taylor conducted an extensive survey sample by questionnaire. The response, he wrote,

> throws a terrifying light on the educational deficiencies of those who queue up outside Britain's 4000 cinemas. Was it unreasonable to expect that adult film-goers would be able to spell the more straightforward Christian names? John was repeatedly spelt Jhon, Katharine appeared as Kathreen, Robert as Roburt and George as Gorge. One man (age group 25–34) wrote 'Gerage Sanders' and on the next line 'Geroge Formby', thus misspelling the same name two ways consecutively. Surnames were equally baffling (Robert Taler was a common variant), while the more complicated names pro-

duced countless variations, some unrecognisable (e.g. Greeter Garboo, Ingrim Bergem, Doref Lormore, Jhirra Holduck and Laurall Bascall).[12]

One of the threads in the debate over the quality of the cinema was the influence of Hollywood over the British public. At the end of the war the British film industry was in better shape than ever. Ealing Studios were in their prime, and elsewhere there were outstanding critical and popular successes such as Laurence Olivier's *Henry V* (1944); David Lean's *Brief Encounter* (1946); and Carol Reed's *The Third Man* (1949). But the majority of feature films shown in Britain were imported from the United States, and the two main distribution chains, Rank and ABC, had close ties with Warner Brothers and Twentieth Century-Fox respectively. Some protection was given to the indigenous film industry by the quota system, whereby at least 20 per cent of the first features shown had to be British productions. But Hollywood took the lion's share.

The sociologist J. P. Mayer published in 1948 a collection of 200 'motion picture autobiographies' compiled for a competition by cinema addicts. The fans clearly did not think of themselves as pro-British or pro-American but had complex likes and dislikes on both sides of the Atlantic. The response was discriminating and it would be an exaggeration to claim that British audiences were 'under the spell of Hollywood'. But economics ensured a steady predominance of American films and on the whole they were popular.

At an impressionable age, two-thirds of the British people were subject to a powerful image of the United States as an alternative society. Here was a land that appeared to be sexy but romantic, wealthy but classless, aggressive but idealistic – and at all times brimming over with vitality and ambition. How far British attitudes were influenced by all this is still very difficult to judge. Was the dazzling image of the United States dismissed as irrelevant to the realities of British life? Was it, at most, a passing obsession of adolescence? Or did it lodge in the mind and quietly shape expectations of the future?

It is impossible to say with any certainty, but two of our witnesses suggest the variety of response to American films. Terry Alford says:

> The types of films we used to go see were mainly American musical types of film, you know these big extravaganza types, with Betty Grable and June Havoc where they always finished up with a big balustraded staircase and they'd come

prancing down these stairs with all these furs and there would be a dramatic song and all reach up to the heavens. I used to find them quite boring really but I used to go along with my mother 'cause she used to think they were absolutely fantastic ... but I used to like more the English films especially the English comedies and also the English dramatic films. The character acting was so superb and we could identify ourselves with the characters because they used to portray the times we lived in whereas the American films were all candyfloss and superficial.

But Joan Marwood comments:

I hated British films because they were all men in them, they were awful and they were all about stiff-upper-lip men, which was worse, anyway they were all war films ... No I only wanted to see Bette Davis sliding down a staircase or Greer Garson having a stiff upper lip in a beautiful dress.

Whether deep or shallow, the cultural influence of Hollywood was largely a matter of indifference to the Labour government. But they blundered into a battle with Hollywood from concern over the extent of Britain's trade deficit with the United States. In August 1947 Hugh Dalton, the Chancellor of the Exchequer, slapped a heavy duty on US films in order to reduce imports and conserve dollars. Hollywood retaliated by refusing to send any more films to Britain. The subsequent film war was an unequal contest and in March 1948 Harold Wilson, as President of the Board of Trade, skilfully patched up a deal to allow the return of American films. But the sudden withdrawal of protection threw the British industry into a crisis of profitability. Wilson attempted to rescue it by setting up in 1949 the National Film Finance Corporation, a bank with an initial budget of £5 million to finance British productions. The British industry was just about kept afloat but never looked as though it would displace the influence of Hollywood.

American entertainment, though not to everybody's taste, was a much needed stimulus and morale-booster. In April 1947 the stage shows of two new American musicals, *Oklahoma* and *Annie Get Your Gun*, opened in the West End. Followed soon afterwards by *Carousel* and *South Pacific*, they took the British by storm. *Oklahoma* broke box-office records with takings of one and a quarter million pounds. Jennifer Chorley, who took a delight in most of the arts and was a founder member of the English Opera Group, reflects on the success of the American musical:

It came at a particularly drab time in England – austerity, utility, rationing and cuts and crises of every sort – and the lovely colour, and vitality, and beautiful music, everybody just lapped it up ... I don't think the impact of the American musicals was necessarily because they were American, but because they were so vital and because they produced such an escapism from what we were going through.

'Death to Hollywood!' Thus, half in jest, spoke John Maynard Keynes in a broadcast of July 1945. He was explaining to listeners the purpose of the newly founded Arts Council of Great Britain, of which he was chairman. 'We look forward', said Keynes, 'to a time when the theatre and the concert hall and the art gallery will be a living element in everyone's upbringing, and regular attendance at the theatre and at concerts a part of organised education.'[13]

Keynes's words remind us of a neglected theme in the history of the 1940s: the movement to raise the moral and cultural standards of the general public. The Welfare State had a very practical basis in the improvement of material conditions, and many a politician looked no further than that. But in the philosophy of social reform, material benefits were secondary to the ultimate ideal of a better way of life. In their different ways, Bevan, Beveridge or Keynes all believed in a society where service to the community would be a more powerful motive force, and the community in return would enlarge and enrich the life of the citizen. 'Service' and 'citizenship' were the key terms, forever on the lips of social reformers.

How quaint and obsolete such words sound today. Consumer society and pressure-group politics have overtaken them. The ethical principles of the 1940s have almost been forgotten and history students know only the types of benefit proposed by the Beveridge plan. Another reason for amnesia is, perhaps, that attempts to diffuse the values of middle-class improvers were never very successful.

Social reformers in the 1940s expressed much concern over the problems of youth. Little did they realise how little there was to worry about but they worried all the same. Great efforts were made to 'improve' the minds and morals of adolescents. In the opening months of the Second World War, anxieties about the disruption of family life and loss of parental control led the government to proclaim, as it was called, the 'Service of Youth'. The Exchequer provided a 50 per cent grant to assist the many voluntary youth organisations in the setting up of youth clubs and the clubs duly multiplied. The momentum was maintained after the war and, taking the decade as a whole, public expenditure on the youth service rose from £175,000 in 1939–41, to £1,800,000 in 1949. By this time there were 240 full-time youth organisers in England and Wales.

It would be foolish to belittle the work of the youth clubs but the majority of young people did not enrol in them. A report for the Cadbury Trust on the leisure activities of post-war adolescents in Birmingham dolefully reported that they whiled away their time in amusements instead of improving themselves:

> It has astonished us that the standard of writing and spelling among so many young people should be so poor, and that the reading of so many should be limited to 'comics'. It is almost astounding that in the list of radio programmes to which these young people listen there should only be one mention of the Third Programme and only one mention of religious services.[14]

Reading such comments, one realises that the evangelical mission of the Victorians to the masses was far from exhausted by the mid-twentieth century.

The establishment of the Arts Council in 1945 reflected a similar ideal, best expressed in the phrase 'Art for the People'. The Arts Council originated in 1940 as a private foundation known as CEMA – the Council for the Encouragement of Music and the Arts. With theatres and orchestras disrupted and art galleries closing down, the function of CEMA was to improvise emergency alternatives and so help to sustain civilian morale. On this basis the Treasury agreed to assist CEMA with an annual grant fixed initially at £50,000, and rising by 1945 to £175,000.

CEMA won a mass audience for drama, classical music, painting and sculpture. The secret of its success was that it literally took art to the people, that is out into the provinces and into popular venues. Exhibitions, concerts and plays were taken into the factories and the air-raid shelters. In 1945 the Coalition government decided that CEMA should be put on a permanent footing and granted a royal charter as the Arts Council of Great Britain. Keynes, the prime mover in its creation, was appointed as the first chairman.

Between 1945 and 1949 the Arts Council's annual grant crept up from £235,000 to £575,000, and its influence over the arts grew. But at the same time the audience for the arts contracted. For a while, the spirit of CEMA haunted the corridors of the Arts Council. A number of exceptionally well-attended art exhibitions suggested that the new popular audience had come to stay: 250,000 people went to see a collection of Spanish paintings in the winter of 1946–7, and the Van Gogh exhibition in the winter of 1948–9 was seen by more than 350,000. Yet the temporary wartime bridge between the arts and the masses was in fact crumbling. The unorthodox wartime arrangements for taking the arts into the factory canteen or town hall were superseded. When factory concerts ended in April 1946 the Arts Council appointed 'industrial music organisers' to set up clubs which workers could attend outside the workplace. The clubs flopped and the music organisers had to be redeployed. After the war, the Arts Council concentrated naturally enough on the support of permanent organisations such as Covent Garden, the Old Vic, the big orchestras and the leading provincial theatres. It was still the aim of the Council to make the arts available to a wider audience, especially in the regions. But inevitably the arts based themselves after 1945 on a regular constituency of enthusiasts.

The Arts Council was influential in the commissioning of new works of art, and likewise in the funding of new arts festivals including Aldeburgh (1945), the Cheltenham Contemporary Music Festival (1945), and the Edinburgh International Festival (1947). But these are topics that properly belong to the history of music, opera and the theatre and rate only a footnote or two in the history of mass entertainment. Not that culture had necessarily to be one thing or the other. Between the two worlds of Beethoven and Bing there existed a kind of no man's land known as the jazz scene.

Jazz began to catch on in Britain during the slump. From 1933 onwards little knots of enthusiasts began to form rhythm clubs and listen reverently to 78 rpm records of the great American jazz musicians. Though many club members were musicians or would-be musicians, no live music was performed and it would have been considered sacrilegious to dance. The aim of the clubs was to heighten the enjoyment of the music by critical discussion and the exchange of expertise. The social appeal of jazz, which at this time was a male preserve, was mainly to white-collar employees in and around London: upwardly mobile self-made men for whom high culture was too remote and Tin Pan Alley too unintelligent. As Francis Newton, alias Eric Hobsbawm, puts it, 'If H. G. Wells had been in his teens in the early 1930s, he would have attended rhythm clubs.'[15]

During the war, the enthusiasm began to spread, drawing in women and appealing more broadly to young people from a variety of social backgrounds. Joan Astelle, who began to go to club meetings at that time, recalls:

When rhythm clubs first started all we did was to sit about just listening to the records ... Somebody with a slightly larger collection than anybody else would do the recital, with such names as 'The Trombone in Jazz' or something like that – it was an excuse to play your best records to the audience.

John Basnett, who started to attend rhythm clubs in the Manchester area during the war, describes how they began to move on from the playing of records:

A rhythm club was usually ... a room above a pub where people who dug jazz or swing would go and get together ... There'd be a radiogram there and they'd play their records to each other. As time went by people started bringing instruments and started playing together and then from that they started a little band and then more people would come along to listen to it and that's how it expanded into a jazz revival.

In 1944 the first influential British jazz band appeared when George Webb and his Dixielanders began to blast out the New Orleans sound at the Red Barn, a pub in Bexleyheath. Among the audience at the Red Barn was Joan Astelle, who explains:

After the Red Barn, clubs came to London, but there were two really famous ones. There was Mac's Rehearsal Rooms in Windmill Street and 100 Oxford Street. They became enormously popular, packing in the crowds, both, as I recall, underground, getting tremendously hot and steamy and in those days before deodorants, quite nasty.

As Humphrey Lyttelton points out, there was nothing peculiarly British about the jazz revival. The same thing was happening at about the same time in San Francisco, in Paris, and in Melbourne, Australia. In 1947 Graham Bell and his band came over from Australia and gave a new impetus to the jazz scene. Though the rhythm clubs now featured live bands there was still no dancing. Humphrey Lyttelton takes up the story:

Graham Bell came into this scene with his band of extrovert Australians and he didn't like it at all, it wasn't his idea of fun, and so it was through him that a club started up in Leicester Square in London which catered for dancing. And I remember that the people, the regular jazz buffs who used to come along and sit through the thing thought this was absolute heresy. To do what in fact they used to do in New Orleans, in the early part of the century, was blasphemous ... But the dancers won out, and all through the 1950s it was an era of jazz for dancing.

The young people who listened or danced to jazz were only mildly rebellious, and there was a wild incongruity between the passing bohemianism of British adolescents and the black subculture of oppression, violence and prostitution, soulfully expressed in the music of New Orleans. But even in the British context, jazz did express dissent. The spontaneity of jazz was a protest against commercial convention. It was, says John Basnett,

> A rebellion against swing music. Although we know that swing stems from jazz ... it really is a different kind of music. If it's a big band then it's arranged, and although the solos of course are the same as in jazz music, improvised solos, in swing music you will probably get a trumpet section, three or four in a trumpet section, two or three trombones playing arrangements ... the bands were getting bigger and bigger and there was a kind of feeling among people like myself to get back to a small band again, to the real collective improvisation.

The informality of jazz made it the natural vehicle for young people impatient of social convention. Humphrey Lyttelton comments:

> There was a general feeling of people wanting to do something different, and there was also a feeling with the young people, especially young people who had gone to art schools where you know they are normally radically minded. They didn't want to be regimented, and all the things like the clothing at the club, the do-it-yourself dancing, dance styles and things, arose I think from the fact that people didn't want just to be told what to do.

From its beginnings in Britain, the jazz scene had links with the Left. 'Few of the leading revivalist bands', writes Francis Newton, 'were without some Communists.'[16] For others, the jazz revival had no political implications. Joan Astelle, for example, says that for her there was no motive of rebellion in following jazz: she just liked the music. But as she goes on to explain, jazz clubs were bound up with a nonconformity of style:

> There were special clothes that you wore, very informal clothes, not the sort of clothes that you would wear to the Hammersmith Palais or anything like that. This was the open-necked shirt and the corduroy trousers, the rather arty look ...

In the eyes of the older generation – like Joan's father, who detested it – the jazz revival did have dangerous connotations. The atmosphere of the jazz clubs was freer than that of the dance-halls: there were no MCs parading the floor to keep an eye on the dancers. As in orthodox dance-halls, no drink was sold on the premises, but at 100 Oxford Street drink could easily be brought in from the pub next door.

The leisure-patterns of the post-war years bespeak a healthy, wholesome, orderly and somewhat repressive society. Young people knew nothing then of the deadly cocktail of drugs, demoralisation and unemployment, so freely available to them in the 1980s. The main solvent of the old order was to be consumerism, bringing with it a passion for private pleasures, a high risk of dissatisfaction, and a temptation to consume things that were harmful as well as things that were good. In the 1940s pleasures were unsophisticated and the boundaries of rebellion were set by under-age drinking, pre-marital sex, and a sweaty night out at 100 Oxford Street. As Humphrey Lyttelton remembers:

> Mothers used to ring me up and say they were extremely worried, their daughters had expressed the intention of coming to my club. They used to ring me saying, 'What sort of place is it?', and they were very worried. So I used to say, 'Well, the only thing you're likely to get hung up on in 100 Oxford Street is Tizer.' Whether or not their doubts were assuaged by that, I don't know!

6

SCHOOLDAYS

Teachers know the problem of trying to occupy an unruly class and keep it out of mischief. A similar problem confronted the managers of parliamentary business in 1943. There was very little for backbench MPs to do in wartime but make a nuisance of themselves criticising the government. In the New Year of 1943 Labour MPs got hold of a first-class issue, the Beveridge Report, and mounted a parliamentary rebellion against the government's half-hearted response to its proposals. The air at Westminster was thick with flying inkwells, drawing pins were discovered on ministers' chairs, and there was excitable talk in the dorm of a revival of party politics.

Fortunately for ministers assistance was at hand. Since 1940 the Board of Education had been drafting a very long and complex bill for a reform of State education. Suddenly a new-found enthusiasm for the Bill was evident in the Whips' Office and it was allocated an early place in the parliamentary timetable. As the then President of the Board of Education, R. A. Butler, wrote in his memoirs, the beauty of the bill was that it would 'keep the parliamentary troops thoroughly occupied; providing endless opportunity for debate, without any fear of breaking up the government'.[1]

An ambitious and complex agenda for reform: yet as welcome to Conservatives as to Labour or Liberal politicians. That was the peculiar character of the 1944 Education Act. The aim was to expand a patchwork of existing schools into a unified system of education, advancing in step with the development of the child from the ages of two to eighteen. The very young would be looked after in nursery schools. The school-leaving age would be raised from fourteen to fifteen, and part-time education in county colleges would continue until the age of eighteen. But the outstanding feature of the Act was the pledge to introduce free secondary schools for all children over the age of eleven or twelve, in place of the elementary schooling hitherto experienced by nearly 90 per cent of the population.

It would have been impossible to fulfil the aims of the Act without a reorganisation, from top to bottom, of the government of education. The Board of Education obtained much stronger central powers of direction over the local authorities, and was upgraded in status to a Ministry. The number of local education authorities was reduced from 315 to 146, and the new authorities were to organise within their boundaries all stages of education except for the universities. The religious denominations were manoeuvred into a new concordat with the State, and many of their schools transferred to the control of the local authorities. Following the Act, the Burnham Committee, the representative body in charge of pay negotiations for teachers, had to be reorganised and new scales of pay negotiated.

Once all the nuts and bolts of a new administrative framework were in place, it remained only to carry out the proposals by finding the extra teachers, the extra schools, the extra equipment, the extra capital, and the extra finance required: a colossal exercise. As R. A. Butler remarked, the full implementation of the Act would require a generation. Little wonder, then, that Ellen Wilkinson and George Tomlinson, Attlee's two Ministers of Education, had most of their work cut out organising the physical reconstruction of schools and classrooms. When Labour fell from power in 1951, the work was still a long way from complete.

The administrative momentum of the 1944 Act determined the pattern of change after 1945. Apart from a vocal body of dissenters in the Labour Party, who campaigned for the introduction of comprehensive schools, the goals of educational policy were seldom questioned and the attention of school managers was fixed on such practical issues as the installation of new toilets or the requisitioning of an emergency hut to cope with the increased number of children consequent on the raising of the school-leaving age.

Striking through the mass of detail in the Act, with its five sections and 122 clauses, we come to a psychological basis of great simplicity. In the 1940s, respectable opinion in all parties regarded the expansion of education as self-evidently desirable. Society was to be criticised for failing to make education more widely accessible. But there was little sign that the nature of education was subject to critical scrutiny. Like pure air or water, it was an unproblematical good. Even the conflict over comprehensive schools was primarily a dispute over the distribution of a social service rather than the content or efficacy of the service itself. The lack of strictly educational innovation in the 1940s was the silent clue to much of the action.

Like the Beveridge plan of social insurance, the Butler Act was a rationalisation and expansion of existing services. State education between the wars consisted of two systems running in parallel, but increasingly mixed up together. The elementary schools, inherited from the Victorian era, were free and compulsory and still retained their essential character as schools intended for the instruction of working-class children in the three Rs. Children entered school at the age of five and continued in elementary education, often in the same school building, until the statutory school-leaving age of fourteen. In 1938, 88 per cent of all children between five and fourteen were at a public elementary school.

Compared to the grammar school, the elementary school was a lower form of life. But it had a tendency to grow and develop more complex ambitions. By the 1930s the best of the elementary schools were a long way removed from their humble nineteenth-century beginnings. In 1926, the Hadow Report on the education of the adolescent recommended that elementary schoolchildren over the age of eleven should be separated from the younger children and be given more advanced instruction in senior classes or separate senior schools. This was a recognition that elementary schools should reach beyond the three Rs to equip children with practical knowledge and skills. By 1938, nearly half of the children in elementary schools were in 'reorganised' senior classes, or separate but related senior schools.

The oldest of the elementary schools, dating back to the era before State education, had been founded by the churches. The great majority were Anglican but 12 per cent were Roman Catholic and a handful nonconformist. In the State elementary schools religious instruction was non-sectarian; but the church schools instructed children in the teaching of the denomination to which they belonged. Allegedly they were administered under a system of 'dual control' with the local authorities. But the phrase was misleading, since the local authorities had very little control over the schools despite a legal obligation to pay the lion's share of the costs. Surprising as it may seem, church or 'voluntary' schools comprised more than 50 per cent of all the elementary schools in England and Wales. But as they were stronger in rural than urban areas, and tended to be smaller schools, only 30 per cent of elementary pupils attended them.

In the 1930s the prospects for the voluntary schools were bleak. They were falling behind the council schools and in many cases literally crumbling to pieces. Though the local authorities paid the running costs, including the salaries of teachers, the churches remained liable for the cost of repairs and improvements to the buildings. All too often they could not afford it. By 1925, 521 church schools were on the Board of Education's black list of schools with defective premises. The Hadow proposals for the reorganisation of senior classes, which at the very least meant a new classroom if not a new building, were very difficult for impoverished voluntary schools to implement. By 1939, 62 per cent of the older children in council schools were in reorganised classes, but only 16 per cent of the children in church schools.

So far the elementary schools have been described as though they were a self-contained system from which there was no exit. But at the age of eleven plus some pupils did move on to more advanced schooling elsewhere. In the industrial areas there were a number of junior technical schools, attached to a technical college, and intended to prepare children to take up a local trade. But the most common exit from elementary school was by scholarship to a grammar school.

Every year the most promising elementary pupils of around the age of eleven or twelve would be entered for an examination held by the local authority, and the successful candidates would be awarded a scholarship entitling them to a free place at a grammar school. Under the Education Act of 1918 at least 25 per cent of places in the grammar school had to be reserved for scholarship children, and the tendency was for the percentage to increase. By 1938, almost half of the secondary school places were taken by children who had won a scholarship from the elementary school.

The competition was intense, a sign of the pent-up desire of so many working-class families to emancipate their children from manual labour. For unlike the elementary schools, the secondary schools prepared children to sit public examinations. The School Certificate was the indispensable qualification for a range of white-collar and middle-class employment, and indeed for entrance to university. But if the door to social mobility was ajar, it was only just. Only 11·3 per cent of children ever entered a grammar school. And of all elementary schoolchildren in 1938, only 12 per cent moved on at the age of ten or eleven to secondary schools. The grammar schools, meanwhile, were increasingly confused institutions with a dual purpose and a double standard. On the one hand they were recruiting by competitive examination a broadening stream of academically clever boys and girls from working-class homes. But the other half of their pupils consisted of the children of middle-class parents who were admitted because their parents paid a fee. In this way, the secondary schools catered for the less affluent middle classes who could not afford to send their children to private boarding schools.

The outstanding features of the pre-1943 system were the relative inferiority of the mass of the schools and the relative exclusiveness of a grammar-school education. The overriding aim of educational reformers was to provide a good secondary education, though not necessarily of a grammar-school type, for all children. From 1918 it was the policy of the Labour Party that all pupils be transferred at the age of eleven from elementary to secondary school and remain there until they were sixteen. Instead of two different types of education based on social class, there would be two different stages of education related to age: primary and secondary. The Hadow Committee of 1926, appointed by the first Labour government, recommended a clean break in the education of all children at the age of eleven and a division between primary and secondary phases – hence its proposals for the reorganisation of the senior classes of elementary schools, already touched on.

Conservative governments between the wars did not advance in a straight line towards secondary education for all. Nor did the Conservative Party ever commit itself on the point. But under the leadership of Baldwin and Chamberlain, the Conservatives were a party of progress in the social services, finance permitting. Public expenditure on education rose from £65·1 million in 1919–20 to £107·5 million in 1939–40. In 1936, the Baldwin administration passed an act for the raising of the school-leaving age to fifteen on 1 September 1939. In principle, this marked a long step towards universal secondary education but there was an important escape clause. Exemptions were to be granted in the case of children leaving school for 'beneficial employment'. How big a hole this would have knocked in the scheme must remain a matter of speculation. For on 1 September 1939 Germany invaded Poland, the Act was suspended, and hundreds of thousands of schoolchildren were evacuated with their teachers to reception areas in the countryside. The prospect of educational reform was overtaken by the imminent possibility of educational breakdown.

The immediate consequence of war was the disruption of education. Schools were evacuated from the urban areas and put up in makeshift accommodation in the countryside. Since evacuation was a voluntary activity, the truancy officers were unable to enforce attendance. Younger teachers were called up and older colleagues called back from retirement. The *Luftwaffe*, the V1 and the V2 took their toll and by 1945 some 20 per cent of school buildings were damaged or destroyed.

What the Nazis sought to destroy, social reformers were determined to recreate. As the balance of class relations tilted in favour of organised labour, and a Coalition government signalled a change of tone in social policy, the education lobby seized its opportunity. The pressures for educational change were activated by leading officials of the Board of Education, most of whom had been evacuated to Bournemouth in September 1939. There, at the Branksome Dene and Durley Dean hotels in the winter of 1940–1, they drew up a set of proposals for post-war educational policy and embodied them in a confidential pamphlet known as the Green Book. The President of the Board of Education, Herwald Ramsbotham, was even then one of the most obscure of all political figures, and later passed into honourable oblivion as Lord Soulbury. But it was he who took the decisive step of circularising the Green Book to interested parties in the educational world. The traditional processes of consultation, one of the unwritten elements in the constitution, were under way, and memoranda began to pour into Bournemouth. Though not yet published, the contents of the Green Book were extensively leaked to the press, and propaganda for educational reform encouraged.

In July 1941, Ramsbotham was replaced at the Board of Education by R. A. Butler, a young Conservative politician of great subtlety and perseverance. Butler himself was the offspring of a famous academic dynasty with an unbroken tradition as Cambridge dons since 1794. While Butler exemplified the academic élite, his junior minister, the Labour politician James Chuter Ede, was a former elementary schoolteacher from a background of religious nonconformity. The alliance between the two symbolised the forward march of the educational profession.

Without the political skills of Butler and Chuter Ede, there would probably have been no Education Act in wartime. Educational reconstruction was impossible unless the potentially explosive religious issues were defused. Secondary education for all would require heavy expenditure on the school buildings owned by the churches, but the churches could not afford it. The churches would demand greater financial support from the Treasury and the local authorities. But this was certain to be opposed by religious nonconformists, who had always resented 'Rome on the Rates', and the National Union of Teachers, which stood for the transfer of the church schools to the State and the abolition of denominational instruction. If, therefore, the State were to increase its support for the church schools, the churches would have to pay a price, losing some or all the independence of their schools. To this, the Roman Catholic Church was fiercely opposed. And the Church of England, while ready to enter the lion's den, demanded a controversial *quid pro quo*: the extension of religious teaching in the State schools.

To cut a long story short, Butler and Chuter Ede devised a religious compromise. The voluntary schools were offered two alternatives as 'controlled' or 'aided' schools. Where the managers of a school were unable to meet half the cost of the necessary alterations and improvements, effective control of the school was to pass to the local authority, but with safeguards to protect its denominational character. In a case where the managers could pay more than half the cost, the school would retain its existing independence.

With the religious issue settled, the way was clear for the introduction of free secondary education for all. (In theory, at least, Scotland had already introduced universal secondary education in September 1939: but as the history of Scottish education in the twentieth century has yet to be explored my remarks will be confined to education in England and Wales.) The consensus of opinion on the point was overwhelming. Accordingly, the Education Act provided for the transfer of all adolescents to separate secondary schools, and the abolition of all fees in the grammar schools. But the Act was silent on the critical issue of the type of secondary education to be provided.

R. A. Butler had, however, appointed a committee under Sir Cyril Norwood to report on the secondary school curriculum. The Norwood Report, published in 1943, argued in favour of a tripartite system of grammar, modern and technical schools. Such a system, the committee argued, would correspond to a natural division of aptitudes among children. Pupils with academic ability would attend a grammar school. Pupils with a capacity for skilled manual work would attend a technical school. And pupils whose interest was in the immediate and the concrete would best be served by the modern school. The Norwood Report fitted admirably with the preconceptions of the men from the Ministry and was at once adopted as official doctrine. The change of government in 1945 made no difference. As Toby Weaver, a civil servant who arrived at the Ministry of Education in 1946, puts it:

There was a general belief, I believe totally false, that children were divided into three kinds. It was sort of Platonic. There were golden children, and silver children, and iron children. The golden children were capable of going to a grammar school, they had minds, they could have abstract thinking. The technical children, the silver children so to speak, were technically orientated, and all the rest, they couldn't handle ideas, they had to have concrete notions.

Anyone who conceives that social reform in the 1940s was dominated by abstract thinking should reflect on the Norwood Report. On the face of it, the report proclaimed a theory of education: three different types of ability should be provided for in three different types of school. In fact, the committee's conclusions were conservative. The three types of school were already in existence. The grammar and the technical schools were to continue providing the kind of teaching they had in the past. The 'modern' schools would be upgraded versions of the elementary schools, modelled on the best practice of the more advanced teachers. The social assumptions were no less transparent and realistic. The grammar schools would equip children for middle-class employment. The technical schools would prepare the skilled working class. The modern schools would look after the mass of children bound for unskilled work.

No less conservative was the report's reliance on intelligence testing at the age of eleven plus as the means of selection for the 'appropriate' secondary school. The intelligence test had become standard practice between the wars in the selection of elementary schoolchildren for the grammar school. In the 1940s it was at the height of its prestige as an allegedly objective test devised and propagated by psychologists. The conventional wisdom was challenged, but with little success, by the supporters of comprehensive schooling. The phrase 'comprehensive school' only passed into general usage after 1945. Between the wars, the term 'common school' (or in Scotland, 'omnibus school') was the normal expression. A variant of this was the concept of the 'bilateral' or 'multilateral' school, with two or three 'sides' – grammar, modern and technical – housed in the one institution.

The movement for comprehensive or multilateral schools won a measure of support in the 1930s. The most dedicated supporters of the idea were the National Association of Labour Teachers, who lobbied hard to convert the Labour Party. In 1942, the annual conference of the party did indeed pass a lengthy resolution on education which included a declaration in favour of multilateral schools and, in February 1943, a Labour Party deputation urged R. A. Butler to provide for them in the Education Bill. Butler responded by leaving the door open. The Bill did not specify the type of secondary education to be provided but left the decision to the local authorities, subject to the approval of the Ministry. Or in other words, there was all to play for. No sooner was the Act through Parliament than the education committee of Labour-controlled London County Council decided, in July 1944, to include comprehensive schools in its plan of post-war development.

On paper, the Labour Party was committed by the conference resolution of 1942 to the multilateral concept. But it is doubtful whether the party in general felt that the problem was urgent or central. The little band of educational specialists had the general support of the TUC but the issue failed to catch fire. As the Fabian socialist Margaret Cole recalled in 1966, the multilateral argument was of marginal significance – 'an esoteric idea, moved by enthusiasts, till almost the 1950s'.[2] Another handicap of the multilateralists was the diversity of opinion within the party. Many Labour stalwarts still cherished the grammar schools as élite institutions through which the bright working-class child could rise in the social scale. They were opposed to the abolition of grammar schools, instead they wanted them thrown open to all on the basis of academic competition. Herbert Morrison, the party's chief electoral strategist in the run-up to the general election of 1945, was opposed to multilateral schooling and had been heard to remark that there were not many votes in education. The section on education in the party manifesto of 1945 was intentionally vague and brief.

While the Labour Party wobbled, the officials of the new Ministry of Education were quite clear what they wanted. They were strongly in favour of the tripartite system recommended in the Norwood Report. The Permanent Secretary, Maurice Holmes, ruled in favour of selection at the age of eleven with a review at the age of thirteen. In 1945, R. A. Butler authorised the publication of a pamphlet, 'The Nation's Schools', which set out once more the case for 'three broad types' of school to meet the 'differing needs of different pupils'. On multilateral or comprehensive schools, the pamphlet stated:

> While enterprise and experiment are certainly to be encouraged, it would be a mistake to plunge too hastily on a large scale into revolutionary change which would entail some losses that are clear and offer gains the values of which for this country are perhaps somewhat uncertain.[3]

There matters rested until the election of a Labour government in July 1945 and the appointment by Attlee of Ellen Wilkinson as Minister of Education.

Ellen Wilkinson was Minister of Education for only eighteen months. During the final twelve months it was known to people close to her that she was in poor health and in February 1947 she died of a drug overdose. None the less her influence was decisive in the organisation of secondary education. She took office at a crucial moment when fundamental decisions had to be taken. Had she been so-minded she could have pressed for the development of the multilateral or comprehensive school. The change could not have been accomplished in one fell swoop or without powerful opposition. But with socialism at the flood-tide and much party sentiment behind her, she could have taken the risk. As David Rubinstein has pointed out, a number of local authorities, including London, Coventry and Reading, were eager to plan along comprehensive lines:

> These early plans indicated that a considerable measure of support for comprehensive education existed in England and Wales, and this sentiment would have been greatly strengthened by a strong lead from the Minister. Instead she led her troops in an entirely different direction, insisting that it would be 'folly to injure' the grammar schools, which were the 'outstanding achievement' of the State educational system.[4]

The new Minister pressed the local authorities to adopt the tripartite system of the Norwood Report. As very few local authorities proposed to build technical schools, the practical outcome was a dual system of grammar and secondary modern schools. Here and there, the Ministry allowed local experiments in comprehensive education, but elsewhere the pressure was for conformity. Herbert Hughes, better known as Billy Hughes, was Ellen Wilkinson's Parliamentary Private Secretary:

> One of my jobs as PPS actually was to go down and talk to the local authority in Coventry and so on, where the local authorities wanted to introduce multilateral schools, and one had to go and argue the pros and cons of multilateral schools or separate schools with them. The Ministry's policy under Ellen was to accept experiments in multilateral schools, but she wanted the difficulties to be faced. The sort of difficulties were, ought a multilateral school to be a very large building catering for a very large number of children? Would you have one multilateral at the east end of the town catering for the

working class, another multilateral in the west end of the town catering for the middle class?

The first comprehensive school in Britain was at Windermere in 1945, and the first local authority to operate a completely comprehensive system was Anglesey. The explanation was practical rather than doctrinal. A convenient way of providing secondary education for all in a sparsely populated rural area was to transfer the older children from village schools to the nearest grammar school and extend it, rather than build a separate secondary modern. Of the other local authorities planning to introduce comprehensive schools, few had reached the point of opening one by 1951. The London County Council created a dozen quasi-comprehensive schools in 1947 by grouping neighbouring schools under a single headmaster. But by 1952 there were fewer than a score of fully-fledged comprehensives in England and Wales.

Why did Ellen Wilkinson take the line she did? A number of explanations present themselves. She was a scholarship girl from a Methodist home in Manchester and might be expected to believe in the grammar-school system. Once a fiery socialist on the left of the Labour Party, she had fallen in love in the late 1930s with Herbert Morrison, the quintessential moderate, and moved into the Morrison camp of step-by-step reformism. Never having specialised in educational issues, she tended to rely upon the guidance of her Permanent Secretary, John Maud, and other leading officials. Cecil Denington, a leading light of the National Association of Labour Teachers, says of her:

> She didn't know her subject. She relied entirely on officials, when you went on a delegation she was surrounded by officials and she tried to wriggle out of anything she could. Well, one can quite understand how a minister who doesn't know the thing from A to Z is bound to find themselves in difficult situations and try to avoid them as best they can.

It is plain from Betty Vernon's biography that Ellen Wilkinson was nevertheless uneasy at the Ministry of Education. She had qualms over the official view that the 70 per cent of children in secondary moderns should be cut off from academic learning. 'Can't Shakespeare mean more than a scrubbing brush?' she wrote. 'Can't enough of a foreign language be taught to open windows on the world a bit wider – I learnt French verbs saying them as I scrubbed floors at home.'[5]

In private she was inclined to be more radical than in public, a conclusion borne out by the recollections of her junior minister, David Hardman, who writes:

> The Minister wanted to eliminate the direct grant list, the response being protests in my ear from Labour backbenchers who had important DG [direct grant] schools in their constituencies. She also ventured the opinion that public schools should be taken into the State system and even the universities. Nothing came of all this though I heard Herbert Morrison describing the idea as 'female tantrums'.[6]

Whatever the Minister's private doubts, she was swept along by the administrative revolution in progress at the Ministry. In the view of the officials, the goals of policy were already settled: the level of educational provision was to be raised for all children from the ages of two to eighteen. The time for policy-making was over and the time for implementation had arrived. On 1 April 1945 the main provisions of the Butler Act had come into force. The new education authorities were in place and starting to draw up their plans. The new powers of the Ministry were ready to be exercised. The priority was to get the administrative wheels turning and begin the physical reconstruction of the schools.

Top of the agenda was the raising of the school-leaving age, which Butler had deferred for two years to 1 April 1947. Though elementary schools had officially ceased to exist on 1 April 1945, and were now classified either as primary or secondary schools, nothing had changed physically except, perhaps, for a fresh coat of paint with new wording on the school notice-board. One of Ellen Wilkinson's first acts was to pledge that the deadline of 1 April 1947 would be met. But it was touch and go whether the promise could be fulfilled on time. Places would be required in school for another 391,000 children. But how were they to be accommodated and who was to teach them?

Wartime preparations came to the rescue. The Ministry had estimated in 1944 that an extra 70,000 teachers would be needed and the quest for additional teachers began with the adoption in May 1944 of the Emergency Training Scheme devised by Sir Gilbert Flemming, a senior official of the Board. It would have taken several years to expand the supply of teachers by the normal route of a two-year course at training college for suitably qualified applicants. With the consent of the teaching unions, professional constraints were temporarily relaxed. Emergency teacher-training colleges were to be set up wherever suitable premises could be found, and staff were enrolled to provide a one-year course. Applications for teacher training were to be invited from men and women about to be demobilised from the armed forces or civil defence. In June 1945, eligibility was extended to men and women working in war industries. The customary academic qualifications were no longer essential but applicants were expected to give evidence of some background in education and culture – terms of reference delightfully framed to allow interview boards the maximum scope for selection by rule of thumb.

One of those who applied to join the scheme was Kathleen Taylor, who had left school at fourteen, spent four years in the forces, and was working as a shop assistant in Carlisle. As she explains:

> At that time I was twenty-five and I decided that I wasn't going to be married so if I was going to be single for the rest of my life, I may as well have a really worthwhile job ... To get on the course I had to go and face a board of about six people and they all asked me lots of questions, about teaching children, and gave me situations – how would I cope with such a situation and would I be in the classroom all the time, or did I think I'd be outside with them, and then I was sent into a room and told to write an essay ... they all read it and a week or two later I was accepted for the course, but found that I had a whole year to wait before I could actually go to college.

At the emergency training college she met her future husband and after their marriage they moved up to Cumbria where they both taught.

Another recruit to the ETS was George Limburn, who went into teaching because his attitudes had been transformed by his experiences in the Army. Before the war, he had worked in a high-class grocery and provision store in Tunbridge Wells. After six years in the Army he was loath to go back to his old job:

> I left school at fourteen, but I think I can count my six years' war service as an education in various things. I was in Signals and I studied electronics to a great extent and radio ... I did a lot of instructing during the war, both in signals and electronics, radio telephony and radio telegraphy and so on and also with small arms, and got to enjoy instructing and teaching, and thought that I would like to do this when the war ended, if I survived ... I learned about the Emergency

Training Scheme in the newspapers, but I'd also by that time met a very attractive young lady and she was a teacher and had been talking to me a very great extent about teaching and I think that's what really persuaded me to go and train as a teacher. I married her eventually of course!

For the first two years or so, the Emergency Training Scheme teetered on the brink of fiasco. Applications poured in, reaching more than 1000 a week at the end of 1946. By this date more than 37,000 men and women had been accepted for training. But there was nowhere for most of them to be trained. The local authorities, charged with finding the premises and the staff for the emergency colleges, were failing to deliver. Ellen Wilkinson and the Ministry were 'overwhelmed with abuse from all sides'.[7] In 1946, Toby Weaver was transferred from the War Office to the Ministry of Education and given the job of hunting for suitable premises:

> I was told when I arrived that within two years I'd got to find enough buildings for twenty-five emergency training colleges, and I rushed all over the country looking at hotels, decayed primary schools, country houses, hutted camps, industrial hostels, a lunatic asylum and after endless struggle we found the buildings and adapted them with the help of all the other government departments. There was a great feeling of enthusiasm and teamwork, money didn't seem to worry people, we just got down to it. It was a very exciting period.

By the end of 1947, at the height of the scheme, there were no fewer than fifty-four emergency training colleges in operation. As the wheels began slowly to turn, criticism abated but the scheme never did work out as well as had been hoped. By 1951, 35,000 teachers had been through the scheme and into the schools. Though the figure fell far short of the original estimate of the 70,000 required, the contribution they made was substantial. In 1950, for instance, the total number of male teachers, in all types of State school in England and Wales, was 87,840: the Emergency Training Scheme produced 23,000 between 1945 and 1951.

It is interesting to speculate on the impact of the ETS teachers on the schools. They brought to the classroom a wealth of experience denied to colleagues whose whole lives had been spent in the educational system. Though more than half possessed School Certificates or some equivalent qualification, they had been selected mainly on grounds of personality rather than of academic record. The

ETS opened the profession to a mixed bag of unacademic types –
diamonds in the rough, and graduates of the University of Life. The
effect on the schools must have been bracing. Toby Weaver observes:
'You ask whether it diluted the profession. I remember somebody
asking that, and the answer was, "Yes – a jolly good thing to dilute
water with whisky." '

George Limburn, who first began his teaching career in Lough-
borough, found that established teachers welcomed new blood into
the profession:

> The established teachers of course had been through a very
> hard time and I think they were more grateful to see an inflow
> of new teachers to lighten the burdens which they'd been
> bearing all through the war. For example, I think discipline
> had suffered during the war because the shortage of teachers
> and the influx of people from the big cities and towns had
> made life hard and difficult for them. They received us very
> well ...

Not everyone was so fortunate. Mary Sumser-Ali, who had left
school at fourteen to work in the offices of a boot and shoe company
in Norwich, was among the civilian intake to the scheme. After she
had completed her training, she taught first in a grammar school and
then at a secondary modern. Asked how the established teachers
reacted, she replies:

> Most of them regarded us very doubtfully. They thought, I
> suppose rightly, that one year's intensive training didn't make
> up for the two years they had been required to do, and I think
> we had to prove ourselves.

The last word on the subject may be left to Harold Dent who, as
editor of the *Times Educational Supplement* for many years, was in a
good position to form an overview. He writes that when he
undertook a tour of secondary schools in 1952:

> Several Heads went out of their way to tell me, without my
> asking, what excellent work some of their emergency-trained
> teachers were doing, and in particular what marked initiative
> they were showing. It was not unusual to find the
> emergency-trained teacher occupying a key post in a modern
> school, especially on the arts and crafts side.[8]

New buildings were in as urgent demand as new teachers. If the school-leaving age were to be raised on time, nearly 400,000 new places would be needed by the time the full effect of increasing numbers was felt in the autumn term of 1948. But how were 5000 extra classrooms to be found at a time of chronic shortage in building labour and materials? As in the case of temporary housing, the solution was to order prefabricated buildings from the Ministry of Works. A standard type of hut was devised with a concrete floor and walls, metal windows and corrugated asbestos roof. The huts were manufactured in the factory, packed into a box and delivered to the school premises. HORSA – the Hutting Operation for the Raising of the School-leaving Age – was the educationalists' version of Overlord. Everything had to be ready for D-Day, the first day of the autumn term of 1948. HORSA huts began to appear in school playgrounds or backyards and, though the operation missed its target, 3583 extra classrooms were ready in September 1948. Meanwhile, cantering alongside HORSA came SFORSA: School Furniture Operation for the Raising of the School-leaving Age.

In the midst of all the preparations a hitch occurred. The Chancellor of the Exchequer, Hugh Dalton, recommended that the raising of the school-leaving age be postponed from April to September 1947. The shortage of capital for investment, and the pressing demands of the labour market for juvenile labour, were persuasive factors. But once postponed the momentum of the emergency programme would be lost, and the Ministry was poised on the edge of a slippery slope leading to indefinite postponement. In January 1947 the issue was put to the Cabinet. Billy Hughes recollects:

> When the crucial question came of the Cabinet threatening to postpone the raising of the school-leaving age, I was rushing around the Labour backbenchers getting them all to threaten that they would revolt if the date was postponed and luckily I managed to mobilise enough support to help Ellen fight her battle.

The Cabinet decided in favour of Ellen Wilkinson, but she did not live to see the decision carried out. Three weeks later she died and Attlee appointed in her place another Lancashire Methodist – George Tomlinson. On 1 April 1947 the school-leaving age was raised to fifteen as planned.

Tomlinson made little change in policy. Having left school at the age of twelve to enter a cotton mill as a weaver, he had worked his way up through trade unionism and served on the education committee of Lancashire County Council. Having also lately organised, as Minister of Works, the emergency programme of school huts, he was a natural choice to succeed Ellen Wilkinson. Renowned for his mastery of the common touch, Tomlinson practised a disarming style of politics in which contentious issues were buttered over with lashings of Lancashire warmth and humour. Billy Hughes tells a characteristic tale of Tomlinson in action:

> George Tomlinson came down to a meeting in my constituency, and everybody was there, all the bishops were there on the platform, and George started off. He said, 'I went to Eton the other day, and I sat next to Dean, and he were a nice chap were Dean, and he said to me, "What do you think is the best school in the country?" So I looked at him and said, "Christian Methodist." "Why is that?" says Dean. "Because I went there, like thou thinks Eton's the best because thou went there."' That was typical of George Tomlinson, he could keep a meeting in roars of laughter for hours on end.

Tomlinson remained at the Ministry of Education until the end of the Labour government in October 1951. During this period the National Association of Labour Teachers continued to win ground within the party and, in July 1951, the National Executive declared comprehensive schooling to be the official party policy. But in the meantime the dichotomy between the secondary modern and the grammar school became firmly established. The drive for comprehensive schooling was delayed until the return of the next Labour government in October 1964.

In post-war policy the emancipation of pupils and staff from cramped quarters and inadequate facilities was the highest long-term priority. Regulations issued by the Ministry in March 1945 laid down new standards for school premises and buildings. Every primary and secondary school was to have a playing field. Every secondary school was to have an assembly hall, dining room, gymnasium, library and a room for arts and crafts. Minimum requirements were laid down for the size of classrooms, playgrounds and overall sites. Every school was to have a radio and a film projector.

A wonderful prospectus, but how to drive it through? In 1946, a young civil servant, Antony Part, returned to the Ministry after war service on the general staff of 21st Army Group. Having risen by the age of thirty to the rank of Lieutenant-Colonel, he had marked himself out for important responsibilities and was put in charge of the Ministry of Education's Buildings and Priorities Branch. He says:

> There had to be some quite strong leadership from the Ministry of Education, if only to get the limited materials and authorisations for labour which were required, and in those days there was a much greater belief in two things. One was the close and confident partnership between the Ministry and the local education authorities, a matter of traditional pride to both. The other was a belief in those days that there was such a thing as creativity in the public sector.
>
> So here what you had was in fact a very young team, all of us really in our early thirties, taking this whole operation in hand and really getting stuck in ... We turned the whole administrative system inside out and said, 'What do the local education authorities need that they must have?' They must know how many schools they can build in a year, they must know how much materials they can get ... so we were really clearing the decks for the local education authorities, we even employed regional priority officers, headed by a Major-General and a Captain RN, who went round fighting, literally fighting for the Ministry of Education against the Ministry of Works.

The completion of the entire school building programme within a five-year term of office was impossible. The Attlee government therefore decided to restrict new school building to three categories: the replacement of schools blitzed during the war; schools for new housing estates; and extra primary schools to cater for the increased infant population resulting from the 'baby boom' of 1942–7. As the categories implied, primary schools had the edge in the building programme. Of 1176 new schools completed or under construction by the end of 1950, 928 were primary schools and only 248 were secondary schools.

One of the most interesting changes in the life of schools after the war was the revolution in their design. In 1949, for the first time, an Architects and Buildings Branch was created in the Ministry. This was a great innovation. In the past, the design of school buildings had been a matter for local authorities and their architects to settle between them. The object of the new Architects Branch was to design and build, as prototypes for adoption by the local authorities, prefabricated schools to brighten the environment and match the practical needs of teachers and pupils.

The roots of many post-war phenomena can be found in the influence of the Citizen Army of the war years. The Architects Branch derived from a camouflage unit in the Army, whence it was transplanted to the schools building programme in the county of Hertfordshire, and from there to the Ministry. The architect David Medd tells the beginning of the story:

> I came from a particular unit in the Army, where I spent the last two years of the war – the Camouflage Development and Training Centre, which was responsible for making and designing all kinds of devices for deception. I was working with an architect there called Stirrat Johnson-Marshall who came to be Deputy County Architect in Hertfordshire in 1945. He was very influential because he really understood the role of the public architect in national building pro-grammes after the war, both in Hertfordshire and later at the Ministry of Education. Our experience in the Camouflage Development and Training Centre was extremely relevant to that. We had a small unit where we were concerned with the kind of devices and what kind of theatre of war they were going to be in, we had workshops and we designed and made prototypes. We were connected with industry so we had to get these devices made in quantity, and we were responsible for training the troops in the use of these devices ...

As Medd points out, Hertfordshire was ripe for development after the war. The LCC was building a number of housing estates for Londoners whose homes had been destroyed in the Blitz, and new towns were planned at Hatfield, Hemel Hempstead and Stevenage. The demand for new schools was pressing but materials were scarce and building costs high. To cut through the difficulties, the County Architect's Department pioneered the design of schools which could be constructed in batches from mass-produced compo-nents. Apart from the basic principle of prefabrication, there was no similarity with the HORSA scheme. The aim of the Hertfordshire programme was to construct permanent schools designed by architects to satisfy functional and aesthetic requirements.

The Hertfordshire architects turned their back on the school buildings of the 1930s and started again from first principles. David Medd explains:

> It would have looked silly to have had great big globular light

fittings hung on brass chains. It would have looked silly to have huge towering windows with acres of inaccessible ironmongery on them. It would have looked silly to have had radiators occupying the wall space where there should be furniture. It would look silly to have complicated plumbing under all the basins, the kind of City and Guilds higher-grade spaghetti stuff, we wanted something different all round ... we wanted furniture which children didn't have to raise their arms to get over the desk or from which their legs didn't swing off the floor, window-sills low enough so the children could see out. So everything was looked at afresh.

The Hertfordshire experiment inevitably came to the notice of Antony Part in the course of his school building drive. He admired the design principles of the schools and, a crucial consideration, the success of the operation in reducing costs. Stirrat Johnson-Marshall was accordingly invited to set up an Architects' Development Group at the Ministry.

In the following decades, the new principles of school design became general throughout the country. As moving spirits in the change, neither David Medd nor Antony Part are unbiased witnesses. Each argues strongly that the experiment has proved to be a success. David Medd says:

I think it had a liberating influence. You didn't walk down a corridor into a room and see forty desks and a blackboard. You had colourful circulation areas with pots of flowers and children's pictures in them and bright colour and light furniture which you could move about. You could model the interior to your requirements, it wasn't a set-piece you had to conform to.

Asked what he considered special about the new schools, Antony Part replies:

Certainly the colour, the informality, the murals, the good design generally, the idea that schoolchildren were not natural vandals, but could be exposed to good design and would benefit from it, and that did turn out to be true. I went into an old school in Gateshead and I went into the loos for the kids. They had these little loos, very low and damn great partitions up to eight feet and then on top of that a steel grid between that and the ceiling. I asked them what the hell the steel grid was for and they said it was to stop the little blighters crawling over the top. They must be full of gymnasts in Gateshead!

So much for the shape of things to come. Between 1945 and 1951 the realities of change were modest and even humble where the great majority of schools were concerned. The term 'elementary school' had officially ceased to exist on 1 April 1945. But in January 1952, some 5107 all-age elementary schools, mainly denominational schools in the countryside, still survived in all but name. Meanwhile, the old senior elementary schools for children over the age of eleven were reclassified as secondary moderns. Teachers who had gone to bed as elementary teachers on 31 March 1945 awoke as secondary teachers on the following day. But the secondary moderns never succeeded in shaking off their main inheritance from the elementary schools: the belief that they were inferior to the grammar schools.

Ellen Wilkinson held out the prospect of 'parity of esteem' between the two types of school. But her rhetorical attempts to gloss over the social distinctions involved were unconvincing:

> Not everyone wants an academic education. After all, coal has to be mined and fields ploughed, and it is a fantastic idea that we have allowed, so to speak, to be cemented into our body politic, that you are in a higher social class if you add up figures in a book than if you plough the fields and scatter the good seed on the land.[9]

The educational aims of the secondary modern had always been rather vaguely defined. Evidently it was not intended to serve the academic purpose of the grammar school or the vocational purpose of the technical school. But what, then, was it for? In 1947, a Ministry of Education pamphlet, 'The New Secondary Education', displayed Ellen Wilkinson flannelling desperately on the subject. In a foreword completed shortly before her death she wrote:

> The schools must have freedom to experiment, room to grow, variety for the sake of freshness, for the fun of it even. Laughter in the classroom, self-confidence growing every day, eager interest instead of bored conformity, this is the way to produce from our fine stock the Britons who will have no need to fear the new scientific age, but will stride into it, heads high, determined to master science and to serve mankind.[10]

The pamphlet maintained that a secondary modern education was intended to develop 'out of the interests of the children'. It was recommended that some conventional subjects such as English and mathematics should be taught but the main aim should be to encourage practical activity and experience. Here was the very same advice the Ministry had been dishing out to the elementary schools ever since the Hadow Report of 1926. It was symptomatic of educational reform in the 1940s that curriculum development should occupy so little of the Ministry's attention. Britain had no centralised State philosophy of education. Under the 1944 Act, the only compulsory subject laid down in secondary education was religious instruction. Everything else was left to tradition and the judgement of head teachers.

The diversity of schools makes it hard to generalise. In social insurance, health or housing, common standards were applied throughout the country. Every widow was entitled to the same old age pension, every NHS patient to the same GP and hospital services, and the quality of the service was evened out as far as possible. But in State education, a double standard was entrenched, and within each type of school standards varied greatly.[11]

In England and Wales in 1950, two-thirds of the children of secondary school age, numbering more than a million pupils, were in secondary modern schools. In the early days, the most enterprising of the secondary moderns tried to innovate by gearing the curriculum to 'projects' or 'centres of interest' – a survey of the local neighbourhood, for example, or the exploration of a theme such as transport or housing. The main stimulus to change was the need to work out a curriculum for children staying on an extra year at school. At Rotherfield Secondary Modern, near Henley-on-Thames, the head-master, Mr Frederick Anson, decided to encourage role reversal between the sexes. The girls were taught how to mend a fuse or a broken tap while the boys learnt how to bake a cake. As Mr Anson explains, there was no radical intent. His idea was simply that, when they grew older and married, the wife would be able to cope if the husband were ill and vice versa. He saw his job as equipping children for the practical realities of adult life, including work in a rural area:

> I felt that we must associate what we were taking with the area so, for example, in maths we did a lot of surveying, we had our home-made theodolite and chain and we went around the school for a good quarter of a mile, and we surveyed. In those days there were a lot of hayricks and cornricks around us because we were rural, so they did a lot of measuring of the thatching of ricks and things like that.

Harold Dent, in the course of his travels among secondary modern schools, found many similar examples of initiative by the staff:

> I remember particularly one girls' school in Yorkshire –
> housed in shocking premises – where the work of the entire
> school had been organised in a series of four progressive
> projects each lasting a year: 'Ourselves and our homes',
> 'Ourselves and our districts', 'Ourselves and our country',
> 'Ourselves and our world'. The work was brilliant, its range
> immense, and its academic standard as high, age for age, as
> that of many grammar schools.[12]

After a first flush of enthusiasm, the experimental phase in teaching began to die down. In general, teaching by project proved too ambitious a concept for either pupils or teachers to sustain and by 1952 there was a rapid trend back towards the reintroduction of handicrafts and vocationally biased subjects. These had long been one of the strengths of the more advanced elementary schools, with boys specialising in woodwork, metalwork and gardening, and girls in cookery, needlework or secretarial work. Now they formed the staple of the curriculum in the majority of secondary modern schools. Perhaps it was because of the emphasis in the modern schools on manual skills that the secondary technical school, the third type of secondary school projected in post-war planning, proved to be a non-starter. The number of such schools actually began to decline.

Another development in the early history of the secondary moderns was a bid by some of the more ambitious schools to enter the academic stakes. When the secondary moderns began, they did not enter pupils for School Certificate, the existing type of public examination, as it entailed whole classes of children being entered for whole groups of subjects. As Jean Watkins, an appreciative pupil of Rotherfield Secondary Modern, remembers:

> We didn't have CSEs or O levels or A levels, we came out
> with a little piece of paper which was just our school report,
> and that was what you showed your employer when you
> went for a job. How you'd behaved at school – which
> probably was quite a fair assessment of your character and
> what you were able to do, rather than leaving everything to
> just one exam on one day.

Others were far from content with the system. The opening of all grammar-school places after the war to competitive examination made many parents reluctant to accept the relegation of their children to the secondary modern. In 1951, a new type of examination, the General Certificate of Education, was introduced. Now it was possible for individual pupils to be entered for individual subjects. Parents responded by demanding that secondary modern teachers prepare children to take GCE O levels.

By entering even a minority of their pupils for public examinations, secondary modern schools were in effect challenging the validity of the system of segregating children into different schools at the age of eleven. But for the time being, the grammar schools reigned supreme in the State system.

The top flight of grammar schools enjoyed a special status of loose association with the State. Known as direct grant schools, they received public money direct from the Exchequer instead of through the local authority. Practically independent of the State system, they were institutions half-way in character between a maintained grammar school and a public school. When the Labour government came to power in 1945 there were 232 direct grant schools on the Exchequer list and, as we have seen, Ellen Wilkinson would have liked to abolish the list altogether. But in the end she chose a middle course. Direct grant schools were to be allowed, as before, to charge tuition fees but new strings were attached to the grant. Fearing State control, thirty direct grant schools opted for independence, thus swelling the ranks of the public schools. Other direct grant schools were struck off the list and altogether the number of direct grant schools was reduced from 232 to 166.

In the ordinary grammar schools there was a hint or two at first of reaction among the teaching staff against the Butler Act. Talk of 'parity of esteem' between the different types of secondary schools led grammar school teachers to fear that their own schools would be levelled down. The new Burnham pay scales of 1945, fixed under the Coalition government, abolished the differential between the salaries of elementary and grammar school teachers. This was to be a major source of grievance, rumbling on for several years. Ellen Wilkinson's policy of turning the screw on the direct grant schools was also unpopular, since many local authority grammar schools looked up to their prestigious cousins as the guardians of grammar-school standards.

In the short term, at least, anxieties were misplaced. George Tomlinson and his junior minister, D. R. Hardman, followed Ellen Wilkinson in the warmth of their tributes to the grammar-school sector. One hundred and seventy per cent more was spent on books and other educational materials in the grammar schools than in the secondary moderns. The vast majority of secondary-modern pupils left school at fifteen while the grammar schools invested heavily in sixth form education and most pupils stayed on until the age of eighteen. The grammar schools in 1945 were about to enter a brief golden age of academic superiority and social prestige, bolstered by the faulty mystique of the eleven plus examination.

In 1945 the Crown Film Unit was commissioned to make a film entitled *Children's Charter*, depicting the grammar school of the future. Dorchester Grammar, a day school for boys in the county town of Dorset, was selected as a model and much to the delight of the pupils the spring term was disrupted by the activities of the film crew. Among the boys was Don Culver, who had been admitted as a scholarship entrant in 1943. As he recalls, the Butler Act did have one immediate consequence for boys already enrolled in the school:

> I was there for a year or two when the Butler Act began to bite and then to our pleasant surprise text books were provided free. I think that was really the only major change which we as small boys felt. All of a sudden the end of school year bargaining in the corridors, selling your text books and buying text books of the year into which you were rising, had suddenly ended, and books appeared with the school bookroom stamp inside, and of course to parents this was not a negligible relief.

The long-term effects on the school, Mr Culver argues, were more dramatic:

> The Butler Act ended fee-paying entry to the school. The entry to the school became entirely eleven plus – scholarship boys as they would have been termed in the old days – so that the academic standards increased enormously as a result. You no longer had the incubus, as it were, of the fee payers who got into the school simply because Dad could afford the fees. These boys went off to the secondary modern school now because they couldn't get through the eleven plus. It's a sad reflection really that for those of us who were more able, the grammar school system was a brilliant success. We were, as it were, the élite, even in a small country town. Everything was done for us. We got pushed on and we hope delivered the

goods eventually in academic terms. But the penalty for that was that those who did not get through the gate at eleven went off elsewhere and, on reflection, looking back, provision for them was nothing like as affluent as it was for us.

The abolition of fees in the grammar schools was intended to create an élite of meritocrats recruited purely on the basis of ability, and irrespective of social origins. After 1945, the proportion of working-class children attending grammar school did in fact increase, as Floud, Halsey and Martin showed in their study of two contrasting areas, south-west Hertfordshire and Middlesbrough. Up to 1945, Watford Grammar School in Hertfordshire never allocated more than the statutory minimum of 25 per cent of places to scholarship children, despite pressure to do so from the local education authority. Hence in the period 1934 to 1938 only 16 per cent of the children were the sons of manual workers. The abolition of fees in 1945 transformed the character of the school and by 1950 to 1953 the working-class intake was up to 42 per cent. Middlesbrough, having pursued a more liberal policy of free places in the past, was less affected. The working-class intake rose from 46 per cent in the period 1935 to 1938 to 54 per cent in the period 1948 to 1951.[13]

The change in the social tone of the grammar schools was sufficient to alarm a rearguard of old fogeys without going far enough to satisfy the theoreticians of social equality. In 1950, one observer complained:

The grammar school now includes among its pupils a much higher proportion of children from poorer homes. Some of these children come from homes which are barely literate and where a book is an unusual phenomenon ... Others have very low standards of cleanliness and appearance; some seem to have had very little training in social behaviour; even table manners may leave much to be desired. Children like these have very little to give to the social or cultural life of the school; the school itself has to provide much which, before the war, would have been regarded as the normal contribution of the home.[14]

The grammar schools were more vulnerable to attack from educational radicals. Children from a middle-class background, with the stimulus of parental encouragement and know-how behind them, still had a much higher chance of entry to grammar school than their working-class contemporaries. The eleven plus examination was to some extent an arbitrary bureaucratic device, since the percentage of grammar-school places available varied widely from one part of the country to another. In spite of its scientific aura, the intelligence test was, to say the least, a fallible instrument. Children coached in advance scored higher than children taking the test for the first time. Nor were the people who set the papers as intelligent as they thought they were. They assumed, for example, that there was one correct solution to every question. Cecil Denington, who was teaching in London, saw how cultural bias crept into the assessment:

> The IQ test used to have an answer list and you couldn't depart from this answer list. Now I was teaching at the back of King's Cross at the time and I remember well one of the multiple choice questions, 'What does the word conviction mean?' And the answer was 'Belief'. But of course everybody put the word 'Guilty', which was one of the choices, and around that area you would expect it to be 'Guilty' and not 'Belief'. But there you are, they had to lose a mark over that.

The subversion of the grammar schools did not begin in earnest until the mid-1950s. When the Conservatives returned to power in 1951 they inherited a flourishing and outwardly secure grammar-school system. Another ancient seat of learning still going strong in the 1950s was a fictional creation: Greyfriars School, the home of the legendary Billy Bunter. Restored to life on television by the actor Gerald Campion, the fat owl of the remove roamed the corridors explaining, 'Gosh, you chaps! Leggo! Yarooo!' In fact, as in fiction, the public schools cast an old spell over a new generation of parents and children.

In the 1930s the future of the public schools was clouded by financial anxiety, and the wartime spirit of 'fair shares' seemed to foreshadow the reduction of privilege. In a history of the public schools published in 1941, E. C. Mack observed that 'England is at this moment literally seething with plans for reform of the public schools.' The most likely outcome, he predicted, was that the public schools would have to accept State money, a measure of State intervention and the introduction into their ranks of 'the best elements of the working class'.[15]

Little of this came to pass. The public schools decided to take the initiative and press for reform on their own terms lest it be forced on them from outside. In 1943, they persuaded R. A. Butler to appoint a committee under a Scottish judge, Lord Fleming, to report on the relationship between the public schools and the State system. The Fleming Report of July 1944 recommended that public schools offer a minimum of 25 per cent of their annual admissions to children awarded a scholarship by the local authority. Privilege would make a graceful bow in the direction of democracy and obtain, in return, a new source of income. A scheme to disarm the critics while balancing the books was just what the public schools had been looking for, and they hastened to accept the recommendations of the report.

Then came the Labour landslide of 1945. Oliver Van Os, who was a housemaster at Eton, describes the reaction there:

> I think a shudder did run through and people would say, 'We can't see how anyone who believes in the public schools can support the Labour Party,' etc., etc. It didn't worry me because I thought it was all my eye and I didn't think they would abolish the public schools because they were educationally so good. The good ones, that is. The bad ones are frightful. Beyond measure.

As events proved, the Labour government had no more desire to abolish the public schools than to proclaim a republic. As nearly a quarter of Labour MPs had been educated in public schools, and Attlee brought to the premiership a reverence for the old school tie quite lacking in Churchill, fundamental change was out of the question. For want of a better policy, Ellen Wilkinson sought to implement the Fleming Report. But with a few exceptions here and there, local authorities declined to take up the places offered. The most important disincentive was the high cost to a local authority of paying for a place at an exclusive boarding school. Much better, it was felt, to spend the money on local schools.

In ones and twos a tiny number of pupils were transferred from grammar school to public school under the Fleming scheme. The experiment made no mark on the history of education but it is interesting to find out how the participants coped with a potentially awkward situation. A miner's son, Malcolm Davies, won a scholarship to Shrewsbury, a school of about 500 boys under the headmastership of John Wolfenden. The experiment worked out well. In the early months he was mocked by the other boys for his working-class accent and ridiculed as an 'oik', but gradually the class difference paled into insignificance. As he recollects:

> Boys are fairly cruel and there was a tendency to look down on you and to make you feel a little bit inferior, but it doesn't

last for very long because you all have to go through the same process. We used to have a fagging system, we called it dowling, you were all cleaning somebody else's shoes. You all had your homework to do, you all had to go on a run and you all had to do this, that and the other, and in some things I was better than others, so eventually you finish up coming out top in something and then you've got the respect of the people you're with, and it doesn't really matter whether you're top in maths or whether you're good at running.

Malcolm Davies specialised in mathematics, physics and chemistry with the idea of going into industry. When it was time for him to leave school, the Public School Appointments Bureau arranged an interview for him with United Steel Companies:

I was shown around the steelworks and they said, 'What sort of job do you think you would be good at?' I said, 'Something to do with the sciences, maybe as a chemist,' and they said, 'How about metallurgy?' And I didn't even know the word at that stage. So I said, 'What's it like?' and they said, 'Well, it's a bit like chemistry, you know, but a bit different.' So I became a metallurgist and went along to the local night school and took qualifications in metallurgy and then transferred into sales about twelve years ago.

The top public schools, like the governing class whose children they educated, were skilful in assimilating talented individuals. At Eton, which offered places to a small number of boys from Hertfordshire and Dorset, Oliver Van Os used to interview and select prospective pupils. At the same time, he was responsible as a housemaster for the welfare of scholarship entrants in his house. In his experience, the main problem for the newcomers was homesickness. Unlike their peers, the scholarship boys had never been away to prep school and were unprepared for the break with home. Class differences were awkward but not insuperable:

I don't think the Fleming boys ever felt left out, but they were selected very carefully as good mixers and tolerably good at games, so they had a lot of points of contact. I think they may have felt left out when boys were boasting about holidays on father's yacht or something like that, whereas down in Dorset there was no yacht belonging to father anyway.

Indirectly, the Attlee governments did the public schools much good. Heavy defence commitments overseas ensured a steady demand for places at boarding school for the sons and daughters of the officer class. Meanwhile, middle-class parents who could no longer get their children into grammar school because of the eleven plus might well send them to a public school instead. The fees charged by the public schools were rising, and middle-class incomes were under pressure. But in 1949 Roy Lewis and Angus Maude could write in their study, *The English Middle Classes*:

> In the last two or three years the middle classes have made it abundantly clear that they still greatly prefer the private schools of all kinds. Indeed, they seem to have evinced a growing faith in the public schools which (judging by their waiting lists) are all set fair for a further period of prosperous activity.[16]

The great achievement of the 1940s was to prepare an agenda for increased investment in education at all levels. The provisions of the Butler Act took twenty or thirty years to implement and some still await implementation. But as a percentage of national income, educational expenditure rose from 2 per cent in 1939–40 to 2·7 per cent in 1949–50 and to 4·1 per cent by 1964–5. Though the Butler Act did not deal directly with universities, it made possible the long-term expansion of higher education. In 1939, there were 50,000 university students in Great Britain; by 1950, 80,000; by 1970, 235,000.

The flaw in the programme of educational expansion lay concealed for a long time. It was radical in its ambition of creating an interlocking education system but woolly in its analysis of the purposes of education. Beyond the general idea of spreading enlightenment and doing something for the working classes, there was more rhetoric than precision. Social equality was pursued, if at all, in such a muddled fashion that little was done in education to break down the psychological barriers between 'Them' and 'Us'. The relationship between education and the economy was left to sort itself out piecemeal, with a report here and an initiative there. There is no point in belabouring the politicians of the 1940s for complacency. They were conscious of a great advance but unaware of tomorrow's discontent. Looking back, Denis Healey comments:

> I think the big failure of all post-war governments has been to produce an educational system which enables us today, for example, to move into the new technologies as fast as our competitors are moving ... the whole school system's been

dominated by the values of the early nineteenth-century public schools and to some extent that's been true of the universities as well, and I think that it's clearly inadequate for economic success in the modern world.

Lord Eccles, who as Sir David Eccles was Minister of Education from 1954 to 1957, remarks:

What we've got now is based on the assumption that between the age of five and sixteen you could teach the average child as much as they want for the rest of their lives. Well, once you've got the scientific revolution, technology and all that, that's absurd, because the skills and everything else are changing all the time and you must have a system which enables people to keep up with the changes and we haven't got it. We're still hopelessly behind in what you might call adult education, for instance. Very sad.

7

BRITAIN CAN MAKE IT

Jobs were plentiful after the war. Full employment ruled, and with it trade union power on the shop-floor of industry. A spirit of release from the war effort and emancipation from the work disciplines of the 1930s was abroad in the factories, mines and shipyards. In a leading article of January 1946, *The Economist* wrote of 'the universal reluctance to do a hard day's work, to which almost every employer of labour could at present testify'. In May, the journalist and author J. L. Hodson, who kept in close touch with business opinion on his travels around Britain, noted in his diary:

> A works manager in Sheffield repeats what I have heard elsewhere – that the men are about 70 to 75 per cent as efficient in output as pre-war. He says, 'They feel, "We've won the war, haven't we? Are we to go on slaving for ever as if the war was still on?"' They worked not less than fifty-six hours a week for six years.[1]

Labour's victory in the general election of 1945 was itself the expression of pressure from below for a higher standard of living and better working conditions. Simultaneously the bargaining power of the trade unions was increasing: membership rose steadily from 6,298,000 in 1939 to 8,803,000 in 1946. The scene appeared to be set for a mighty clash between labour and capital, marked by industrial strife and sharp antagonisms between government and business.

In the event, conflicts were muted or transient. Between 1945 and 1950 about 9·5 million working days were lost through strike action, compared with 178 million days between 1918 and 1923.[2] As for relations between the government and businessmen, Sir Raymond Streat, Chairman of the Cotton Board, was to write subsequently, 'It is a matter of history that there was very little hostility and virtually no obstructiveness in industry at large towards the Socialist government.'[3] This was too bland a verdict but in certain areas of policy the understanding between business and the government was undoubtedly close. The extra demands of working people were somehow absorbed by industry and government with a minimum of drama. How and why did this happen?

Western Europe in 1945 stood at the threshold of a long boom. The output and profits of industry were rising. Until the early 1950s expansion was overshadowed by a balance of payments problem between western Europe and the United States. For Britain the threat was particularly acute and the government, fearful of another great slump, bombarded the public with propaganda about the economic crisis. More will be said of this later, but for the present the outstanding fact to be borne in mind is that the blow never fell. The industrial boom carried on.

Whether in home or overseas markets, foreign competition was a minor problem for British industry in the immediate post-war years. The economies of Germany, Italy and Japan had been temporarily overwhelmed. The demand for British products was greater than industry could satisfy and order books were full. The war had served as a stimulus to science-based industries such as chemicals, electronic engineering and aircraft. These now formed the most advanced sector of the economy. Traditional manufactures, meanwhile, were enjoying a phase of remission from long-term decline. With German and Japanese shipyards in ruins, the world turned once more to British yards. Similarly, the output of steel rose from 12·7 million tons in 1946 to 16·3 million in 1950. In 1951 Hugh Gaitskell, the Chancellor of the Exchequer, officially opened the largest and most modern steel plant in the British Isles, the Abbey Works at Port Talbot. The coal industry, nationalised in 1947, took over many inefficient pits. But so urgent was the demand of other industries for fuel, that financial constraints were relaxed and coal was mined at almost any cost. In 1950 the National Coal Board's 'Plan for Coal' therefore proposed to increase output up to a target of 250 million tons a year by 1960.

British manufacturers still enjoyed a high reputation abroad. In the late nineteenth century British firms had pioneered the bicycle and gone on to export it throughout the British Empire, South America and the Far East. Between 1939 and 1945, 90 per cent of production stopped as the industry was turned over to munitions but after the war demand was as strong as ever. In 1948 Phillips, one of the four main British bicycle manufacturers, appointed Ken Collins as an overseas representative and for his first sales mission sent him to India. Arriving in Bombay after a journey by sea via the Suez Canal, he booked in at the Taj Mahal hotel:

To the best of my knowledge no dealer knew I'd arrived although they knew I would be coming to India. And so the next morning my intention was to go down to the Bazaar, but I was awoken by banging on the door. Went to the door in my pyjamas and there's a manager of the hotel requesting that I leave the hotel, the hotel was crowded by cycle dealers wanting to see me. I looked out the door and there, far as the corridor went, there was possibly 200 or more [of] these Indian dealers.

So many dealers in India, Africa and the Middle East were crying out for supplies that the company's main problem was to decide which of them should be allowed to place an order, a state of affairs that was to continue until the early 1950s.

A similar experience of buoyant overseas demand, this time in western Europe, is recalled by Sir Arthur Bryan, who joined the potters Josiah Wedgwood as a management trainee in 1947. The pottery trade, Bryan emphasises, did have to compete with countries such as France, Italy and Germany, which were very keen to re-establish themselves in world markets. But having won the war, British exporters had the edge:

[On] my first visit to Europe as a representative of the firm, we were gods in Europe, the British. Every door was open for us. You had to deliver, of course, it was no use just being a smiling, pretty face, but the introductions to the markets of the world were of the highest order and it was great in those days to be in the market representing a good firm with a quality product.

British industrialists were reaping the benefits of a seller's market. So, too, were British workers in the market that most concerned them – the market for labour. Manpower (and, as Churchill remarked, 'manpower embraces woman') was in short supply. The restrictive practices of trade unions had something to do with this, and so did government policies. The raising of the school-leaving age reduced the supply of juvenile labour. Peacetime conscription, regularised by the National Service Act of 1947, whisked young men into the forces for eighteen months, a period extended to two years after the outbreak of the Korean War in 1950. The new military and welfare states, generated by the war, increased the size of the civil service from 580,000 in 1938 to 972,000 in 1950. Regional policy ensured the opening of new factories in pre-war areas of mass unemployment, such as Tyneside and south Wales. But the fundamental cause of labour shortages was the industrial boom.

So acute was the manpower problem in key industries and services that the government sought out reserves of foreign labour. About 100,000 workers were recruited by government agencies in Ireland, swelling the Irish-born population of Britain to 1,000,000 by 1951. After a century or more, the Irish were a familiar presence and well integrated into the labour movement but the resettlement of Poles, another transfusion from a fiercely Roman Catholic and nationalist culture, was a social innovation, hotly opposed in some quarters of the trade union world.

During the war, about 190,000 Poles had served alongside the British armed forces and afterwards many had no wish to return to a Stalinised Poland, while others were debarred from doing so. In May 1946 the Foreign Secretary, Ernest Bevin, announced that the Polish forces would be demobilised. Those who wished to remain in Britain would be entitled to enrol in a new organisation, the Polish Resettlement Corps, to prepare them for re-entry into civilian life. By the end of 1948 the Ministry of Labour had found employment for some 45,000 Poles, principally in the building, textile, catering, coal and agricultural industries.

The eligibility of the Poles for employment was conferred on them as a right, in recognition of their part in the war. On a quite different footing were the 'European Voluntary Workers', recruited by officials of the Ministry of Labour from displaced persons' camps in Germany and Austria. They were selected strictly according to their qualifications for specific job vacancies. Yet another category of foreign worker, with the lowest status of all, were German prisoners of war who were pressed into service as farm labourers.

The list was variegated but in fact Britain made little use of immigrant labour by comparison with its continental neighbours. In the view of the economist Alec Cairncross, the relative shortage of labour in Britain was one of the factors retarding the rate of economic recovery:

> In nearly all the European countries except Sweden and Switzerland there was a large reserve of labour that could be drawn upon continuously as expansion proceeded ...
>
> It was not only that these additions to the industrial labour force gave expansion a longer run and more thrust but that an elastic labour supply made it easier to maintain labour discipline and plan the use of labour with more assurance.

While the trade unions in Britain were remarkably accom-
modating under conditions in which they enjoyed unpre-
cedented bargaining power, the average British management
still had to spend far more time in struggling with labour
problems than their competitors on the continent.[4]

Full employment and union power tended to restrict the
authority of management and inflate wages. James Rochford, who
described in Chapter One his return to Salford after demobilisation,
took a labourer's job with a firm of engineers manufacturing railway
wheels. What most impressed him as a young labourer was the
powerful grip of the unions representing the skilled machine men,
and their determination to preserve restrictive practices:

> The union set a quota on each machine. So if you produced
> too much, you got tapped on the shoulder. If a machine man
> said, 'Look, I've got a house to pay for and I've got four or
> five kids, I'm going to do this,' he suddenly found that the
> overhead crane was passing him, not to offer him any gear.
> And he couldn't find his slinger to fetch his gear. And once
> he'd been taught a lesson and he started conforming, then he
> got his gear again.

Changes in the nature of work were complicated by demarcation
disputes between unions. Rochford was detailed to work as an
assistant to an engineer called Bernard, and moved to a part of the
shop where a mysterious new machine was lying idle:

> So I said to Bernard, 'What's that machine there?' 'Oh,' he
> said, 'it's been there about five or six months. It balances
> wheels in one operation. You put the wheel in and it balances
> it, weighs it, checks it, see? Instead of it being moved all over
> the shop, being checked and balanced, it does all the
> operation in one go.' And the firm had got it from America. I
> said, 'What's the problem?' 'Oh,' he said, 'the engineering
> union said they should work it, the ETU [Electrical Trades
> Union] said their man should work it, the iron and steel
> blokes' federation said their man should work it, and they
> couldn't agree on who should work that machine.' Finally
> they decided that two union members opposite would work it
> together on two different shifts. Two on one shift, two on
> another, so that was four different unions working it.

Taken out of context, trade union attitudes are easy to satirise but
the historical background has to be taken into account. The unions

looked back to the unemployment of the 1930s and beyond that, in the engineering trades, to prolonged battles with the employers reaching back to the late nineteenth century. Their tactics were profoundly defensive and based on the assumption that wages and employment were precarious. The trade union movement was founded on the principles of pessimism and resistance and was slow to adapt to conditions of full employment.

In the absence of an incomes policy, full employment tended to create wage inflation – pay rises in excess of the general increase in output. Philip Masheder, last encountered in the opening chapter of this book as a convert from Kipling to socialism, took up a job as a foreman in his uncle's printing works. Soon afterwards his uncle died and left him as the owner of the firm. Once in charge, he began to see the question of wages and costs from the employers' point of view:

> Labour was that short, good printers were at a premium and the owners hadn't got the sense to see that they were being strung along over wages. You could open a *Manchester Evening News* every night and you would see adverts for printers required. In those days it was shillings and half-crowns and two bob. And for another half-crown a week a man that was earning, shall we say, five pounds fifteen shillings and sixpence a week would come and work for me for five pounds eighteen shillings. And so you took him on and you'd just got him settled down nicely, he got to know you, you got to know him, and the next thing was, there's a, 'I'm very sorry, I'm leaving you.' 'Oh God, why? What's the matter? What's gone wrong?' 'Well, I can get more money somewhere else.'

Where firms were in competition, workers did not need to be highly skilled or even unionised to drive a hard bargain. They could shop around from one company to another. Mrs Mary Law was a single girl in her teens, working as a sewing machinist in Manchester. She and her friend Rita were inseparable workmates and used to move together from one firm to another, wherever they could get the best price for piecework: 'You just moved around, where the money was. Somebody would say, "Oh, you can earn good money at such a place." And you just got up and you just went down the street and went somewhere else.'

Eighty per cent of workers were covered either by an agreement between unions and employers or by statutory regulation of wages and conditions. The entrenched positions of labour were so strong that no prudent employer was likely to conduct an anti-union offensive. But it would be a mistake to assume that employers in the 1940s regarded union interests as conflicting with their own. The sociologist Ferdinand Zweig, who conducted an inquiry into restrictive practices in four different industries in 1948 and 1949, concluded that it was very hard to define what a restrictive practice was. What an economist might term a restrictive practice, an employer might regard as an essential element in good industrial relations:

> Many managers, especially in large-scale establishments, would feel lost without unions, feeling that they have in the unions lines of communication right to the bottom, natural and responsible spokesmen of their men, and means of consultation and participation without signs of paternalism.[5]

Industrial relations between 1945 and 1951 still retained some of the spirit of co-operation that had been developed during the war through Joint Industrial Councils and Joint Production Committees. From the beginning of 1947, the Labour government encouraged the revival and extension of these arrangements.

The Labour government's approach to industry was shaped by two main imperatives. One was the commitment to the nationalisa-tion of industry, a partisan objective with origins reaching far back into the history of the labour movement. The other was the drive to raise industrial output, a matter of expediency and consensus thrust on the government by the post-war crisis in Britain's trade. It was never clear how the two imperatives were related. Sometimes they overlapped, sometimes they conflicted and sometimes they operated in isolation.

In fulfilment of the pledges given in the election manifesto of 1945, the Attlee governments embarked on the most extensive programme of nationalisation ever undertaken in Britain. Coal, gas, electricity, the railways and canals, long-distance road haulage, civil aviation and iron and steel were all taken into public ownership. In total, two million employees were added to the public sector.

The aims of nationalisation were ambiguous. To an extent now difficult to grasp, industrialists and managers were convinced by wartime experience of the need for a measure of State planning, and were ready to endorse the compulsory reorganisation of ailing industries in fuel and transport. In 1945, for instance, a committee under Geoffrey Heyworth, the chairman of Unilever, recommended the public ownership of the gas industry. More often, business opinion preferred some form of State regulation stopping well short of outright nationalisation. But no matter: the capitalist case for the reform of basic industries lent respectability to Labour's case for nationalisation. Herbert Morrison, the politician chiefly responsible for shaping and presenting the programme, sought to justify each measure on its merits as a means of improving the efficiency and utility of the industry concerned. Always keen to attract white-collar support to the party, he talked in managerial terms attuned to advanced business opinion. While this was the view of the planners, the main body of the labour movement, accustomed to a trade union outlook on the world, thought in terms of the advance of class interests. As the official historian of nationalisation, Sir Norman Chester, writes, 'A major aim, some would say the major aim, of those who advocated nationalisation, was the improvement in the status and conditions of those employed in those industries.'[6]

The prospects for a higher standard of living were persistently overshadowed by fear of another great slump, and though the crash never came, the drive to prevent it was the overriding theme of industrial policy. As a trading nation, Britain depended for its livelihood upon imports of food and raw materials. But in 1945 Britain was deeply in debt. Two-thirds of its export trade and a quarter of its overseas investments had been sacrificed to the war effort. Massive sterling debts had been incurred in Egypt and India, owing to their use as military bases. Britain was living on credit extended by the United States under Lend-Lease.

In August 1945 Japan surrendered. To the astonishment and dismay of the British government, President Truman abruptly cancelled Lend-Lease. It was estimated in Whitehall that in order to meet Britain's deficit, an economic miracle would have to be wrought. Or in plain terms exports would have to be increased to a level 75 per cent above that of 1939. To achieve this would take several years and in the meantime there was no alternative but to seek additional credit from the United States.

As long as the Americans were prepared to refloat the British economy, all might yet be well. But there was no guarantee that they would. Lord Keynes led a delegation to Washington in search of a loan but the negotiations were long and painful. The terms proposed by the United States, though generous by normal peacetime criteria, came as a shock to the government and the House of Commons. After all the sacrifices Britain had made in the common cause, it seemed unjust that the United States should charge 2 per cent interest on a loan. A worrying condition was attached. The British had to agree that within a year of the granting of the loan, sterling was to become freely convertible into dollars. In December 1945 the government reluctantly accepted the terms as the best they could get, though Congress did not ratify them until the following July.

A breathing space had been obtained. But the balance of payments problem was poised like an axe over Britain's recovery. Unless output and exports were expanded fast, the loan would run out and the axe fall, slicing through the Welfare State and the standard of living. Perversely, there were also risks in expansion. The revival of the British economy stimulated the import of food and raw materials from the United States: wheat, petrol, cotton, tobacco and so on. But as there was very little Britain could sell to the United States in return, there was a danger that precious dollar reserves would vanish. In the spring of 1947 – by which time Britain was purchasing a prodigal 42 per cent of its imports from the United States – the dollars obtained under the loan agreement began to melt like snowflakes in the sun. When convertibility came into play in July, investors converted vast quantities of pounds into dollars and drained away all but the dregs of the loan. In August the Chancellor of the Exchequer, Hugh Dalton, announced the suspension of convertibility.

The currency crisis shook the government to the core and temporarily shattered its reputation. But in the autumn the Cabinet began to stage a recovery, led by Sir Stafford Cripps. Attlee moved Cripps from the Board of Trade to the newly created Ministry of Economic Affairs, with the responsibility for framing a coherent strategy for boosting exports and restoring the balance of payments. Aided by a small planning staff under Edwin Plowden, Cripps revelled in the task. None the less he might have been unable to carry it through but for the chance resignation of Dalton from the Treasury in November. Attlee appointed Cripps in his place. As Chancellor of the Exchequer he was now able to draw all the various threads of economic policy into his hands. In Cripps, industry found a new leader with a fervent message of recovery through consensus, productivity and the export drive.

A lengthy excursion into the history of the Labour governments has been unavoidable at this point, since Whitehall was omnipresent in the affairs of post-war industry. But let us turn to the experience industry had of government.

The greatest test of the government's industrial policies occurred in the coal industry. In 1945 the shortage of coal was a fundamental economic problem. Other industries could only expand to the extent that coal supplied the fuel, but output had fallen from 231 million tons in 1939 to 175 million in 1945. As all the coal produced now had to be jealously reserved for the home market, Britain had also lost a valuable export trade. At 10 Downing Street, in January 1946, Douglas Jay sent a minute to Attlee reminding him that 'the lack of coal exports is already depriving us of Swedish timber for housing and acutely needed Argentine wheat. It will also be a counsel of despair to have to face the critical foreign exchange year of 1947 without coal exports.'[7]

The coal industry was an archaic branch of capitalism, indefensible by the standards of twentieth-century business organisation. Ownership of the industry was dispersed between 950 separate firms, many of them too small to afford the capital necessary to modernise the pits. Industrial relations in the majority of coalfields were notoriously bitter, the wounds of the past having never healed. 'Whenever you start a conversation with the miner on the pits,' wrote Ferdinand Zweig in 1948, 'he invariably begins by telling you about the Coal Strike of 1926.'[8]

In 1944 the Tory Reform Committee had condemned the structure of the coal industry and recommended a reduction of the number of companies to between forty and sixty and the introduction of regional planning. The following year, a government-appointed committee led by Sir Charles Reid, a mining engineer, itemised the inefficiencies of the industry and placed the responsibility on the employers. Reid did not recommend nationalisation, to which he was opposed, but a statutory central authority with powers to effect mergers and plan production.

There was no possibility that the Attlee government would accept a half-way house. The miners had been calling for nationalisation since 1918 and so had the Labour Party. Emanuel Shinwell, the Minister of Fuel and Power, proceeded to draw up a plan of nationalisation modelled on Herbert Morrison's device of the public corporation. On 1 January 1947, over 800 colliery companies and 1500 pits were vested in the National Coal Board. The flag of the NCB was hoisted at the pithead and notice-boards proclaimed, 'This colliery is now managed by the National Coal Board on behalf of the people.' At some collieries the miners struck out the word people and wrote, 'Miners'.

Within a few weeks of nationalisation a severe fuel crisis occurred. During the summer and autumn of 1946 the Ministry of Fuel and Power received several warnings that coal stocks at power stations were perilously low. Shinwell, always self-confident, brushed the worries aside. 'Everyone knows there is going to be a serious crisis in the coal industry,' he declared in October 1946, 'except the Minister of Fuel and Power.'

At the end of January 1947, wintry conditions of exceptional severity set in. Snowstorms brought the railways and the movement of coal to the power stations to a halt, and blizzards prevented the sailing of coal ships along the east coast. On 7 February Shinwell announced to a stunned House of Commons that the power stations were running out of coal stocks. As from the following Monday there would be no electricity at all for industrial users in selected regions and consumers would be forbidden to switch on electric heaters for three hours each morning and two each afternoon. Four weeks of power cuts followed and nearly two million people were temporarily thrown out of work. Greyhound racing, television and the production of magazines were stopped. No reasonable observer could blame nationalisation, which had been running for only three weeks when the crisis occurred. The weather could be blamed in part as a stroke of bad luck. But Shinwell and the Ministry were responsible for the lack of coal stocks at the power stations.

The fuel crisis was a spectacular revelation of the importance of coal production as a service to the rest of the economy. The most urgent priority was a higher volume of total output: costs were a secondary consideration. Financial constraints were relaxed as the NCB pushed ahead with the introduction of new machinery. Campaigns were mounted to recruit workers to the mines and increase productivity. But here we need to glance back at the predicament inherited by the Coal Board.

During the war the number of workers in the industry fell from 773,000 to 694,000. Young men had gone into the forces leaving an ageing population of miners in run-down pits. Output per miner fell from 302 tons per year to 259 tons, and absenteeism was rife. The problem after the war was that the younger generation in mining areas were reluctant to join the industry. Owing to the success of regional policy, the mining areas were mushrooming with new factories offering more attractive employment. Miners were near the top of the league table of industrial earnings but the nature of the job was still so dangerous and oppressive that wages alone failed to attract a large enough number of school-leavers. 'The fathers discourage their lads as much as possible,' wrote Zweig, 'and I often heard vows that their lads should never go down.'[9]

The new Labour government appealed to the miners to work

harder. But on a visit to the Durham coalfields in August 1945, J. L. Hodson commented on the lack of incentive to work:

> They are asked to get more coal and thus earn more money at a time when there are precious few goods in the shops they can buy with the money anyhow, and when income tax is very high. Failing goods to buy, they've bought leisure – by absenteeism ... I asked a miners' leader, who impressed me by his grasp and alertness, honesty and frankness, what proportion of the Durham men would work a lot harder out of pure loyalty to the Labour government and thankfulness that the pits are going to be nationalised at some future time. He said he thought about 10 per cent.[10]

In coal as in other undermanned industries one potential resource to be tapped was the labour of the Polish Resettlement Corps. When the idea was first put to Shinwell in 1946 he rejected it on the grounds that the miners believed the Poles concerned to be fascists. The real bone of contention was, in fact, the traditional fear of immigrant labour. But opinions changed. The leaders of the NUM, keen to assist a Labour government, agreed in principle to the employment of the Poles. As preconditions, the NUM stipulated that the recruits must join the union and sign an undertaking agreeing that their jobs were conditional. If for any reason miners had to be made redundant, the Poles would be the first to lose their jobs. Local branches of the union also retained a right of veto, and some pits refused to accept Polish workers.

By December 1948, 7000 Poles had joined the industry. Among them was Walter Kobak, who served during the war with the Polish Parachute Brigade. While stationed in Fife he married the daughter of a local miner and, having returned to Scotland after the war, decided to follow his father-in-law into the industry:

> To start with it was really very hard physically and mentally. Mentally because I went into a pit that was a closed shop, meaning that all the people who worked in that pit came from that particular village. And of course there was resentment of me coming in and probably taking away [someone's] job. Not at the time, because there was plenty of work, but his son probably was in danger of not being accepted in that pit because I would work until I was sixty-five years of age. Through time, of course, it became better, because we were hard workers – well, I can only speak for myself. I was a hard

worker and I was gradually being accepted as a good
worker, not as a Pole. Then of course, with me being able to
express myself a little better, I tried to point out to them
that down below, when there is a fall, it doesn't say, 'I'm
not going to fall because I've got a Britisher underneath me,
I'll fall now because there's a Pole,' and of course the boys
understood that. Down below we were all black, dirty, and
you couldn't recognise a Pole from – from a Chinaman.

The National Union of Mineworkers maintained that the best
way to recruit extra workers was to make the job more attractive. In
January 1946, the union's general secretary, Ebby Edwards,
addressed to Shinwell a series of proposals for better conditions,
known as the 'Miners' Charter'. Apart from such items as improved
earnings and safety, the most important demand was a five-day
week with no reduction in pay. This, the NUM argued, would
reduce absenteeism. Shinwell and the Cabinet, on the other hand,
feared that it would reduce output. However, in April 1947 a five-
day week was introduced. One of the main principles on which the
agreement rested was that miners would do a fair day's work on
each of their five shifts, which would involve a reassessment of the
work to be performed. Sometimes this involved an increase in the
stint, or measured stretch of coal the miner was asked to clear from
the face to the conveyor-belt. The sequel revealed that industrial
relations were as combustible under the NCB as they had been
under the old owners.

In August 1947, 132 men at Grimethorpe colliery in Yorkshire
went on strike. The dispute began when a chargehand at the
colliery, Eddie Cook, was summoned to his manager's office and
asked to sign an agreement to extend the stint the following week
from twenty-one feet to twenty-three feet. Eddie Cook refused to
sign:

I says, 'I'm sorry, I can't sign it, not without the consent of
the union.' He said, 'Well, I'm sorry, it's got to happen next
week.' I said, 'Well, the boys will not stand for it.' And that
was the last time we worked for the next five weeks.

The bosses used to work like that. They were the boss
and what they said you were supposed to do. They wouldn't
come to you in a proper manner and say, 'Why don't we
have a meeting about it?' 'cause then we could have got the
union in and had a proper meeting about it and then turned
it down if we didn't want it.

The strike spread as other Yorkshire miners came out in sympathy and by September forty-six pits were affected. After mediation by the NUM, the Grimethorpe strikers agreed to go back to work on condition that a fact-finding committee of five miners be appointed to discover why the men objected to the extension of the stint. The committee, which included Eddie Cook, discovered that according to the men's contract the coal should have been prepared for them in advance by boring and shot-firing. But as they were having to delay while the coal was prepared, and help prepare it themselves, they were unable to complete a longer stint in a day. The management withdrew the proposed contract and the men were vindicated.

Grimethorpe had been owned prior to nationalisation by the Carlton Main colliery company. The previous managers, reappointed by the National Coal Board, were still in place. Continuity of management at local level was the rule rather than the exception in the early days of the NCB, a fact that explains why industrial relations were slow to change. Yet looking back, Eddie Cook regards nationalisation as a watershed. At Grimethorpe, new machinery revived and sustained the profitability of the pit and working conditions were transformed. Whereas before miners had had to walk to the coalface, an underground journey of up to three miles, the NCB introduced paddy trains to transport them to the spot. As for the relationship between the miners and the management, Eddie Cook says:

> After nationalisation it altered altogether from private enterprise. The bosses and the men were more together and you could talk to them differently as though a barrier had been taken down. It was a lot easier to talk to a boss and a lot easier to get a bit of cash out of them as well.

The five-day week, the ultimate source of the trouble at Grimethorpe, failed to improve output sufficiently and at the urgent request of the government the NUM agreed to restore Saturday working, this time at overtime rates. With the introduction of new machinery on a lavish scale, output per man shift rose from 2·7 tons in 1945 to 3·17 tons in 1951. But shortages of manpower persisted. After a temporary surge of recruitment following nationalisation, the drift away from the industry recurred. By 1951 the number of men leaving the pits was outstripping recruitment and the labour force had fallen back to the level of 1946.

Judged in economic terms, nationalisation was an advance but not a breakthrough. The same goes for its impact on industrial relations. Working conditions greatly improved. Within ten years of nationali-

67–9 *above left*, R. A. Butler, the author of the 1944 Education Act; *above right*, Ellen Wilkinson, Minister of Education 1945–7; *below*, George Tomlinson, Minister of Education, opens a new primary school at Hollingbury, Brighton, November 1948

70–1 Role reversal: *above*, girls doing woodwork at Queensbridge Secondary Modern School, 1950; *below*, domestic science at Arnos Secondary Modern School, Southgate, 1950

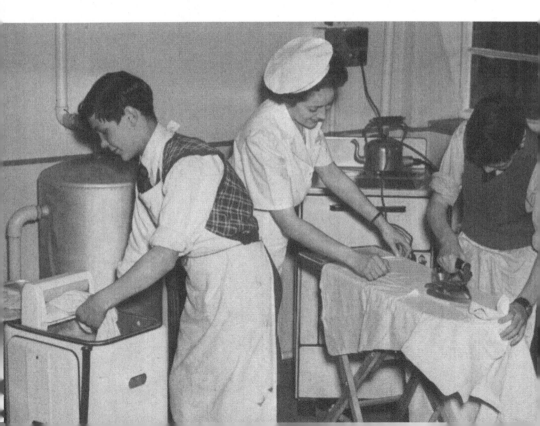

72 Emergency training of teachers at Trent Park, Cockfosters, home of the late Sir Philip Sassoon, 1947

73 Temporary school accommodation for children from new housing estates at Chigwell, 1948

74　George Tomlinson attends an exhibition of new techniques of school-building, 1948

75　The new principles of school design: Templewood Primary School

76 A model living-room on show at the Britain Can Make It exhibition,
1946
77 The streamlined bicycle arrives at the Britain Can Make It exhibition

78 Mass-production of radio-receivers, 1947

79 Sir Stafford Cripps encourages the setting-up of a working party for the Nottingham lace industry, 1946

80 The inauguration of the National Coal Board at Murton Colliery in January 1947: *left*, Emanuel Shinwell, the Minister of Fuel and Power; *right*, Lord Hyndley, chairman of the National Coal Board

81 The great freeze-up of 1947

82   Propaganda for the export drive, 1947

83–4 *right*, Appealing to women workers: a poster with a revealing slant; *below*, The motor industry's export drive

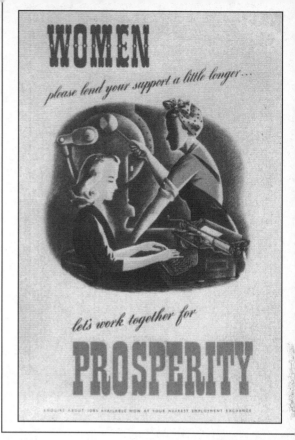

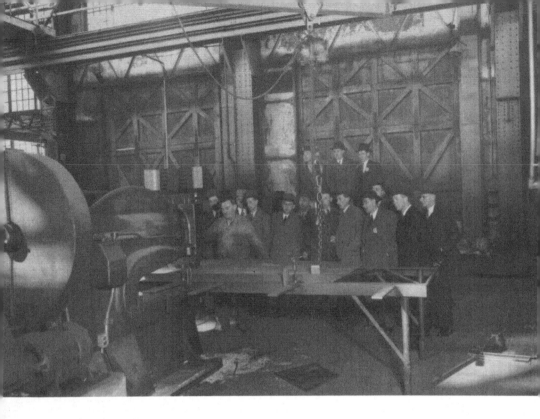

85 Learning from the Americans: a team from the British locomotive industry visits the Eddystone plant at Philadelphia, 1950

86 The Brabazon I at Bristol, 1947

87   The Festival funfair and Pleasure Gardens at Battersea, 1951

88-91 *opposite above*, Herbert Morrison having his palm read by Mrs Vaughan Williams; *opposite below*, The King and Queen's visit to the South Bank; *right*, The Festival logo designed by Abram Games; *below*, The Emett railway at Battersea

92　The Skylon at night
93　The South Bank with the Dome of Discovery in the foreground

94 The transport exhibition at the Festival: a locomotive destined for export to India

95 A display of kitchen units at the Homes and Gardens pavilion

96   The South Bank packs up, October 1951

sation, the number of deaths from accidents had been halved. But vague expectations of a psychological transformation in the pits were confounded. Greater consultation between workers and management eased the tension but failed to efface old differences of outlook. When the sociologists Dennis, Henriques and Slaughter made their study of the Ashton colliery in Yorkshire in the early 1950s, they reported:

> National Coal Board officials complain bitterly that any change they introduce is greeted with mistrust, even if its advantages to the men would seem to be immediately obvious. When the National Coal Board or any other employer talk about the need for 'economies' the workers expect attacks on their wages. If cubic capacity is introduced for measurement of coal production in place of the old weighing system, suspicion immediately comes to the fore and the men worry how much they are going to lose. Scores of examples could be given of the prevailing idea among workers that any suggestion emanating from the management, since it is designed for greater profit, is an underhand attack.[11]

By a historical irony, of which observers were blissfully unaware in the 1950s, the nationalised coal industry was fated in a later epoch to be the scene of the most bitter and brutal industrial conflict since 1926: the miners' strike of 1984–5.

In coal, as in other branches of industry, the Labour government discovered how difficult it was to influence the behaviour of wage-earners in conditions of full employment. In peacetime compulsory powers over labour were unacceptable except as a temporary expedient. Nor could the government afford to set off a wages spiral by the offer of juicy incentives to particular groups of workers. For the lack of a substantial carrot or stick, the government was obliged to fall back on publicity, propaganda and appeals for voluntary co-operation.

In the spring of 1946 the government launched a production campaign across the whole of industry, with the aim of communicating to the shop-floor the state of the economy and the necessity of higher output. Douglas Jay, who witnessed the start of the campaign from the Prime Minister's office, contributed the memorable slogan, 'A Fair Day's Work for a Fair Day's Pay.' Posters, leaflets and documentary films were released over Britain like a string of balloons.

The fuel and convertibility crises of 1947 led to an intensification of the campaign. In March, Cripps came to the fore with a series of press conferences to launch the government's new *Economic Survey for 1947*, the first coherent attempt to explain the aims and methods of economic planning. 'We Work or Want,' posters proclaimed from the hoardings. That summer, a special appeal was directed towards women.

During the war the government had conscripted women into industry and raised the total number of women going out to work to nearly eight million. But as ordnance factories closed, many women workers returned to the home and the number at work had fallen, by June 1947, to six million. Now the government was keen to attract women back to work to expand key industries and services. There were 42,000 vacancies for women in the clothing trades, 16,000 in the cotton mills, and so on: a grand total of more than 92,000 women was required. In June 1947 the Minister of Labour, George Isaacs, initiated a publicity campaign in seventy-two selected districts to encourage women back to work.

The proportion of married women going out to work was higher than it had been before the war, and could have been raised substantially if the government had been prepared to open more day nurseries. But on this issue, Isaacs was cautious. He stressed that his appeal for assistance did not apply to mothers with young children, and acknowledged the view that a housewife's first duty was to the home. With this proviso, he begged housewives to think carefully about the possibilities of employment, and do the best they could. The results of the campaign were disappointing. 31,000 women were recruited, leaving nearly two-thirds of the vacancies unfilled.

The tone of official propaganda is one of the most revealing aspects of the period. The public were jollied along as though they were rather backward children at school. *Women Must Work*, a Central Office of Information film released as part of the campaign, depicted a father, mother and small boy pleading for more consumer goods. The dialogue ran:

> Father: 'I want a pair of trousers.'
> Mother: 'I want a new chair.'
> Small Boy: 'I want lots of soldiers.'
> All Three (in unison): 'We want more everything.'

At this point, the voice of an unseen, upper-class male broke into the proceedings with a message from on high:

> All right. All right. You want more goods. But you really can't have them until we have produced more. And we can't

produce all we want unless a lot of you women come back into industry. And they're needed now. If you can manage to take up work you will be helping the country, making new friends and putting more money in your bag.

The cotton industry, one of the most stricken of the 1930s, was the scene of several recruitment and production drives. With Japanese competition temporarily in abeyance, and the government keen to encourage the revival of exports, the mills were hungry for labour. As they depended mainly on female workers, the campaigns were principally directed towards women. In the summer of 1948, sixty-one weaving mills in the town of Nelson took part in a drive to increase production by 10 per cent. The employers co-operated with the Ministry of Labour and the Central Office of Information in a call for greater effort at work and new recruits to the industry. Ferdinand Zweig describes the methods employed:

> Each mill had its own target and target posters were set up in the mills. Progress bulletins were issued and delivered to each mill. A copy of the government short *Economic Survey* and a questionnaire, which asked for offers of help and labour, were sent to each house. A travelling exhibition of fine fabrics was arranged to serve as a campaign liaison unit. In the centre of the town a Nelson's Column was erected, which was floodlit every evening, and showed the target of production and actual percentage increase each week.[12]

The results of the campaign were modest. Young married women, complaining of the lack of nurseries, were reluctant to take up work. Due to better time-keeping and a reduction in absenteeism, production was increased by about 4 per cent but this was less than half the gain expected.

In peacetime, exhortations to work hard for the sake of the nation lacked the moral authority they had possessed during the war. The rhetoric of economic crisis was at odds with the popular experience of abundant employment and better working conditions. Worse, there was a hectoring element, an implicit criticism of the working classes as lazy, and a veiled threat of penalties to come unless they pulled their socks up. Having observed the production campaign in the weaving mills of Nelson, Zweig concluded that most workers did not respond, or resented the insinuation that they were not already working as hard as they could. He noted a similar reaction in the pits. 'The more I hear about the economic crisis,' a miner told him, 'the more I am convinced that the wheel will be turned against us, and that conditions in the mines will get worse.'[13]

As a writer in the *Listener* observed, trade union leaders, generals, Lord Mayors and economists were flogging the British public with words. For the speakers the experience was therapeutic, a release from the anxieties of responsibility. But they should ask themselves a question:

> How does it feel to be in the audience? To be a docker or a cotton worker or a miner? The speaker, frustrated because output has not risen to the extent of his hopes, or because there have been strikes, bad time-keeping and absence, sets about his audience ... But how does it feel to be threatened, to be told that, 'There is a small minority among you who are traitors to the national cause'?[14]

Propaganda to ginger up work discipline in the factories achieved little. But indirectly it assisted industrial policy in another direction. It contributed to the process whereby the leaders of the trade unions were drawn into collaboration with the government in imposing wage restraint on their members. The trade union leaders of the 1940s were oligarchs with great, though never unqualified, authority over the rank and file. The propaganda campaigns over the economy reinforced their alliance with the Labour government and taught them to view the problems of economic management in the same way as ministers. When Cripps took charge of economic policy at the end of 1947, one of his first initiatives was to invite the trade unions to adopt a policy of voluntary wage restraint, to be coupled with the restraint of salaries and dividends. Strong opposition was expressed by some trade unions, notably the AEU and the ETU, but on 24 March 1948 a conference of trade union delegates voted in favour of a wages freeze by 5,421,000 to 2,032,000. A voluntary policy for the restriction of wages, salaries and dividends was sustained over the next two years, but collapsed in 1950. Douglas Jay, who joined Cripps as Economic Secretary to the Treasury in December 1947, and frequently had to speak at regional production conferences, points to the link between propaganda and pay:

> We used to have meetings of a couple of hundred people, and run through the story of how the war had been paid for and all the losses inflicted on us, and the effort to repair those and what the government was doing. Of course it did finish up with the moral that it was impossible to grant 25 per cent and

30 per cent pay increases every year as we should wish, but if we could keep them at a reasonable level then we could keep down the increase in the cost of living, which was kept down to 3 or 4 per cent a year, except in 1951, when of course the Korean War produced a world rise in raw material prices which forced it up to 10 or 11 per cent.

The partial incorporation of trade union leaders in the government led to sporadic revolts by the rank and file against their new masters. The Communist Party, for its part, had significant enclaves of support and was keen to undermine the hegemony of right-wing trade unionists such as Arthur Deakin, the General Secretary of the Transport and General Workers' Union. A rash of unofficial strikes occurred between 1948 and 1951. Coinciding with the Cold War, the strikes were attributed, with or without proof, to Communist wrecking tactics. The government, applauded by the big battalions of the TUC, took firm action, employing soldiers to break strikes in the docks and the power stations.

So much, within the brief compass of a chapter, for the situation of the worker in post-war industry. But what of the employers? As was remarked earlier, some took a rosy view of the state of industrial relations while others grumbled but accepted the realities of trade union power. Otherwise their main concern was to re-establish their companies on a basis of peacetime profitability, and the circumstances were propitious.

Haunted by the trade deficit, the government exhorted companies to export more of their products. The message was not always well received. In November 1945 Cripps, as President of the Board of Trade, addressed a dinner of the Society of Motor Manufacturers and Traders. He told them that instead of producing for a protected home market, they should export at least 50 per cent of their vehicles. British consumers would have to go without. At this there were boos and shouts of 'No' and 'Tripe'. Cripps retorted, 'I have often wondered whether you thought Great Britain was here to support the motor industry, or the motor industry was here to support Great Britain.'[15]

As long as the apparatus of economic controls remained, the government was virtually in a position to compel companies into export markets. Sir George Farmer, at that time Secretary of the Rover motor company, describes the position of the firm immediately after the war:

The two major preoccupations were on the one hand exports, and on the other hand shortages of materials. The two were linked together because [the] government, rightly or wrongly – wrongly in my view – decided that they were only going to allocate scarce materials to those motor manufacturers who could produce exports. So much so that the number of cars one was allowed to sell into the home market was a strictly limited and a very small number, and those cars were sold only to people who were able to obtain special certificates of need, by doctors and people of that sort. We'd virtually no exports before the war. We were a very small manufacturer making about 10,000 or 11,000 high-quality, luxury cars a year aimed at the home market. We did have a few exports but they were virtually negligible, so we found ourselves in a highly dangerous situation. Had we not been able to find some way of getting exports quickly we were virtually going to get no steel.

Such was the position when Sir Stafford Cripps entered the picture. Of all the leading members of the Labour Cabinet, Cripps was the only true intellectual. In the course of his career there were periodic upheavals in his mind when one set of political ideas was exchanged for another, but whatever the view he took, he could see the road ahead with intense clarity and moral conviction. His experience as Minister of Aircraft Production during the war persuaded him that the way forward lay through industrial consensus and a planned economy. He was to pursue these principles for the rest of his career, fortified by a devout Anglican belief that he was inspired by the Almighty.

A chemist by training, Cripps was thrilled by the techniques of modern industry. No other Labour politician won the confidence of industrialists to the same extent. Always accessible and interested in their problems, he radiated a lofty Victorian sense of high public purpose. There was never the faintest suspicion that he was industry's man, or anybody else's for that matter.

Cripps was to play an important part in one sector of the motor industry – the development of the Land Rover. Maurice Wilkes, a director of engineering at the Rover company, was using one or two old jeeps on his farm in north Wales. As they kept breaking down he decided to instal Rover engines, thus hitting on the prototype of the Land Rover. Sir George Farmer continues:

We were particularly fortunate in that Sir Stafford Cripps – and one doesn't want to bring politics into this in any way – was a very far-seeing and a brilliant chap. He was President of the Board of Trade at that time [and] expressed a wish to come down to the works and see what we were doing. Fortunately at that stage we had just made the first small experimental batch of these vehicles which used extensively non-rationed materials, particularly aluminium. He accepted the representations that we made to him that here was something new for the British motor industry which had a future not only for exports but for agriculture. He gave it his full support and indeed when he became Chancellor of the Exchequer he specifically exempted Land Rovers from purchase tax. So we were able to do what the Japanese and the Germans did, and what any manufacturer who wants to export successfully does, we were able to build up at least a modicum of a home market from which we could then go out into the world and export. So that when I finished in 1973, we were exporting to no less than 176 different countries.

The Labour government's policy of diverting the motor manufacturers into export markets worked wonders for the balance of payments. Between 1945 and 1952, when the restrictions on domestic production were lifted, nearly two million cars were sold abroad. But the long-term prospects for an efficient motor industry were damaged. British firms were bounced into the mass production for overseas markets of cars designed for the home market in the late 1930s. As Peter Pagnamenta and Richard Overy have written, no time was allowed for the research of overseas markets and the design of appropriate models:

> There was little time to test them for foreign conditions, and they proved to be too underpowered for the sustained long runs of North America, not tough enough for the dust and corrugated mud roads of Africa or South America, and to have the wrong springing for the paved surfaces of Europe.[16]

In short, British cars proved unsuitable and unreliable. As the French and German industries recovered in the 1950s, they began to sweep aside the British competition.

In spite of the assistance given by the government to the Land Rover, Sir George Farmer regards the government's use of controls after the war as short-sighted. What was needed, he argues, was a partnership between industry and government for long-term planning. Sir Arthur Bryan, speaking from his experience of the pottery industry, strikes a different note. Production for the home market, he explains, was restricted to plain, white utility goods at fixed prices:

We put in machinery and churned out thousands of cups, saucers and plates a day. The clever purchaser selected the fine producers, the famous names, and would pick up excellent china and earthenware at what were known as utility prices. A tea saucer was four shillings and seven pence per dozen, for example, and we used to churn them out by their thousands of dozens each week, and that utility period lasted until 1953.

Bryan argues that by obliging the industry to sell abroad in difficult markets, government controls had a salutary effect:

I was one of the recruits after the war that had a great admiration for the controls and regulations that the government of the day brought in, and encouraged manufacturers in our industry to concentrate on the important markets, the dollar markets in particular, and that's what we did. If there hadn't been controls at that time, I'm quite convinced that the manufacturers of the day would have sold to the easiest market at the biggest profit.

Cripps, who took a keen interest in the fortunes of the pottery trade, was also known for his encouragement of industrial design. In 1945 he persuaded British manufacturers to take part in a post-war exhibition demonstrating their latest products. Organised by the Council for Industrial Design, the 'Britain Can Make It' exhibition opened in September 1946 at the Victoria and Albert Museum. Six thousand products by 1300 firms were displayed to wondering crowds tantalised by the sight of fascinating but unavailable new household goods. Reserved for export, they would not be seen in shops at home for several years to come.

Sir Arthur Bryan formed a high estimate of Cripps:

Sir Stafford Cripps was, of course, much denigrated in the 1940s, and through Josiah Wedgwood I saw another Stafford Cripps. I saw a man that had encouraged industry to concentrate on good design. I saw a man who was brave and took action on industry [that] made him very unpopular. I think he did an extremely powerful and useful job in bringing Britain out of a wartime economy into a relatively free economy with some government controls.

When the economic strategies of the Labour government collapsed in 1947, Cripps tried to replace them with a programme of voluntary long-term planning agreed by both sides of industry. For a time, both industrialists and trade unionists rallied to his support. But the decision of the government in the autumn of 1948 to go ahead with the nationalisation of iron and steel provoked a hostile reaction in business circles. Unlike the industries previously nationalised by Labour, iron and steel was an expanding and profitable giant, a sturdy specimen of advanced capitalism. The decision to nationalise it set ideological alarm bells ringing, and the approach of a general election tended to range business openly on the side of the Conservatives. The leading employers' organisation, the Federation of British Industries, abandoned the cautious and moderate stance it had adopted since 1945, and started to attack the government.

Between 1945 and 1951 British industry staged a spirited recovery. By 1951 industrial production was up 50 per cent on 1946 and exports were up 67 per cent. The standard of living, deliberately held back in order to free resources for industrial growth, was little changed but full employment had been maintained. Presented as curves on a graph, the industrial record looks impressive. It compared well at the time with the rates of recovery achieved by the other nations of western Europe. Not until the 1950s was it apparent that British industry was advancing at a more sluggish pace than its competitors.

The reasons for the decline of British industry have been much debated and it is not my intention, in closing this chapter, to open up that enormous subject, still less to gloss over it with a couple of neat generalisations. But for those who are interested, one neglected post-war episode deserves attention. Again the instigator was Cripps. In the 1930s Cripps, like most people on the Left, looked to the Soviet Union as a model of socialism in practice. Whether he still retained a residue of faith in Russia after 1945 is an intriguing question. He certainly developed an admiration for American industry.

In June 1947 the US Secretary of State, George Marshall, proposed a programme of economic aid to restore the prosperity and stability of Europe: 'Marshall Aid' as it was known thereafter. One of the objectives of the Marshall Aid programme was to increase the productivity of European economies, and so help them reduce their dollar deficits. In July 1948 Cripps proposed to the chief American administrator of the programme, Paul Hoffman, that an Anglo-American Productivity Council should be set up so that British industry could learn from the American example: productivity in the United States was known to be much higher than in Britain. In true Crippsian style the Council was composed of representatives of both management and workers. The British half of the Council featured a familiar roll-call of sponsors from the TUC, the Federation of British Industries, and the British Employers' Federation. One of the main activities of the Council was to organise visits by teams representing specific British industries to investigate the techniques of their American counterparts. In all, forty-seven such teams visited the United States, drew their comparisons and returned home to file their reports. As the final report of the Committee makes plain, the exercise enabled the British teams to draw up an inventory of everything that was wrong with the organisation and attitudes of British industry.

The first British delegation to cross the Atlantic represented the Steel Foundry Association. Among the party, which travelled in style on the *Queen Mary*, was Eddie Daybell, who was working for a foundry in Letchworth as Chief Methods Engineer and Assistant Foundry Manager. He was impressed by what he found:

> It was very interesting to see that technically we were very close to what they were, we kept in touch by literature and that sort of thing. Whereas when it came to the shop-floor working, we found that they were much more efficient in putting their ideas into practice on the shop-floor and getting productivity than we were. I don't say they were working harder, but they got better results because they were working more efficiently.

The American foundries, Mr Daybell continues, had more mechanical aids. But their main advantage was better communications between workers and management:

> It was interesting to note that every morning at nine o'clock the manager, the foreman and the works engineers all met together to discuss the snags of the day previous and what could be immediately done to put them right. So they weren't left to the end of the week to put things right.
>
> We found that if you went on to the shop-floor, to talk to the operators of the machines or the various people who were doing various operations, you found that each workman knew exactly why he was doing it, what he was doing and what would happen if he didn't do it correctly. So the people on the shop-floor were fully as conversant with the manufacture of the castings as the management were.

Another member of the delegation was Douglas Aston, an employer. In his opinion the most important single factor in the team's findings was that attitudes, particularly among the trade unions, were different in the American industry:

> There was never any, as far as we could see, resistance [from the unions] to the introduction of machinery to save manpower and to save effort. In America the application of power in its widest sense, that is to relieve the drudgery, or to speed the job, was universally accepted. I think I can best describe the union attitude to you by telling you of the time I walked through one of the plants to be confronted by a huge placard on the notice-board, issued by a trade union, the CIO [Congress of Industrial Organisation] and this said, 'The greatest crime a company can commit against its employees is failure to make a profit.' There was a belief, as I said, from top to bottom that high productivity begets success, individual and collective.
>
> One of the other things of importance in this connection, I think, is the fact that in the American foundry industry they were dealing with just two unions, the CIO, that's the Congress of Industrial Organisation, and the AFL, which is the American Federation of Labor. Now you just imagine in a British company, and this obtains today, you're dealing with a minimum of six or seven plus. The net result is that you have leap-frogging of wage claims and management is beset throughout the year, struggling with wages, industrial problems, industrial relations problems.

The findings of the British delegations were distributed to the industries concerned and discussed at conferences but it is difficult to believe that radical changes resulted.

Instead of a weighty conclusion, here is a small, illuminating footnote. When the Steel Foundry team returned home, Cripps expressed a desire to see three of its members – the leader of the delegation, a technician and a craftsman – to hear their comments. Eddie Daybell was invited to attend as the technician, and Ben Travers, a moulder from Sheffield, as the craftsman. Eddie Daybell recalls that for half an hour Cripps listened carefully to what they had to say. Then he asked a question. If productivity led to better profits, how should the profits be distributed?

> So we said we thought that any extra profits which accrued from better productivity should be shared between the management, who had provided extra money for machinery

and facilities, the customer, he should have a share, and the workmen should have a share. They should find a little bit extra in the pay packet. But we were surprised when Sir Stafford didn't agree with us at all. He said, 'I don't agree to the men having extra money in their pay packets. I think that if a man put up a good performance on the shop-floor and you found that he was doing a good job, then he should be given a medal. Then everyone else would try and emulate him to have the medal.' Now we didn't agree with this, of course, at all, and I asked Ben, who was from the shop-floor, 'What do you think?' He said, 'Well, he wants to think what my wife would think about that. She would like to see a little bit extra in the pay packet. And I am sure the people of Sheffield would soon tell him what he could do with his medal.'

8

FESTIVAL TIMES

One by one different subjects have been explored in earlier chapters. Now is the time to look back over the road from 1945 to see how far the British had travelled, and where they were going to by 1951, when the Attlee government fell. One extraordinary event acts as a signpost along the way. On 2 May 1951, in a speech from the steps of St Paul's Cathedral, King George VI inaugurated the Festival of Britain. Conceived as an official celebration of Britain's recovery from the war, the Festival ran for five months. Eight million people visited the main attractions in London, the South Bank Exhibition and the Festival Pleasure Gardens. Regional and travelling exhibitions spread the Festival spirit around the country, and every town and village was invited to arrange its own festivities. The Rank Organisation, joining in the fun, announced a Miss Festival of Britain competition, with a world tour for the lucky winner. A mixture of cultural high jinks and Butlin pleasures, the Festival had few solemn messages to impart. But whimsical constructions such as the Skylon, or Rowland Emett's Far Tottering and Oyster Creek Railway, did perhaps have something important to say: that the good, grey forties were over.

Two general elections took place on either side of the Festival. In February 1950 the Labour Party scraped home with its overall majority cut to a bare five seats. After an agonising second term punctuated by the outbreak of the Korean War in June 1950, the commitment of British troops to fight alongside the Americans, the launching of an enormous rearmament programme, and a crisis with Iran that almost led to another war in the summer of 1951, the government staggered into a general election in October 1951. This time the Conservatives, led by Churchill, were returned to power with an overall majority of seventeen.

In the social history of Britain after the war the two general elections, and the transfer of power from Labour to Conservative, made very little difference. At most the victory of the Conservatives accelerated trends that were clearly marked out under the previous government. There was no second watershed like that of 1945, when social and electoral change coincided. The interest of party politics at the end of the 1940s lies in the fact that in their different ways the two main parties lacked ideological purpose. One cycle of social change was coming to an end, and another was beginning. Neither party disputed the fact and neither party intended to challenge the trend. To the sorrow of Labour, the radicalising effects of the war and the landslide victory of 1945 were petering out. To the joy of the Conservatives, the private sector and consumer society were reviving. But the Labour Party could find no means of reviving the impetus for social change. And the Conservative Party had no intention of reversing the reorganisation of society already accomplished under Labour. An era of structural change in British society was at an end.

From 1942 to 1948 popular expectations were focused to a remarkable extent on the making of the new Welfare State. Governments were under pressure to ensure jobs, homes, health services and social security for all. In 1946, parents began to collect weekly family allowances, at the rate of 5s. per week for the second and every subsequent child, from the post office. Pensions were more than doubled, rising in the case of a retired couple from 20s. to 42s. a week. On 5 July 1948, as was seen in Chapter 4, the National Health Service came into effect. But so too did the new system of comprehensive National Insurance. Henceforth the possession of a National Insurance card entitled the holder, in return for a weekly contribution, to sickness and unemployment benefit at the new rates, maternity and widow's benefit, the retirement pension and a death grant to cover funeral expenses.

The visions and promises of the war years were turning into bureaucratic fact. At the newly-built offices of the Ministry of National Insurance on the outskirts of Newcastle, the records of the insured population were stored on 25 million separate ledger-sheets, housed in 100 rooms. There were 650,000 Smiths on the books, of whom 8000 bore the most plain and honourable of English names: John Smith. On that same 5 July, work began at the 992 local offices of the Ministry as the staff handled claims for benefit and passed on inquiries to headquarters.

Beveridge himself had been excluded from the sphere of social policy ever since 1942, when the publication of his Report gave rise to a new consensus between the Conservative and Labour Parties. The consensus was that Beveridge, being too big for his boots, should be sent out like little Lord Lundy to govern New South Wales – or the mid-twentieth-century equivalent. In 1948 Beveridge was chairman of the Development Corporation of the New Town of Newton Aycliffe in County Durham. None the less, 5 July 1948 was Beveridge Day. His was the philosophy, and by and large the plans, that were put into effect. The social security system as envisaged by him was to be a collective exercise in self-help and self-respect. The poor were to be emancipated from the stigma of means-tested benefits. Like everyone else, they would obtain equal rights in return for equal contributions.

It was recognised that even under the new social security system, some people would fall through the net. However high the rate set for retirement pensions the elderly were at risk from the effects of inflation, and family allowances were too low to meet the needs of certain families. For such residual cases, as they were then regarded, the National Assistance Board was created to administer benefits on the old principle of the means test. In the optimistic dawn of 1948 it was expected that in time fewer and fewer people would have to depend upon National Assistance for support, since poverty was about to be extinguished. In 1936 Seebohm Rowntree had estimated, in a social survey of York, that 31·1 per cent of the working-class population were living in poverty. Repeating the survey in 1950 he put the figure at 2·8 per cent.

What more could be done? In health, social security and education, electoral promises had been redeemed. Though there were still pockets of unemployment here and there, the total number of unemployed never rose above half a million except for a week or two during the coal crisis of February 1947. Only in housing were the benefits predicted from State action yet to materialise. On a number of occasions Bevan predicted that by the time of the next election, the housing shortage would have disappeared. But he was mistaken, and the Conservatives exploited the issue vigorously, with a pledge in October 1950 to build 300,000 houses a year.

As the elements of the Welfare State fell into place, popular expectations shifted. The government could no longer afford to increase the level of benefits and services. In 1945 a vision could be set before the public of a cornucopia of rights and benefits to come. By 1950 there was no more that a responsible politician could offer. The message of the Labour government after July 1948 was indeed one of restraint and economy in the social services.

Once in possession of the new Welfare State, the majority of the British people had no intention of surrendering the rights they had won. But the main purpose of the Welfare State was to prevent poverty and guarantee a steady flow of income from the cradle to the grave. The problem for the British in the late 1940s was not so much lack of income (though the middle classes complained of high taxation), as lack of things on which to spend their money. Once the Beveridge Report was implemented there was nothing to shield the Labour government from the full force of the popular clamour for more consumer goods. Labour politicians had been inclined to interpret the 1945 election result as a mandate for public goods and services. Whether as dogmatists bent on socialism, or high-minded improvers of the masses, they were slow to recognise that voters hankered after the New Look or 'pleasure motoring'.

The trend towards a consumer society was no invention of the 1940s. The mass-production of cheap luxuries for the working classes dates back to the late nineteenth century. The sale of vacuum cleaners, three-piece suites, radios, record-players, cameras, bicycles, and so on, flourished between the wars. During and immediately after the Second World War, the Anglo-American alliance, and the dependence of the British on American aid, may well have introduced an accelerator: the vision of the American way of life, spread out like a banquet before the wondering gaze of the British. The historian Angus Calder has suggested that during this period American popular culture, and the spirit of the New Deal, were particularly influential in imbuing the younger generation with new ideals.[1] While hard proof is inevitably lacking in such matters, the link is highly plausible when applied to the revival of the consumer spirit in Britain.

In 1955 Hugh Gaitskell claimed to detect an Americanisation of British society. For this he was berated by J. B. Priestley, who wrote:

He is now trying to tell us what we were trying to tell him even before the war ended ... He sees himself as a serious man who must restrict his attention to serious matters, the sort of stuff that finds its way into the City columns of *The Times*. It would never occur to him to take a look at *Mabel's Weekly* or *Filmfans' Pictorial*. It is now some years since certain sections of the popular press, still pretending to be more British than the Union Jack, began to treat London as a suburb of New York. The theatre publicity of 1945 and the mood of the electorate in 1955 are linked together; the trouble is, that so few people give both of them some thoughtful consideration.[2]

Next to Priestley's comments may be placed the recollections of two of the witnesses quoted earlier in the book. Both testify to the magical power exercised by images of America in austerity Britain. Terry Alford remarks, 'America, at the time, seemed to be a land of everything, you know, a land of milk and honey, where there's us poor little English people, or British people, had virtually nothing.' Vera Mather adds:

> I think that the English teenager was influenced greatly by Hollywood. At the cinema you saw all these wonderful clothes and you tried to imitate them the best you could on your allocation of clothing coupons. You got girls that imitated Dorothy Lamour, Hedy Lamarr, Rita Hayworth. Ginger Rogers was a favourite of most girls and she made a film about a girl with a sweater, I don't know the title, but you know all the girls afterwards started wearing sweaters, it was amazing.

Labour ministers may not have reflected on the influence of the American way of life, but as professional politicians they responded to the pressure for derationing and decontrol. Harold Wilson, adept at publicising himself and catching the popular mood, was photographed in March 1949 tearing up his clothes ration book. With a little more luck and better electoral timing, the Labour Party might well have won a general election in 1949 and gone on to preside over the 'affluent society' of the 1950s. As the party of full employment and the Welfare State they were increasing their working-class support as they entered the 1950s. It was the redistribution of seats, the defection of middle-class voters in marginal constituencies, and the erratic relationship between the number of votes cast and the number of seats won in the British electoral system that deprived Labour of office.

But let us keep away from the quicksands of psephology. The transfer of power from Labour to the Conservatives was not inevitable but it was appropriate. To most Conservatives, the restoration of a thriving free market (albeit in a mixed economy), with a society geared to advertising, supermarkets, mortgages and commercial television, was a positive ideal, gleaming with promise. Younger Labour politicians, like Wilson or Gaitskell, may have been ready to adapt. But the older leaders, such as Attlee himself, and indeed Bevan, were increasingly out of sympathy with the times. On 3 October 1951, three weeks before the general election, Attlee addressed his party conference at Scarborough. The language he spoke was unchanged from 1945, or indeed 1935. He saw the future as a continuation of the past:

We know the kind of society we want. We want a society of free men and women. Free from poverty, free from fear, able to develop to the full their faculties in co-operation with their fellows; everyone giving, and having the opportunity to give, service to the community; everyone regulating his own private interests in the interests of others, in the light of the interests of the community; a society bound together by rights and obligations – rights bringing obligations, obligations fulfilled bringing rights.

Attlee still held to the old public school ideal, common among families with a hereditary commitment to the Empire or the Army, of a society dedicated to service rather than competition for wealth. History was not on his side. Cultural change was rapidly undermining the high rationalist humanism of late Victorian social reform. At Newton Aycliffe, the aged William Beveridge was marooned among a community consisting mainly of young married couples of the skilled working class. Tolerant but rather perplexed, Beveridge hoped that the occupational character of his neighbours would lend itself to cultural advance:

> This, I hope, is going to mean that, as the town grows, common activities on the intellectual and artistic side will develop with more than usual speed: organisation of libraries, community drama, debating societies, art societies, voluntary service of all kinds – everything that calls for use of leisure in doing things rather than passively enjoying things.[3]

The civilising mission of the upper middle class, which seemed to have come so close to success during the Second World War, in the heyday of CEMA and ABCA, was falling on hard times. The Arts Council had lost the common touch. ABCA was re-created in 1946, with a five-year grant from the Carnegie Foundation, as the Bureau of Current Affairs. Detached now from the Army, but retaining its former staff and issuing its fortnightly bulletins just as before, the Bureau was perpetuated in the belief that the wartime upsurge of discussion groups and adult education classes would carry over into the peace. It did not. Circulation fell and in a bid to make itself self-supporting the Bureau changed itself into a service for schools. But when the subsidy from Carnegie expired, the Bureau was lost. Its final bulletin was published on 30 September 1951, ten years after the beginning of ABCA, and less than a month before the return of the Conservatives to power. At the height of its influence, ABCA had probably contributed to Churchill's defeat in 1945. Now it was over, and Churchill was back.

Every political party has an ideal to sustain it, or should have. The ideal of the Labour Party was socialism. 'The Labour Party is a Socialist Party and proud of it,' declared its manifesto in 1945. 'Its ultimate purpose at home is the establishment of the Socialist Commonwealth of Great Britain – free, democratic, efficient, progressive, public-spirited, its material resources organised in the service of the British people.' We shall never know for certain how popular the ideal of socialism was in 1945, or how much enthusiasm it kindled. All that can be said is that the three million members of the Labour Party would have described themselves, in one way or another, as socialists, as, doubtless, would many other voters. Nor is the socialism of 1945 readily defined. The most successful political ideals have a mythical quality. They work on many levels from sentiment to theory and lend themselves to continuous reinterpretation.

Socialism in 1945 was a many-sided faith. In Britain it still held the promise and excitement of an untried experiment. There never had been a majority Labour government, nor a Labour government in office at the dawn of a new age: fervent believers had everything to hope for. Yet by 1951 much of the hope was dissipated and the lights of socialism were burning low.

As interpreted by the Attlee governments, socialism meant centralised bureaucratic direction of the economy and the creation of public corporations to run major industries as State monopolies. These policies are often misinterpreted as timid or cautious. Unimaginative they may have been, but Labour ministers were hard-headed politicians ambitious to win and hold economic power for the State. This they achieved. No other British government has extended the frontiers of the State so far or so fast.

Unfortunately for Labour, socialism as a form of bureaucratic power tended to sterilise socialism as a myth of equality and co-operation. Among the first to express disillusion were intellectual allies and sympathisers. During the war, J. B. Priestley had expressed the hope that a new communal spirit would sweep away social divisions. By 1948 he was disgruntled. Everywhere in the world, he maintained, power was being concentrated in the hands of a few. No matter whether they were capitalists, socialists or bureaucrats, their common purpose was to mechanise and reduce popular culture to an inferior pulp:

Their political colouring may be widely different, but they all appear to be inspired by the same horrible vision of life. They all see us slogging away in enormous factories, our heads wagging to *Music While You Work*, enjoying flavourless hash and pep-talks in the canteen, eager for a message from Elmer J. Tweedle or Comrade Tweedle or Sir Westminster Tweedle, congratulating us upon producing more rubbishy goods than ever.[4]

The parallel between the opinions of Priestley and Orwell is unmistakable. Orwell, like Priestley, was a disciple of English literature torn between sympathy for the Labour government and fear of a regimented mass culture. In 1948, of course, he was writing *Nineteen Eighty-Four*. Whatever literary critics might make of the text, it was most easily read as a nightmare vision of the ultimate consequences of State socialism in Britain. As the Cold War set in and Europe divided into two armed camps, middle-class radicals hitherto sympathetic to Socialism began to distance themselves from it, or turn to the Right. Edward Hulton, the proprietor of *Picture Post*, had given a rapturous reception to the Labour victory of 1945. 'I rejoice', he wrote, 'that latter-day Conservatism has been overthrown.' By 1948 his enthusiasm was frozen to ice by fear of Communism and the wholly irrational suspicion that Ernest Bevin, the Foreign Secretary, was appeasing the Kremlin. In February 1950 he published an article explaining to readers why he intended to vote Conservative in the general election. As Hulton swung to the right he grew impatient with the radical outlook of the staff of *Picture Post* and bombarded the editor, Tom Hopkinson, with complaints that the magazine was too left-wing. Finally, in October 1950, he sacked Hopkinson for trying to publish a report by James Cameron about the discreditable treatment of political prisoners in South Korea.

As the work of recent historians has shown, disappointment with the workings of State socialism was strongly expressed within the nationalised industries and the Labour Party. Attlee himself worried over the divorce between management and workers. In a touching memorandum to the Socialisation of Industries Committee in November 1948, he wrote:

There is need in industry of the kind of spirit and leadership which obtains in a good regiment, an *esprit de corps* not only of the regiment, but of the company and the platoon. I am sure that this is necessary in, for instance, the coal industry, where you want the *esprit de corps* of the pit.[5]

When in 1949 the Labour Party came to consider the future of nationalisation, the crisis of faith was apparent. The shopping list of industries for nationalisation betrayed a quiet desperation: industrial assurance, cement, sugar refining, and the wholesale meat trade. With the Federation of British Industries campaigning strongly against the nationalisation of steel, private industry was already regaining the propaganda initiative. The new proposals, by stirring the wrath of the industries affected, intensified the campaign against nationalisation.

Mrs Irene Lovelock and the Housewives' League – still active and urging housewives to burn their ration books – concerted action with the meat traders. The sugar refiners Tate and Lyle teamed up with the free enterprise pressure group Aims of Industry to mount a publicity campaign against the nationalisation of sugar. A cartoon figure, Mr Cube, appeared sword in hand on millions of packets of Tate and Lyle sugar, proclaiming, 'Don't Fence Me In', or, 'Tate not State'. Richard Dimbleby, already well known as a radio reporter, was invited to go to one of Tate and Lyle's refineries and record the opinions of the staff about nationalisation. The views expressed were mixed but a number of the refinery workers declared that although they were lifelong socialists they did not believe that nationalisation would work in the manufacture of golden syrup. Tate and Lyle proceeded to put out a set of twelve records of Dimbleby's interviews. After the general election of February 1950 the shopping list of proposals was quietly dropped. G. D. H. Cole, a veteran socialist of great eminence, summed up the work of the Attlee governments in the tone of a slighted lover grieving over the faults of a party he still loved:

> So we have drifted into a position in which nobody feels any enthusiasm for further nationalisation, and nobody knows what to do about the major part of industry that is left under capitalist ownership and control. We are not able to hand out further expensive benefits in the form of social services, or to raise wages, or to reduce taxation on the smaller incomes so as to increase incentives to higher output. There is, in fact, nothing much left to be done, along the established lines; for it is a formidable task to go on carrying out the measures already enacted, without the aid of a drive of working-class enthusiasm to ease the burden.[6]

G. D. H. Cole was a gloomy old soul. The spiritual aims of late Victorian socialism were unfulfilled. There was to be no socialist commonwealth. Whatever Labour intended in 1945, the outcome was a social democratic Britain. No remedy was proposed for the discontents of workers as producers. Unskilled and semi-skilled work, though sometimes carried on in a sociable setting, remained boring and repetitive, tasks performed for cash alone. Post-war social reform bypassed the issue but offered the working classes more leisure, greater security of income and the distant prospect – in 1951 – of a brave new supermarket. To someone of Cole's outlook, the material compensations could never make up for the lost ideal of working-class participation in the control of industry. Yet as voters, manual workers registered great approval of the work of the Attlee governments.

And so, after six years of Labour government, the social and political structure of Britain had crystallised and the pattern of development was set for a quarter of a century. The Conservative Party, meanwhile, had pulled itself together during its period in opposition. Recognising a fresh historical reality, the Conservatives adapted to circumstances. Lord Woolton overhauled the party organisation. R. A. Butler, with the assistance of the rising young men of the Research Department, committed the party to the maintenance of full employment, the preservation of the Welfare State, and a working relationship with the TUC. Churchill, though belligerent in opposition and unconvincing in the role of social democrat, practised the politics of consensus on his return to power. Though the Churchill government removed the remaining economic controls and denationalised the steel industry, there was no counter-revolution. Churchill founded his peacetime administration on the appeasement of labour.

The heroic phase of post-war history was over and social change moved on from questions of structure to questions of style. The market set the pace as new styles of consumption emerged with new status distinctions to accompany them. And here we come to the significance of the Festival of Britain. A smattering of adult education and elevating purpose was included in the Festival. But in the main it was a visual romp, a revolt – to borrow George Melly's phrase about pop culture – into style.

The pretext for the Festival of Britain was the centenary of the Great Exhibition of 1851. At first the idea was to hold another great international trade exhibition, to be sponsored by Cripps and the Board of Trade with the accent on exports. As in 1851, Britain would show itself off as the workshop of the world. But owing to the heavy cost of staging an international exhibition the government decided that a purely British trade fair would be preferable. In 1947 Cripps passed the project on to the Lord President of the Council, Herbert Morrison, who had the bright idea of turning the event into a popular festival to celebrate the recovery of Britain from the war. With the aid and advice of Max Nicholson, a temporary civil servant of unconventional opinions, Morrison conceived the Festival as an exercise in cultural patriotism accompanied by bread and circuses. In its more earnest aspects, the Festival was intended to commemorate the contributions of the British to the arts of peace. But probably the overriding purpose, in Morrison's mind, was to give the people a splash of colour and pleasure as a relief from austerity. As Sir Max Nicholson explains:

> It had to be a British affair and therefore it had to be rather concentrated on the arts and the sciences. And above all, because Herbert Morrison was in it, he wanted the British people to have fun. He wanted it to be a fun thing, which made it unique I think among all great exhibitions. He wanted the people to participate in it, he didn't want it to be a 'them and us' affair. He wanted the teaching side of it, which was about science and so on, to be played down, and a great deal of jam spread over the pill.

Morrison no doubt had an eye on the electoral implications of the Festival, though no one could have anticipated in 1947 that there was likely to be a general election in 1951. But the Festival was carefully staged as a national event, with royal patronage and a Festival Council representing all parties and a galaxy of famous names from the arts including T. S. Eliot, John Gielgud, and Malcolm Sargent. 'Pug' Ismay, who had been Churchill's representative on the Chiefs of Staff Committee during the war, was prevailed upon to serve as chairman of the Festival Council. This artful appointment had the effect of preventing Churchill, who was known to be hostile, from coming out openly against the Festival.

The Festival Council served as a front. Effective planning was in the hands of a number of interlocking councils and committees which included the Arts Council, the Council for Industrial Design, and a specially constituted Council of Architecture of which Hugh Casson was director. At the apex of the Festival organisation was the director-general, Gerald Barry.

All told, the Festival of Britain was an affair of immense ramifications. A book would be needed to explain the full proceedings. There was no master plan, and the Festival in its final form was the upshot of chance and hectic improvisation. It might have been held at Olympia or Earl's Court but for the fact that both exhibition halls were already booked for the summer of 1951. It might have been held in standardised sheds in Battersea if the government had not rejected the idea. By a supreme stroke of good fortune the chance arose of siting the main exhibition on the South Bank of the Thames between County Hall and Waterloo Bridge.

By exhibition standards the space available – twenty-seven acres – was tiny, and bisected by the railway bridge to Charing Cross. But it was an open space by the river, enabling Casson and his fellow architects to lay it out as a miniature wonderland. Here on the South Bank a long series of pavilions and displays unfolded the story of the land and the people of Britain, and the role of the British in exploration and discovery. The Skylon, a slim, silvery pencil of aluminium and steel, hung in mid-air, or so it appeared from a distance. The Dome of Discovery, the largest dome ever constructed, was perched on slender stilts. Two and a half miles upstream in Battersea, a host of amusements was laid on in the Festival Pleasure Gardens. There visitors could enjoy the firework displays, the Emett railway, the Mississippi Showboat, or a large circular dance-hall held up by the biggest tent pole ever erected.

In a famous essay on the Festival, written in 1963, Michael Frayn argued that it expressed the values of the radical middle classes who planned it:

> The do-gooders; the readers of the *New Chronicle*, the *Guardian* and the *Observer*; the signers of petitions; the backbone of the BBC. In short, the Herbivores, or gentle ruminants, who look out from the lush pastures which are their natural station in life with eyes full of sorrow for less fortunate creatures, guiltily conscious of their advantages, while not usually ceasing to eat the grass.[7]

Sir Hugh Casson does not demur:

> Gerald Barry was our leader. I suppose you would call him a wet now, he was a Hampstead intellectual, he'd been editor of a left-wing paper, he had liberal views. The whole smell of the place was rather like the Workers Education Association. We all had, I suppose in a way, rather naïve views that England could be better and was going to be better – that the arts and architecture and music and healthy air and Jaeger underwear and all these things, which the garden city

movement stood for, were in fact the keys to some sort of vague Utopia.

The narrative of the land and the people, devised by Ian Cox, the Director of Science, to link the exhibits in the twenty-seven pavilions on the site, was laboriously educational. Visitors were advised to follow a plan with a dotted red line taking them all the way from The Land of Britain ('How the natural wealth of the British Isles came into being') to Design Review ('A novel display, with information service, of 25,000 photographs illustrating the wide range of British manufacturers'). Twenty-five thousand photographs to see in the twenty-seventh pavilion? With information service? Might this not be the psychological moment at which to dash off and see Oscar the Rubber Octopus in his tank at the Pleasure Gardens?

That was one side of the Festival. In some ways it was another paternalistic exercise in educating the masses and elevating their taste – yet this shaded easily into advance propaganda for a colour supplement way of life. The architects and designers on the South Bank were propagandising modern styles. The piazzas, terraces, murals and modern sculptures, the chairs with spindly legs and the spidery staircases rising into the air with no visible means of support, were intended as examples for the rest of Britain to imitate.

In so far as the South Bank had a serious message to convey about the state of the nation, it was best expressed by Humphrey Jennings in his very last documentary film, *Family Portrait*. A lyrical celebration of Britain past and present, and steeped in historical romanticism, it is a beautifully made film. The sincerity of the enterprise is impossible to doubt. But viewed in the 1980s it comes as a shock. The tone is one of overwhelming complacency. The celebration of British literary, scientific and industrial triumphs is a cultural equivalent of 'Land of Hope and Glory'. The cosy presentation of British society as a family divided, not by class, but by a rift between the imaginative and the practical sides of the national character is sentimental guff. Jennings' film may be taken as a measure of the sublime sense of insular content reflected in various corners of the Festival. In a whimsical fashion the Festival celebrated tradition as much as change. Though John Betjeman had no part in the Festival, a Betjemanesque affection for Victoriana was evident in the Emett railway, or the section of the South Bank devoted to the English seaside holiday. The middle-class radicalism identified by Frayn was losing its cutting edge.

Not that it mattered to the eight million people who visited the

South Bank and the Pleasure Gardens. (Or did four million people go twice? Statistics are often a conundrum.) Whatever the intentions of the Festival organisers, the Festival worked because, as Morrison had intended, it was great fun. There was open-air dancing every night in the summer on the Fairway of the South Bank. When autumn came, couples danced in their overcoats. The attraction was not the opportunity to dance – for there were plenty of dance-halls – but the environment. Among the grime and ruins of London, the South Bank was an enclave of colour and light, full of attractive novelties. 'It was a gigantic toyshop', said the journalist Patrick O'Donovan, 'for adults.'

On 29 September 1951 the Festival came to an end. That evening, Geraldo and his orchestra played on the Fairway, Richard Murdoch and Kenneth Horne supplied the jokes, and Gracie Fields topped the bill – demanding, it was noted, payment in dollars. 'Auld Lang Syne' and the National Anthem were sung and the crowds melted away, leaving the site deserted. It had never been intended that the exhibition structures should be permanent, but arrangements might have been made to preserve the Skylon or the Dome by moving them elsewhere. When, however, the Conservatives were returned to office, they were keen to remove a monument to the previous administration. Apart from the Festival Hall, which had been planned from the start as permanent, everything was knocked down.

Sir David Eccles, the Minister of Works, took a pleasure in exercising his responsibilities for the demolition. Yet while the Festival may be seen as a last expression of the spirit of 1945, it was more significant in foreshadowing the future. The Festival helped to popularise a new style of living. The television pavilion, or the Homes and Gardens exhibition, the piazzas and brightly decorated restaurants, the accent on youth and fashion after the gerontocracy of the Attlee government, foretold the consumer boom of the later 1950s. 'Work or want' would no longer be the slogan. 'Let's be frank about it,' Harold Macmillan was to say in July 1957, 'most of our people have never had it so good.'

NOTES

Chapter 1: Goodbye to All That

1 Martin Gilbert, *Finest Hour: Winston S. Churchill 1939–1941*, Heinemann, 1983, p. 331.
2 Correlli Barnett, *Britain and Her Army 1509–1970*, Penguin Books, Harmondsworth, 1974, p. 473.
3 Tom Hopkinson (ed.), *Picture Post 1938–1950*, Penguin Books, Harmondsworth, 1970, p. 90.
4 David Niven, *The Moon's A Balloon*, Hamish Hamilton, 1971, Coronet Books, 1972, p. 231.
5 Sheila M. Ferguson and Hilde Fitzgerald, *Studies in the Social Services*, HMSO, 1954, p. 7.
6 *Picture Post*, 12 January 1946, p. 13.
7 Alan Bullock, *Ernest Bevin Vol. 2: Minister of Labour 1940–1945*, Heinemann, 1967, pps 334–5, 354–5.

Chapter 2: Making Do

1 Harry Hopkins, *The New Look: A Social History of the Forties and Fifties in Britain*, Secker and Warburg, 1963, p. 42.
2 James Lansdale Hodson, *The Way Things Are*, Victor Gollancz, 1947, p. 74; John Bonham, *The Middle-Class Vote*, Faber and Faber, 1954, p. 28.
3 British Medical Association, *Report of the Committee on Nutrition*, 1950, p. 52.
4 PRO, PREM 8/1196, Memo by the Minister of Food, 16 May 1949.
5 In Michael Sissons and Philip French (eds), *The Age of Austerity*, Penguin, Harmondsworth, 1964, pps 35–57.
6 *Picture Post*, 19 April 1947. For Anne Scott-James's satirical view of the magazine as a hothouse of radical conspiracies of which she clearly disapproved, see her semi-fictionalised autobiography, *In The Mink*, 1953.

7 Jane Lewis, *Women in England 1870–1950*, Wheatsheaf Books, Brighton, 1984, p. 39.

8 I am grateful to Mrs Lovelock's son, Mr Keith Lovelock, for permission to see the manuscript of Mrs Lovelock's unpublished autobiography, from which details about her have been taken.

9 Edward Smithies, *Crime in Wartime*, Allen and Unwin, 1982, p. 71.

10 Edward Smithies, *The Black Economy in England since 1914*, Gill and Macmillan, Dublin, 1984, p. 110.

11 Smithies, *The Black Economy*, p. 91.

12 Quoted in Mary Ingham, *Now We Are Thirty*, Methuen, 1981, p. 37.

Chapter 3: A Home of Our Own

1 Woolton MS2, Diary for 1 November 1940, Bodleian Library.

2 John R. Short, *Housing in Britain: The Post-War Experience*, Methuen, 1982, p. 42.

3 Michael Foot, *Aneurin Bevan Volume Two: 1945–1960*, Davis-Poynter, 1973, p. 72. I have based my account of Bevan's housing policy on Foot's work.

4 *Who Was Harry Cowley?* Queenspark Book 13, Queenspark Books, Brighton, 1984.

5 Michael Foot, *op. cit.*, p. 78.

6 J. H. Forshaw and Patrick Abercrombie, *County of London Plan*, Macmillan, 1943, p. 3.

7 Michael R. Hughes (ed.), *The Letters of Lewis Mumford and Frederick J. Osborn*, Adams and Dart, Bath, 1971, p. 40: Osborn to Mumford, 7 September 1943.

8 *Ibid.*, Osborn to Mumford, 29 January 1952.

9 Harold Orlans, *Stevenage: A Sociological Study of a New Town*, Routledge, 1953, p. 101.

Chapter 4: From Cradle to Grave

1 Harry Hopkins, *The New Look: A Social History of the Forties and Fifties in Britain*, Secker and Warburg, 1963, pps 130–1.

2 Brian Watkin, *The National Health Service: The First Phase 1948–1974 and After*, Allen and Unwin, 1978.

3 S. Melvyn Herbert, *Britain's Health*, Penguin Books, Harmondsworth, 1939, p. 148.

4 Brian Abel-Smith, *The Hospitals 1900–1948: A Study in Social*

Administration in England and Wales, Heinemann, 1964, p. 406.

5 Lord Hill of Luton, *Both Sides of the Hill*, Heinemann, 1964, p. 42.

6 Brian Watkin, *op. cit.*, p. 19.

7 Michael Foot, *Aneurin Bevan Volume Two: 1945–1960*, Davis-Poynter, 1973, p. 142.

Chapter 5: Living It Up

1 For the life and career of Billy Butlin see Rex North, *The Butlin Story*, Jarrolds, 1962.

2 Woodrow Wyatt, 'Butlin Joys', *New Statesman*, 12 July 1947, p. 27.

3 Diana Rait Kerr and Ian Peebles, *Lord's 1946–1970*, Harrap, 1971, p. 13.

4 Quoted in Charles Barr, *Ealing Studios*, Cameron and Tayleur, 1977, p. 97.

5 Brian Glanville, 'Britain Against The Rest' in Michael Sissons and Philip French (eds), *The Age of Austerity*, *op. cit.*, p. 155.

6 Quoted in S. Seebohm Rowntree and G. R. Lavers, *English Life and Leisure*, Longmans, 1951, p. 124.

7 Cmd 8190, *Report of the Royal Commission on Betting, Lotteries and Gambling*, para. 186.

8 Roger Mortimer, *History of the Derby Stakes*, Cassell, 1962, p. 552. The race was won by Mr John Ferguson's 'Airborne'.

9 Kenneth Morgan, *Labour in Power*, Clarendon Press, Oxford, 1984, p. 304.

10 Pearl Jephcott, *Rising Twenty: Notes on Some Ordinary Girls*, Faber and Faber, 1948, p. 154.

11 Norman Crosby, *Full Enjoyment*, Nicholson and Watson, 1948, p. 22.

12 *New Statesman*, 28 February 1948, p. 372.

13 Eric White, *The Arts Council of Great Britain*, Davis-Poynter, 1975, p. 59.

14 *Eighty Thousand Adolescents: A Study of Young People in Birmingham*, Allen and Unwin, 1950, p. 47.

15 Francis Newton, *The Jazz Scene*, MacGibbon and Kee, 1959, p. 274. I am greatly indebted to this book for my comments on the subject.

16 *Ibid.*, p. 253.

Chapter 6: Schooldays

1 R. A. Butler, *The Art of the Possible*, Hamish Hamilton, 1971, p. 117.
2 Quoted in David Rubinstein, 'Ellen Wilkinson Reconsidered', *History Workshop*, Issue 7, Spring 1979, p. 162.
3 *Ibid.*, p. 165.
4 *Ibid.*, p. 165.
5 Betty D. Vernon, *Ellen Wilkinson*, Croom Helm, 1983, pps 222–3.
6 Mr David Hardman to the author, 15 March 1985. I am grateful to Mr Hardman for permission to quote this letter.
7 H. C. Dent, *Growth in English Education 1946–1952*, Routledge, 1954, p. 7.
8 *Ibid.*, p. 19.
9 Quoted in David Rubinstein and Brian Simon, *The Evolution of the Comprehensive School 1926–1972*, Routledge, 1972 edition, p. 38.
10 Quoted in Dent, *op. cit.*, p. 89.
11 In the making of the programme to which this chapter relates interviews were conducted with several former teachers and pupils and I have drawn on these where appropriate, but as the schools concerned were mainly in rural areas or country towns I have been reluctant to draw inferences for industrial Britain. In any case, a major oral history project, well beyond the resources of a single television programme, will be required to fill the credibility gap between the formal accounts we have of the government and sociology of post-war education, and the realities of daily life in school. The pioneering study by Stephen Humphreys, *Hooligans Or Rebels? An Oral History of Working-Class Childhood and Youth 1889–1939*, Blackwell, 1981, should serve as a model.
12 Dent, *op. cit.*, p. 98.
13 J. E. Floud (ed.), *Social Class and Educational Opportunity*, Heinemann, 1956, pps 29–30.
14 H. Davies, 'The Social Effects of the 1944 Act on the Grammar School', quoted in Floud, *op. cit.*, p. 27.
15 Quoted in John Dancy, *The Public Schools and the Future*, Faber and Faber, 1966, p. 15.
16 Roy Lewis and Angus Maude, *The English Middle Classes*, Phoenix House, 1949, p. 230.

Chapter 7: Britain Can Make It

1 J. L. Hodson, *The Way Things Are*, Gollancz, 1947, p. 168, entry for 27 May 1946.
2 Technically, strikes were illegal under Order 1305, an emergency regulation of July 1940 which remained in force until August 1951. The major unions favoured the order because the provisions for compulsory arbitration assisted unions in obtaining recognition from the employers. All strikes in this period were therefore unofficial, in theory at least. The Order was not a cause of the low level of strikes but a reflection of the power of trade unions to enforce collective bargaining. The Attlee government attempted no prosecutions under Order 1305 until 1950, but efforts to employ the law rapidly discredited it and led to its withdrawal.
3 Quoted in Stephen Blank, *Industry and Government in Britain: The Federation of British Industries in Politics 1945–1965*, Saxon House/Lexington Books, 1973, p. 75.
4 Alec Cairncross, *Years of Recovery*, Methuen, 1985, pps 275–6.
5 Ferdinand Zweig, *Productivity and Trade Unions*, Blackwell, Oxford, 1951, p. 29.
6 Sir Norman Chester, *The Nationalisation of Industry 1945–1951*, HMSO, 1975, p. 745.
7 Douglas Jay, *Change and Fortune: A Political Record*, Hutchinson, 1980, p. 144.
8 Ferdinand Zweig, *Men In The Pits*, Gollancz, 1948, p. 10.
9 *Ibid.*, p. 28.
10 J. L. Hodson, *The Way Things Are*, p. 25, entry for 24 August 1945.
11 Norman Dennis, Fernando Henriques, Clifford Slaughter, *Coal Is Our Life*, Eyre and Spottiswoode, 1956, p. 33.
12 Zweig, *Productivity and Trade Unions*, p. 158.
13 Zweig, *Men In The Pits*, p. 12.
14 Dennis Chapman, 'Flogging Us With Words', *Listener*, 19 August 1948.
15 William Plowden, *The Motor Car and Politics*, Bodley Head, 1971, pps 312–14.
16 Peter Pagnamenta and Richard Overy, *All Our Working Lives*, BBC Publications, 1984, p. 229.

Chapter 8: Festival Times

1 In a paper given to a conference on Britain and the Second World War at the Open University in May 1981.

2 J. B. Priestley, *Thoughts in the Wilderness*, Heinemann, 1957, pps 120–1.

3 *Listener*, 3 January 1952, p. 4.

4 *New Statesman*, 22 May 1948, p. 408.

5 Quoted in Henry Pelling, *The Labour Governments 1945–1951*, Macmillan, 1984, p. 95.

6 *New Statesman*, 12 May 1951, p. 525.

7 Michael Frayn, 'Festival' in Michael Sissons and Philip French (eds), *The Age of Austerity, op. cit.*, p. 351.

PICTURE CREDITS

The author and the publishers would like to thank the following for permission to reproduce the photographs in this book: BBC Hulton Picture Library, 5, 6, 7, 8, 15, 22, 23, 29, 30, 34, 38, 39, 42, 45, 58, 62, 64, 67, 84, 86, 88, 89, 94; BBC Publicity, 65; Design Council, 76, 90, 92, 95; GLC, 35, 36; Henry Grant, 70; HMSO, 33; Imperial War Museum, London, 9, 12, 48; by permission of the *London Standard*, 14; Mansell Collection, 2, 3; David Medd, 75; Ministry of Agriculture, Fisheries and Food, 47; Photo Source, 1, 11, 31, 32, 40, 57, 69, 77; Popperfoto, 4, 10, 16, 27, 37, 43, 44, 59, 66, 68, 80, 87, 93; Press Association, 55; Public Record Office, 41, 83; reproduced by permission of *Punch*, 26; Sport and General Press Agency, 18, 19, 20, 53, 56, 91; Syndication International (*Daily Herald* photograph), 24; Times Newspapers Ltd, 13; Topham, 17, 21, 25, 28, 46, 49, 50, 51, 52, 54, 60, 61, 63, 71, 72, 73, 74, 78, 79, 81, 82, 96; TUC Library, 85.

INDEX

Numbers in italic refer to illustrations.

Abbey Steel Works, Port Talbot, 172
ABC cinemas, 130, 132
Abel-Smith, Brian, 93
Abercrombie, Patrick, 71–2, 73–4, 75, 77–8, 79
Abrams, Mark, 124
Abse, Leo, 14–15
Acland, Sir Richard, 9–10, *11*
Adam, Sir Ronald, 12
Adams, Mrs, 81–2, 83, 85
Adams, Ben, 81, 85
Addison, Lord, 52
AEU, 188
Africa, 173, 191
agriculture, 27, 127
Aims of Industry, 205
Alanbrooke, Lord, 52
Aldeburgh Festival, 136
Alexander, Field Marshal Lord, 52
Alford, Terry, 31, 34–5, 39–40, 49–50, 121, 132–3, 201
Aly Khan, 126, *60*
American Federation of Labor, 195
American Forces Network, 128
Anglesey, 150
Anglo-American Productivity Council, 193–5
Annie Get Your Gun, 133
Anson, Frederick, 161
Anti-Gambling League, 124
The Archers, 127
architecture, 72, 73
Argentina, 38, 180
Army: Camouflage Development and Training Centre, 158; decline of class differences, 4–6, 117; demobilisation, 19–23, 24, 62–3; education, 4, 12–15, 24, 202, *8*, *9*; employment of ex-service personnel, 23–5; NAAFI, 4, 5; numbers at D-Day, 1; political outlook, 18; reunion with families, 21–2; social patriotism, 12
Army Bureau of Current Affairs (ABCA), 12–15, 202, 203, *9*
Army Education Corps, 12, 13

Arnos Secondary Modern School, *71*
Arsenal Football Club, 120, 122
art exhibitions, 135, 136, *64*
Arts Council, 2, 134, 135–6, 207
arts festivals, 136
Ascot, 126
Ashton colliery, 185
Ashworth, Dr, 90, 108–9
Asia, 35
Association Football, 121
Astelle, Joan, 116, 118, 129, 137, 139
Aston, Douglas, 194–5
Attlee, Mrs, 19
Attlee, Clement: 1945 election, 14, 19; 1951 election, 201–2; coal crisis, 180; currency crisis, 179; educational reform, 148, 155–6, 166–7, 169; health service reform, 99; housing policy, 57, 58, 80; industry 204; leisure, 113, *59*; nationalisation, 177; rationing, 30, 36, 42; school building programme, 157; sterling crisis, 37; taxation, 28–9; austerity, 27–9, 37, 44, *14*
Australia, 119–20, 137
Austria, 174
Automobile Association (AA), 45
Auxiliary Territorial Service (ATS), 6, 15
Avery Jones, Sir Francis, 106–7
Avonmouth, 34
Ayr, 115

'baby boom', 56, 157
balance of payments, 172, 179, 191
Baldwin, Stanley, 144
bananas, 34–5
Barlow, Sir Montague, 79
Barlow Report, 79
Barnett, Correlli, 4
Barnsley, 50
Barry, Gerald, 207, 208
Basildon, 79
Basnett, John, 47–8, 129, 137, 138
Battle of Britain, 2

Bee, Philip, 81, 83, 84–5
Bell, Graham, 137
Bermondsey, 45, 75
Bevan, Aneurin, 57, 58–60, 62, 68, 69, 70, 72, 99–103, 110, 111, 134, 199, 201, *34*, *43*
Beveridge, William, 134, 198, 199, 202, *37*
Beveridge Report, 10, 11, 18, 99, 110, 124, 140, 198, 200
Beverley Sisters, 117
Bevin, Ernest, 1, 3, 7, 14, 19–20, 24, 36, 57, 174, 204
Bexleyheath, 137
bicycles, 126–7, 172–3
Birmingham, 56, 71, 135
black market, 6, 28, 32, 44–50, 62, *21*
Blackpool, 115, 118, 128
Blakey, Mary, 32, 42, 44
Blitz, 2, 9, 11, 55, 70, 75, 158, *27*
Board of Education, 140, 141, 143, 145
Board of Trade, 7, 37, 40, 53, 60, 111, 133, 179, 189, 191, 206
Bombay, 172–3
Bond, Clare, 46–7, 104–5
Boodle's Club, 30–1, 33
Botwright, Valentine, 45–6, 48–9
Bournemouth, 109, 145
Brabazon I, *86*
Bracknell, 79
Bradman, Don, 120
bread rationing, 35–7, 42, 53
Brief Encounter (film), 132
Brigham and District Rural Council, 67
Brighton, 65–6
'Britain Can Make It' exhibition, 192, *76*, *7*
British Broadcasting Corporation (BBC), 3–4, 114; Forces Network, 2; Light Programme, 2; Third Programme, 135
British Empire, 172
British Employers' Federation, 194
British European Airways, 61
British Housewives' League, 37, 40–4, 56

British Medical Association (BMA), 37–8, 96–7, 98, 99, 100–4, 107
British Restaurants, 6
Brooke, Rupert, 11
Bruce, Donald (Lord Bruce), 110
Bryan, Sir Arthur, 173, 191–2
building controls, 58–62
Burma, 35
Burnham Committee, 141, 163
Butler, R. A., 9, 18, 140–2, 145–6, 147–8, 151, 166, 206, 67
Butlin, Billy, 115–19, 127, 52

Cabinet, 99, 111, 155, 179, 183
Cadbury Trust, 135
Cairncross, Alec, 174–5
'Cairo Parliament', 14–15
Calder, Angus, 200
Callaghan, M., 65
Cameron, James, 204
Campion, Gerald, 166, 65
Cardiff, 108
Cardus, Neville, 120
Carling, Rock, 100
Carlton Main colliery, 184
Carousel, 133
cars: motor industry, 189–91; petrol rationing, 26, 48–9, 53
Carter, Mrs, 95–6
Casson, Sir Hugh, 207, 208
Central Office of Information, 40, 113, 186–7
Ceserani, Victor, 30–1, 33, 34
Ceylon, 35
Chamberlain, Neville, 79, 93, 144
Chapman, Mrs D., 106
Cheltenham Contemporary Music Festival, 136
Chester, Sir Norman, 178
children: cinema-going, 130; evacuation, 144; food rations, 29, 42; pre-war health services, 89, 91; reunions with fathers, 22; in wartime, 16; see also education; teenagers
Children's Charter (film), 164
Chorley, Jennifer, 126, 133–4
Christianity, 5
Church of England, 117, 142, 146
church schools, 142–3, 145–6
churches, 125, 141
Churchill, Sir Winston, 2, 3, 5, 10, 18–19, 43, 53, 56, 99, 167, 173, 197, 203, 206, 207, 10
Chuter Ede, James, 145–6
CID, 46
cinema, 113, 129–33, 63
civil service, 11, 173
Clacton, 115, 52
class distinctions, 4–8
clothes: black market, 45, 46–8, 21; demob suits, 20–1, 4, 5; jazz clubs, 139; rationing, 6–7, 20, 53, 2, 24, 25; 'Utility' scheme, 7; women's, 50–2, 3, 22, 23
clubs: jazz, 136–9; sporting, 126–7; youth clubs, 135

coal industry, 172, 179–85, 187–8, 80
Coalition government, 3, 18, 19, 135, 145
Cockshott, Dr, 103
Cold War, 189, 204
Cole, G. D. H., 205, 206
Cole, Margaret, 148
collectivism, 9
Collins, Ken, 172–3
Common Wealth, 9–10, 11
Communist Party, 4–5, 68–9, 138, 189
comprehensive schools, 141, 147–8, 149–50, 156
Compton, Denis, 120, 53
Congress of Industrial Organisation (CIO), 195
conscription, 173
Conservative Party, 57; 1945 election, 18–19; 1950 election, 53, 197; 1951 election, 54, 197, 198, 201; and bread rationing, 37; and the British Housewives' League, 43–4; Coalition government, 3, 18, 19; distrust of Army education, 13; educational policy, 140, 144, 166; ends rationing, 54; and the Housewives' League, 40; housing policy, 77–8, 80, 199; opposition to austerity measures, 28, 38; opposition to nationalisation, 193; opposition to rationing, 53; patriotism, 11; and petrol rationing, 49; prescription charges, 111
consumer society, 54, 139, 200, 201
convertibility crisis, 37, 179, 185
Cook, Eddie, 183–4
Corbusier, Le, 73
Corby, 79
cottage hospitals, 93
cotton industry, 187
Council of Architecture, 207
Council for the Encouragement of Music and the Arts (CEMA), 2, 135–6, 202
council houses, 58–61, 63–5, 70, 72, 74–5
Council for Industrial Design, 192, 207
Council for the Preservation of Rural England, 73
Countryman magazine, 127
Countryside Commission, 127
County of London plan, 71
Covent Garden, Royal Opera House, 136
Covent Garden market, 34, 94
Coventry, 71, 149
Coventry Cathedral, 72
Cowley, Harry, 65–6
Cox, Dr Alfred, 102
Cox, Ian, 209
Coxhoe Hall, Durham, 65
Craigentinny, 65

Crane, Marjorie, 21–2, 92
Crane, Peter, 21–2
Crawley, 79
cricket, 119–21, 53, 54
Cripps, Sir Stafford, 37, 38, 53, 60, 81, 111, 179, 185–6, 188–96, 206, 207, 79
Crisp, Dorothy, 43
Crosby, Bing, 128
Crosby, Norman, 131
Crown Film Unit, 164
Culver, Don, 164–5
currency crisis (1947), 37, 179, 185
Cwmbran, 79
cycling clubs, 126–7, 58

D-Day, 1, 3
Dagenham, 63
Daily Express, 50
Daily Herald, 51
Daily Mirror, 9, 14
Daily Telegraph, 65
Dalton, Hugh, 37, 60, 70, 117, 133, 155, 179
Dalton, Dr Katharina, 94, 105–6
dance-halls, 128–9, 138, 139, 208, 210
Davies, Malcolm, 167–8
Davies, Mostyn, 108
Davis, Bette, 133
Daybell, Eddie, 194, 195–6
Deakin, Arthur, 189
demobilisation, 19–23, 24, 62–3, 4, 5, 8
Denington, Cecil, 150, 166
Dennis, Henriques and Slaughter, 185
Dent, Harold, 154, 162
dentists, 86, 89, 91–2, 104, 45
Derby (horse-race), 125–6, 60
Development Corporations, 79, 80
diet: and food rationing, 37–8: food shortages, 32–3
Dimbleby, Richard, 205
Dior, Christian, 51–2
direct grant schools, 163
divorce, 16–17
doctors: consultants, 109; and the establishment of the NHS, 98–9, 100, 107–8; pre-NHS, 88, 89–91, 92, 94; and the reform of the health services, 100–4; specialists, 106–7
Dorchester, 104
Dorchester Grammar School, 164–5
Dorset, 164, 168
Dorsey, Tommy, 128
Duchess of Bedford flats, Kensington, 68–9
Dudley Committee, 70
Dunkirk, 2, 4, 9, 12
Durham, 65, 182, 199

Ealing Studios, 2, 132
East Kilbride, 79

INDEX

Eccles, Sir David (Lord Eccles), 102, 170, 210
economic controls, 27–8, 53, 189–90, 191–2
Economic Survey for 1947, 186, 187
The Economist, 27–8, 68, 171
economy, 26–54; austerity measures, 27–8, 37, 44; black market, 44–50; food rationing, 29–44; 53–4; living standards, 28–9, 37; post-war crisis, 178–9, 185–8; shortages, 26–7
Ede and Ravenscroft, 52–3
Eden, Anthony, 117
Edinburgh, 65
Edinburgh International Festival, 136
Edrich, Bill, 53
education, 17, 140–70, 65–75; Army, 4, 12–15, 24; before the war, 142–4; during the war, 144–5; grammar schools, 163–6; public schools, 166–9; raising of school-leaving age, 151–5, 173; reform proposals, 140–2, 145–51; school-building programme, 156–60, 73, 74, 75; secondary modern schools, 160–3, 70, 71
Education Act (1918), 143
Education Act (1944), 11, 18, 140–2, 146, 147–8, 151, 161, 163, 164–5, 169
Educational Reconstruction (White Paper), 11
Edwards, Ebby, 183
Egerton-Savory, Arthur, 16–17, 20, 23, 24–5, 5
egg, dried, 35, 41–2
Egypt, 178, 12
Electrical Trades Union (ETU), 175, 188
electricity, fuel crisis, 181
elementary schools, 142, 143, 144, 147, 151, 160, 161, 162
eleven plus examination, 147, 164–5, 166, 169
Eliot, T. S., 207
Elizabeth, Princess, 51–2
Elizabeth, Queen (Queen Mother), 82, 89
Emergency Medical Service (EMS), 97–8
Emett, Rowland, 197
employment, 17, 173–7; building industry, 62–3; ex-service personnel, 23–5; shortages, 7, 41; wage restraints, 188–9; women, 16, 17, 50, 186–7, 41, 83
Employment Policy (White Paper), 11
English Opera Group, 133
Epps, Sir George, 110
Epsom, 126
Errington, Bob, 20–1
Eton, 167, 168, 66

Europe, 191, 193
European Voluntary Workers, 174
Exchequer, *see* Treasury
exports, 26, 27, 172–3, 178–9, 189–92, 193, 82, 84, 94

Fabian Society, 148
family: the Housewives' League and, 42; in wartime, 16–17
Family Portrait (film), 209
Far East, 172
Far Tottering and Oyster Creek Railway, 197
Farmer, Sir George, 189–91
fascism, 43
Federation of British Industries, 193, 194, 205
feminism, 40–4
Ferguson, Sheila, 16
Festival of Britain, 76, 113, 197, 206–10, 87–96; aims of, 207; Hugh Casson on, 208; demolition of, 210; Dome of Discovery, 208, 210; educational aspects of, 207, 209; Emett's Railway, 197; entertainment aspects of, 207, 209, 210; Fairway, 210; Michael Frayn on, 208, 209; inauguration of, 197; Mississippi Showboat, 208; Pleasure Gardens, 197; regional exhibitions, 197; siting of, 208; Skylon, 197, 208, 210; South Bank Exhibition, 197
Festival Hall, 210
Fielding, James, 66–7, 68
Fields, Gracie, 128, 210
Filey, 115–16, 117
films, 129–33
First World War, 8, 27
Fitzgerald, Hilde, 16
flats, 73–4, 75, 78
Fleming, Lord, 166
Fleming Report, 166–7, 168–9
Flemming, Sir Gilbert, 151
Fletcher, Bill, 67
Fletcher, Mrs, 67
Floud, Halsey and Martin, 165
food: black market, 45, 46; rationing, 6, 27, 29–44, 46, 53–4, 119, 6, 15, 16
Food Offices, 29, 30, 40, 55
Foot, Michael, 60
football, 120–2, 124, 55, 59
football pools, 124, 125
Ford, Cyril, 82
Ford, Mrs, 82–3, 85
Ford, Thelma, 66
'Formation Colleges', 24
Formby, George, 127–8
Forshaw, J. H., 71
fox-hunting, 125
France, 173, 191
Francis, Mr, 22–3
Franklyn, Mr, 63, 116
Frayn, Michael, 208, 209

Freeman, John, 111
Freeman, Mrs, 115, 128, 129
Frere, James, 52–3
friendly societies, 88
fuel crisis (1947), 180–1, 185
furniture, 27

Gaitskell, Hugh, 111, 172, 201
gambling, 122–5
Games, Abram, 90
Garbett, Dr, Archbishop of York, 117
garden city movement, 73, 79, 83, 84
Garson, Greer, 133
Gas Board, 82
Gateshead, 160–1
Gaumont-British cinemas, 130
general elections: July 1945, 2, 5, 12, 14, 17, 18–19, 28, 57, 171, 12, 13; February 1950, 53, 197, 205; October 1951, 28, 54, 197, 198
A General Medical Service for the Nation, 96–7
General Motors, 36
George VI, King, 19, 197, 89
Germany, 102, 144; displaced persons camps, 174; economy, 172; food shortages, 35, 36; motor industry, 191; pottery industry, 173; surrenders, 2
Gielgud, Sir John, 207
Gilbert, Martin, 3
Glanville, Brian, 122
Glasgow, 4, 121
Glenrothes, 79
Godber, Sir George, 99–100, 112
Goldman, Dr Jacob, 13–14, 107–8
Government Social Survey, 130
Grable, Betty, 132
grammar schools, 142, 143–4, 146–7, 148, 149–50, 156, 160, 163–6
Gravesend, 65
Great Dunmow, 42
Greater London Plan, 71–2, 74, 79
Green Belts, 71, 72, 77
Green Book (educational reform), 145
Greenwood, Arthur, 60
greyhound racing, 122–5, 181, 57
Greig, Teresa Billington, 19
Griffiths, Mrs, 90–1
Griffiths, James, 38
Grimethorpe colliery, 183–4
Guildford, 20–1
Guy's Hospital, 93

Hadow Report, 142, 143, 144, 161
Hampden Park, Glasgow, 121, 122
Handley, Tommy, 2, 117
Hardman, David, 151, 163
Harlow, 79

Harris, Dr Jeaffreson, 104, 107
harvest camps, 119, 127
Hatfield, 79, 158
Havoc, June, 132
Hayworth, Rita, 126, 201, 60
Healey, Denis, 18, 169–70
health centres, 98
health services: pre-war, 88–96;
    reform proposals, 96–102; in
    Second World War, 97–8, 47;
    see also National Health Service
Hemel Hempstead, 79, 80, 81–3,
    84–5, 158
Henderson, Stan, 4–5, 68–9
Henley-on-Thames, 161
Henn Collins, Mr Justice, 81
Henry V (film), 132
Herbert, S. Melvyn, 91
Hertfordshire, 158–9, 165, 168
Heyworth, Geoffrey, 177
High Court, 81
higher education, 169
Hill, Charles (Lord Hill), 98, 100,
    103, 42
Hiroshima, 2
Hobsbawm, Eric, 136
Hodson, J. L., 29, 171, 182
Hoffman, Paul, 193
holiday camps, 115–19
holidays, 114–19, 50, 51, 52
Holidays with Pay Act (1938), 114
Hollywood, 132–3, 134
Holmes, Maurice, 148
Home Front, 117
Home Guard, 3
Hopkins, Harry, 26, 86–7
Hopkinson, Sir Tom, 2, 9, 204
Horne, Kenneth, 117, 210
HORSA, 155, 158
horse-racing, 122, 123–4, 125–6
horsemeat, 39–40
hospitals: consultants, 109;
    during war, 97–8, 39, 40; and
    the establishment of the NHS,
    108–9; pre-NHS, 88, 89, 93–7;
    reform proposals, 96–7,
    99–100; specialists, 106–7
House of Commons, 11, 37, 53,
    56, 68, 102, 103, 140, 178, 181
House of Lords, 81
housewives, 29, 40–4, 89, 186
Housewives' League, 205, 18, 19,
    20
housing, 17, 55–85, 26–36;
    building programme, 56–63,
    69–70, 33, 34, 35, 36; controls,
    58–62; expectations, 15; local
    authority, 58–61, 63–5, 70,
    74–5; new towns, 79–85;
    prefabs, 57–8, 31, 32;
    shortages, 55–7, 199, 26; slum
    clearance, 57, 27, 29, 30;
    squatters, 55–6, 65–9, 28;
    standards, 70; subsidies, 59;
    timber shortage, 61–2, 63;
    town and country planning,
    70–85, 33
Housing Act (1946), 59

Housing Act (1948), 70
Housing Policy (White Paper), 11
Howard, Ebenezer, 73
Howerd, Frankie, 116
Hughes, Herbert (Billy), 149–50,
    155, 156
Hulton, Edward, 204
Hungary, 122
Huss, Jack, 122–3, 124–5
Hyde Park Corner, 66
Hyland, Norman, 91–2
Hyndley, Lord, 80

immigrant workers, 174, 182–3
imports, 26–7, 37, 178–9
income differentials, 8
India, 20, 35, 36, 119, 172–3, 178
industrial assurance companies,
    88–9
industrial design, 192
industrial relations, 175–7, 180,
    183–5, 189
industry, 171–96, 76–86; coal
    industry, 172, 179–85, 187–8;
    controls, 27–8, 191–2; exports,
    26, 27, 172–3, 178–9, 189–92,
    193; fuel crisis, 180–1, 199;
    industrial boom, 172;
    nationalisation, 19, 43, 177–8,
    180–1, 184–5, 193; production
    campaign, 185–9, 193–4; raw
    materials, 27; recovery, 193;
    strikes, 7, 171, 183–4, 189;
    trade unions, 7, 171, 173,
    174–7, 188–9, 195; vocational
    training, 24; see also
    employment
infant welfare services, 97
inflation, 176
insurance, medical, 88–9, 95–6
Iran, crisis with, 197
Ireland, 174
iron and steel industry, 172, 193,
    194–5
Isaacs, George, 20, 60, 186
Ismay, 'Pug', 207
Italy, 172, 173

Jaffe, Dr G., 110
Japan, 2, 26, 172, 178, 187, 191
Jay, Douglas, 8, 36, 180, 185,
    188–9
jazz, 136–9, 62
Jennings, Humphrey, 209
Jephcott, Pearl, 130
jitterbugging, 129
Johnson-Marshall, Percy, 75, 76
Johnson-Marshall, Stirrat, 158,
    159
Joint Industrial Councils, 177
Joint Production Committees, 7,
    177
junior technical schools, 143

Kemsley group, 43
Kensington, 68–9
Keynes, J. M., 9, 26, 134, 135,
    178

Kilbey, June, 126–7
King, Len, 91
Kipling, Rudyard, 5, 11
Kobak, Walter, 182–3
Korean War, 111, 173, 189, 197

labour, see employment
Labour Exchanges, 24
Labour Party: 1945 election, 2, 5,
    14, 17, 18, 19, 28, 148, 171, 198,
    203, 13; 1950 election, 53, 197;
    1951 election, 28, 197, 198,
    201–2; and the Beveridge
    Report, 140; Coalition
    government, 3; economic
    controls, 27–8; employment
    policy, 206; educational policy,
    140, 141, 144, 147–8, 167;
    housing policy, 57, 59, 69, 78,
    79; ideals, 203; industrial
    policy, 177–8, 204, 205;
    nationalisation of coal industry,
    180; and rationing, 53–4, 201;
    and the reform of the health
    services, 99, 198, and the TUC,
    206; and the Welfare State, 206
lace industry, 79
Lake District, 127
Lamarr, Hedy, 201
Lamour, Dorothy, 201
Lancashire, 65, 94–5
Land Rovers, 190–1
Landeau, Mrs, 18
Lansbury, George, 76
Lansbury estate, 76–7, 78–9, 35,
    36
Law, Alice, 105
Law, Mary, 176
Law, Mr, 92–3
Lean, David, 132
leisure, 113–39, 50–64; cinema,
    129–33; dance-halls, 128–9,
    139; gambling, 122–5;
    holidays, 114–19; jazz, 136–9;
    sport, 119–23, 125–7; youth
    clubs, 135
Lend-Lease, 26, 178
Lester, Renie, 67
Letchworth, 79
Lewis, Jane, 40–1
Lewis, Roy, 169
Liberal Party, 18, 140
Limburn, George, 152–3, 154
Ling, Arthur, 3, 74–5, 78, 85
Linsell, Joe, 57–8
Linsell, Mary, 57–8
Listener, 188
Liverpool, 21–2, 51, 56, 65
living standards, 28, 37, 178, 179,
    193
Lloyd George, David, 56, 88
local authorities: education, 141,
    142, 145–6; hospitals, 93, 95–6,
    97; housing, 58–61, 63–5, 70,
    74–5
Local Government Act (1929), 93
Location of Industry Act (1945),
    71

London, 25, 43, 56; architecture, 73; black market, 45–6; Blitz, 2, 9, 11, 55, 75, 158; dance-halls, 129; education, 149; Green Belt, 77; jazz clubs, 137; new towns, 70–1, 72, 79; office building, 78; squatters, 68–9; urban reconstruction, 71–2, 73–9
London County Council (LCC), 58, 64, 71, 72, 74–8, 81, 99, 148, 150, 158
London Electricity Board, 127
London Symphony Orchestra, 117
Lord's cricket ground, 120, 54
Lovelock, Irene, 41, 42, 43, 44, 205, 18
Luton Hoo, 8
Lynn, Vera, 2, 128
Lyttelton, Humphrey, 137–8, 139
Lyttelton, Oliver, 37

Mac's Rehearsal Rooms, London, 137
MacDonald, June, 8, 17, 31–2, 41, 43–4, 52, 18
Macey, John, 15, 64
Mack, E. C., 166
Macmillan, Harold, 77–8, 210
Madrid, 122
Malaya, 35, 36
Manchester, 56, 90–2, 122, 129, 137, 176
Manchester City Football Club, 121
manufacturing industry, 172–4
marriage, in wartime, 16–17
Marshall, George, 193
Marshall Aid, 193
Marwood, Joan, 128–9, 133
Marx, Harpo, 61
Masheder, Philip, 5, 12, 176
Mass Observation, 124
maternity services, 97, 105
Mather, Vera, 31, 33–4, 39, 50–1, 54
Matthews, Stanley, 55
Maud, John, 150
Maude, Angus, 169
Mayer, J. P., 132
Maynard, Bill, 117
MCC, 119
meat: black market, 46; rationing, 30–1, 38–9, 54
Medd, David, 158–9
Medical Planning Commission, 98
Melbourne, 137
Melly, George, 206
Merseyside, 43
middle class: British Housewives' League, 43; education, 143–4, 147, 165–6, 169; holidays, 117; living standards, 28–9; mortality rates, 87; politics, 204; pre-war health services,

88, 95; radicalism, 209; and the reform of the health services, 102
Middle East, 14–15, 20, 173
Middlesbrough, 165
Milburn (footballer), 121
Miller, Glen, 128
Miller, Max, 128
mining, coal, 179–85, 187–8
Ministry of Agriculture, 60, 119
Ministry of Aircraft Production, 190
Ministry of Economic Affairs, 179
Ministry of Education, 141, 146–7, 148–57, 160–1; Architects and Buildings Branch, 157; Architects' Development Group, 159
Ministry of Food, 2, 29–30, 32–3, 35, 37–9, 46, 119
Ministry of Fuel and Power, 180–1
Ministry of Health, 57, 59, 60, 64, 99–100, 101–2, 112
Ministry of Labour, 19–20, 174, 187
Ministry of National Insurance, 198
Ministry of Supply, 60
Ministry of Town and Country Planning, 59, 60, 71, 80
Ministry of Works, 2, 58, 155, 156, 157
Ministry of Works and Planning, 71
Mr Churchill's Declaration of Policy to the Electors, 19
Mitchell, Charles, 61
Monckton, Sir Walter, 69
Monolulu, Prince, 126, 61
Montgomery, Field Marshal, 52
Moran, Lord, 100
Morgan, Kenneth, 127
Morrison, Herbert, 35–6, 99, 148, 150, 151, 178, 180, 207, 210, 88
mortality rates, 87
Mortimer, Roger, 126
Moscow Dynamo, 122
Mothers' League, 40–1
motor industry, 189–91, 84
Movietone News, 39, 66, 67–8
Mucklow, Mr and Mrs, 32
Mumford, Lewis, 73–4
Murdoch, Richard, 117, 210
music, 135, 136–9
Music While You Work, 204
musicals, 133–4
mutinies, 19, 20

NAAFI (Navy, Army and Air Force Institute), 4, 5
·Nagasaki, 2
National Assistance Board, 199
National Association of Labour Teachers, 147, 150, 156
National Coal Board (NCB), 172, 180–1, 183–5

National Cyclists' Union, 127
National Film Finance Corporation, 133
National Government (1930s), 43
National Health Act (1946), 101–3
National Health Insurance, 88–9, 96, 198
National Health Service, 10, 11, 17, 18; costs, 109–12; doctors, 107–8; early days of, 104–12, 44; establishment of, 86–8, 98–104, 198; hospitals, 108–9, 44
National Health Service, A (White Paper), 11
National Parks, 71
National Parks Act (1949), 127
National Service Act (1947), 173
National Socialism, 102
National Union of Mineworkers (NUM), 182, 183–4
National Union of Teachers, 145–6
nationalisation, 19, 43, 177–8, 180–1, 184–5, 193, 203, 204, 205
Nelson, 187
New Look, 51–2, 200, 22, 23
New Orleans, 137, 138
new towns, 71, 72, 73, 79–85
New Towns Act (1946), 71, 79
Newcastle United, 121
Newlove, Clarrie, 59–60, 67
Newmarket, 126
Newton, Francis, 136, 138
Newton Aycliffe, 79, 199, 202
Nicholson, Sir Max, 207
Nineteen Eighty-Four, 204
Niven, David, 14
nonconformists, 145
North America, 191
Northolt, 61
Norway, 26
Norwood, Sir Cyril, 146
Norwood Report, 146–7, 148, 149
Nuffield Provident Hospital Trust, 96
nursery schools, 140

Observer Corps, 26
O'Connor, Cavan, 117
O'Donovan, Patrick, 210
Odeon cinemas, 130
O'Farrell, Talbot, 117
Oklahoma, 133
Old Vic, 117, 136
Oliver, Vic, 117
Olivier, Laurence, 132
Olympia, 20
Olympic Games (1948), 126
100 Oxford Street, London, 137, 139, 62
opticians, 86, 89, 92–3, 104–5, 45
Order of the Garter, 52–3
Orlans, Harold, 84
Orwell, George, 204

Osborn, Frederick, 73–4, 78, 79
O'Shea, Tessie, 117
Overy, Richard, 191
Oxford, 109

Pagnamenta, Peter, 191
Paris, 137
Parkinson, Jenny, 21
Parliamentary candidates, 17
Part, Sir Antony, 6, 156–7, 159–60
Pataudi, Nawab of, 119
patriotism, 11–12
Patten, Marguerite, 33
Peak District, 127
Penguin Books, 12
Penny, Mrs, 82
Peterlee, 79
Petherick, Maurice, 13
petrol: black market, 45, 48–9; rationing, 26, 48–9, 53
Philip, Prince, 51–2
Phillips, 172–3
Picture Post, 2, 9, 20, 40, 60, 204
planning, town and country, 70–85, *33*
Plowden, Edwin, 179
Plymouth, 71
Poland, 144
Poles, 174, 182–3
police, and the black market, 46, 48
Polish Resettlement Corps, 174, 182–3
Poplar, 75–7
Port Talbot, 172
Portal, Lord, 52
Portsmouth, 1, 22
Post Office, 23
pottery industry, 173, 191–2
prefabs, 57–8, *31*, *32*
prescription charges, 111
Price, Mrs, 123
Price, Tommy, 123, *56*
Priestley, J. B., 2, 9, 200, 201, 203–4, *7*
primary schools, 144, 151, 156, 157
Prudential, 88
Public School Appointments Bureau, 168
public schools, 151, 163, 166–9
Pwllheli, 115
Pyke, Magnus, 38–9

Queen Mary, 194
Queensbridge Secondary Modern School, 70
queues, 31, 41

racing, *60*, *61*
radio, 117, 129, 135
railways, 115, *85*, *94*
Ramsbotham, Herwald, 145
Rank cinemas, 132
Rank Organisation, 197
rationing, 28; building materials, 62; clothes, 6–7, 20, 26, 53,

201, *24*, *25*; food, 6, 26, 27, 29–44, 53–4, 119, *16*; petrol, 26, 48–9, 53
Rattray Taylor, Gordon, 131–2
Reading, 149
rearmament, 7, 111
Reconstruction Committee, 10–11
Red Barn, Bexleyheath, 137
Reed, Carol, 132
Reid, Sir Charles, 180
Reinstatement in Civil Employment Act (1944), 23
Reith, Lord, 9, 81, 83
religious education, 142, 146, 161
restaurants, 30–1, 6
rhythm clubs, 136–7
Road Haulage Association, 43
Robledo brothers, 121
Roche, Nurse, 89–90, 109, 110–11
Rochford, James, 23, 24, 175
Rodealgh, Mrs, 51
Rogers, Ginger, 201
Roman Catholic Church, 142, 146, 174
Romford, 45
Roosevelt, Franklin Delano, 26
Rose, Dr Elizabeth, 97–8
Rotherfield Secondary Modern School, 161–2
Rover motor company, 189–91
Rowntree, Seebohm, 199
Royal Air Force (RAF), 20, 26
Royal Automobile Association (RAC), 45
Royal College of Arms, 52
Royal College of Obstetricians, 98, 100, 103
Royal College of Physicians, 98, 100, 103
Royal College of Surgeons, 98, 100, 103
Royal Commission on Gambling, 125
Royal Festival Hall, London, 72
Royal Free Hospital, London, 94
Royal Navy, 115, 116
Royal Scottish Corporations, 98
Rubinstein, David, 149
Ruislip, 61

St Anne's Hospital, Manchester, 92
St Bartholomew's Hospital, 93
Salford, 24, 175
San Carlo Opera Company, 117
San Francisco, 137
Sargent, Malcolm, 207
Scandinavia, 63
School Certificate, 143
School Dental Service, 91
schools, *see* education
Scotland, 31, 68, 79, 146, 147
Scott, Terry, 117
Scott-James, Anne, 40
Scunthorpe, 59–60, 66–7, 68
seaside holidays, 114–15

secondary modern schools, 146–7, 149–50, 156, 160–1, 162, 163, 164
service camps, 65–8, 115–16, 119
'Service of Youth', 134–5
SFORSA, 155
Shakespeare, William, 117, 150
Shawcross, Lord, 62
Sheffield, 171, 196
Shinwell, Emanuel, 29, 102, 180–1, 182, 183, *80*
ship-building, 172
shopping: food rationing, 29–31; queues, 31, 41
Short, John R., 56
shortages, 26, 55–6; *see also* rationing
Shrewsbury School, 167–8
Silkin, Lewis, 71, 79, 80–1
Sinatra, Frank, 128
Singapore, 35
Skegness, 115, 116, 118
Smith, Sir Ben, 35, 36, 41–2
Smith, Frank 121
Smith, Mrs Jessamine, 86
Smithies, Edward, 45
Snoddy, Mrs, 76–7, 78–9
snoek, 38, 39, *17*
Snowdonia, 127
social insurance, 10, 11
Social Insurance (White Paper), 11
social patriotism, 12
social reform, 8–11, 134–5, 145, 147, 199
social welfare, *45*, *46*, *48*
Society of Medical Officers of Health, 98
Society of Motor Manufacturers and Traders, 189
South Africa, 38, 39, 120
South America, 172, 191
South Pacific, 133
Southwark, 45
Soviet Union, 73, 102, 193
Spain, 122, 136
speedway racing, 122, 123, 125, *56*
Spence, Jimmy, 100
spivs, 45, 47, 49–50, *21*
sport, 119–23
sporting clubs, 126–7
squatters, 55–6, 65–9
Stable, Mr Justice, 69
Stallworthy, Sir John, 109
Steel Foundry Association, 194–5
steel industry, 172, 193, 194–5, 205
Stepney, 75, 77
sterling crisis (1947), 37, 179, 185
Stevenage, 79, 80–1, 83, 84, 158
Stevenage Corporation, 81
Stevenage Residents' Protection Association, 80
Stilts, Sylvia, 130–1
stockings, 50
Stockport, 47, 129
Stoke City Football Club, 121
Stokes, Reverend, 83

INDEX

Strachey, John, 36–7, 38, 42, 53, *15*
Streat, Sir Raymond, 171
Street, A. G., 127
strikes, 7, 171, 183–4, 189
Sumser-Ali, Mary, 154
Sunday Graphic, 43
Sweden, 174, 180
Switzerland, 174

Tate and Lyle, 205
taxation, 29, 200
Taylor, Kathleen, 151–2
teachers, 151–4, *72*
technical colleges, 143
technical schools, 146–7, 149, 160, 162
teenagers: cinema-going, 130; education, 142, 143, 146–51; social reformers and, 134–5
television, 114, 181
Templewood Primary School, *75*
theatre, 135
Third Man, The, 132
Tomlinson, George, 58, 60, 141, 155, 156, 163, *69*, *74*
Tory Reform Committee, 180
town and country planning, 70–85
Town and Country Planning Acts, 71, 75
Town and Country Planning Association, 73, 79
trade unions, 7, 171, 173, 174–7, 188–9, 195
Trades Union Congress (TUC), 148, 189, 194, 206
Train, Jack, 117
Transport and General Workers' Union, 3, 189
Travers, Ben, 195, 196
Treasury, 89, 94, 111, 134–5, 145, 163, 179
Trevillion, Fred, *57*
Truman, Harry S., 26, 178
Twentieth Century-Fox, 132
Tyneside, 174

unemployment, 7, 173–4, 176, 199

Unilever, 177
United States: Anglo-American Productivity Council, 193–5, *85*; and the black market, 45; and Britain's economy, 26–7, 178–9, 193; criticism of new towns, 84; dance-halls, 128, 129; films, 132–3; grain exports, 35–6; Lend-Lease, 26, 178; Marshall Aid, 193; musicals, 133–4; popular culture, 200; raw materials, 63
United Steel Companies, 168
universities, 24, 143, 169
upper classes, sport, 125–6
US Congress, 179
'Utility' scheme, 7
Uxbridge, 17

Van Gogh, Vincent, 136, *64*
Van Os, Oliver, 167, 168
Vaughan, Dame Janet, 97, 100
Vernon, Betty, 150
Victoria and Albert Museum, 192
Vigilantes, 66
vocational training, 24
voluntary hospitals, 93–7, 99, 108–9, 111
voluntary schools, 142–3, 146

wages, 7, 28, 176, 188–9
Waites, 61
Wales, 79, 174
War Cabinet, 10
War Office, 111, 153
Ward, Mrs, 94–5
Warner Brothers, 132
Watford Grammar School, 165
Watkin, Brian, 87, 102
Watkins, Jean, 162
Watson, Bob, 61–2
Weaver, Toby, 146–7, 153, 154
Webb, George, and his Dixielanders, 137
Wedgwood, Josiah, 173, 192
Wells, H. G., 136
Welwyn Garden City, 79
Wembley, 82, 121, 122, 123
Wembley Lions, 123
whalemeat, 38–9, 119

Whitehouse, Winnie, 5–6, 25
Wightman, Ralph, 127
Wilkes, Maurice, 190
Wilkinson, Ellen, 141, 148–51, 153, 155, 156, 160, 163, 167, *68*
Williams, Mrs Vaughan, *88*
Williams, William Emrys, 12
Willink, Sir Henry, 99, 100, 125
Wilson, Harold, 53, 111, 133, 201
Wilson, Mary, *24*
Wilson, Susan, 39
Windermere, 150
Wolfenden, John, 167
women: British Housewives' League, 40–4; clothes, 50–2; employment, 16, 17, 50, 186–7; and the establishment of the NHS, 105–6; health insurance, 89, 95; housework, 29
Women Must Work (film), 186
Women's Health Enquiry Committee, 95
Woodlands Sports Club, Gravesend, 65
Woolton, Lord, **41, 53, 55–6, 206**
Woolworth's, 92–3
working class, 1: changing class relationships, 4–6, 8; education, 143, 147, 165, 166, 167–8; and the establishment of the NHS, 106; gambling, 123–4; holidays, 115; housing, 70, 72; living standards, 28, 199; mortality rates, 87; needs and expectations, 3–4, 206; pre-war health services, 88, 89, 90–1, 95–6; production campaign, 187–8; and rationing, 7, 41; sport, 125
Wyatt, Woodrow, 118

York, 199
Yorkshire, 65, 162, 183–4, 185
Young, Ted, 117, 118
youth clubs, 135

Zweig, Ferdinand, 177, 180, 181, 187–8